IMAGES of America

BARBOUR COUNTY

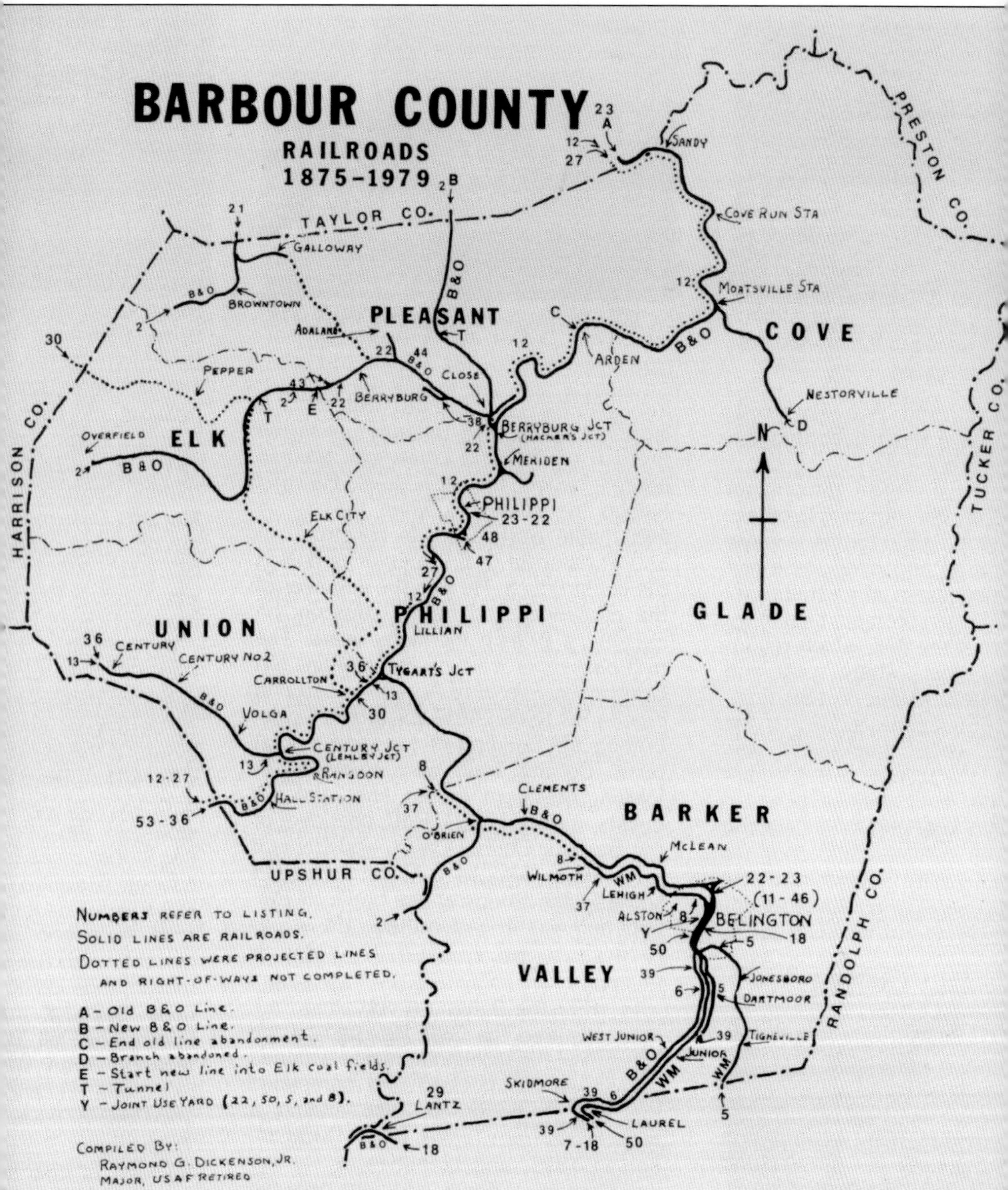
BARBOUR COUNTY
RAILROADS
1875-1979
TAYLOR CO.
PRESTON CO.
TUCKER CO.
HARRISON CO.
UPSHUR CO.
RANDOLPH CO.
PLEASANT
COVE
ELK
UNION
PHILIPPI
GLADE
BARKER
VALLEY
SANDY
COVE RUN STA
MOATSVILLE STA
GALLOWAY
BROWNTOWN
ADALANE
PEPPER
BERRYBURG
CLOSE
ARDEN
NESTORVILLE
OVERFIELD
BERRYBURG JCT
(HACKER'S JCT)
MERIDEN
PHILIPPI
ELK CITY
LILLIAN
CENTURY
CENTURY No 2
CARROLLTON
TYGART'S JCT
VOLGA
CENTURY JCT
(LEMLEY JCT)
RANSOON
HALL STATION
CLEMENTS
O'BRIEN
McLEAN
WILMOTH
LEHIGH
ALSTON
BELINGTON
JONESBORO
DARTMOOR
WEST JUNIOR
JUNIOR
TIGHEVILLE
SKIDMORE
LAUREL
LANTZ
B&O
WM
N
NUMBERS REFER TO LISTING.
SOLID LINES ARE RAILROADS.
DOTTED LINES WERE PROJECTED LINES AND RIGHT-OF-WAYS NOT COMPLETED.
A - Old B&O Line.
B - New B&O Line.
C - End old line abandonment.
D - Branch abandoned.
E - Start new line into Elk coal fields.
T - Tunnel
Y - Joint Use Yard (22, 50, 5, and 8).
COMPILED BY:
RAYMOND G. DICKENSON, JR.
MAJOR, USAF RETIRED

IMAGES
of America

BARBOUR COUNTY

Barbara Smith and Carl Briggs

ARCADIA
PUBLISHING

ISBN 978-0-7385-0570-1

Published by Arcadia Publishing
Charleston, South Carolina

Printed in the United States of America

Library of Congress Catalog Card Number: 00-102554

For all general information contact Arcadia Publishing at:
Telephone 843-853-2070
Fax 843-853-0044
E-mail sales@arcadiapublishing.com
For customer service and orders:
Toll-Free 1-888-313-2665

Visit us on the Internet at www.arcadiapublishing.com

Acknowledgments

First acknowledgment must go to Elza Wilson, who prompted the composition of this book and to whom it is dedicated in recognition of and appreciation for his unlimited support of and dedication to Barbour County.

Major sources of photographs and information were three previously published books: *Light on the Hill* by Richard Withers and Martha Rose Roy, *Milestones: A Pictorial History of Philippi, West Virginia 1844–1994* by Jane K. Mattaliano and Lois G. Ormonde, and *Barbour County: Another Look* compiled by the Barbour County Historical Society. Photographs that are not otherwise credited come from those three books and are used with permission. Individuals who provided other photographs or leads to photographs included Joe and Jane Mattaliano, Peggy Robinson, Patty Marsh, Don Funk, Lars Byrne, Nancy Streets, Don Smith, Joe Kaiser, Amanza Nitz, James B. Keener, Alice "Bonnie" Rowan, James and Robert Califf, Stephen Rautner, Arnout Hyde, Ann Serafin, Neil Irvine, Leonard LoBello, Retta Taylor, Ray Shaw, and Charles Roberts of Barnard, Roberts, and Co., Inc..

In an attempt to make sure to include all areas of the county, newspaper articles were placed in the *Barbour Democrat* requesting pertinent photographs, particularly those of the smaller communities. Telephone calls were also made to people who were believed to have such photos. Within space limitations, as many of those as available and appropriate appear herein.

CONTENTS

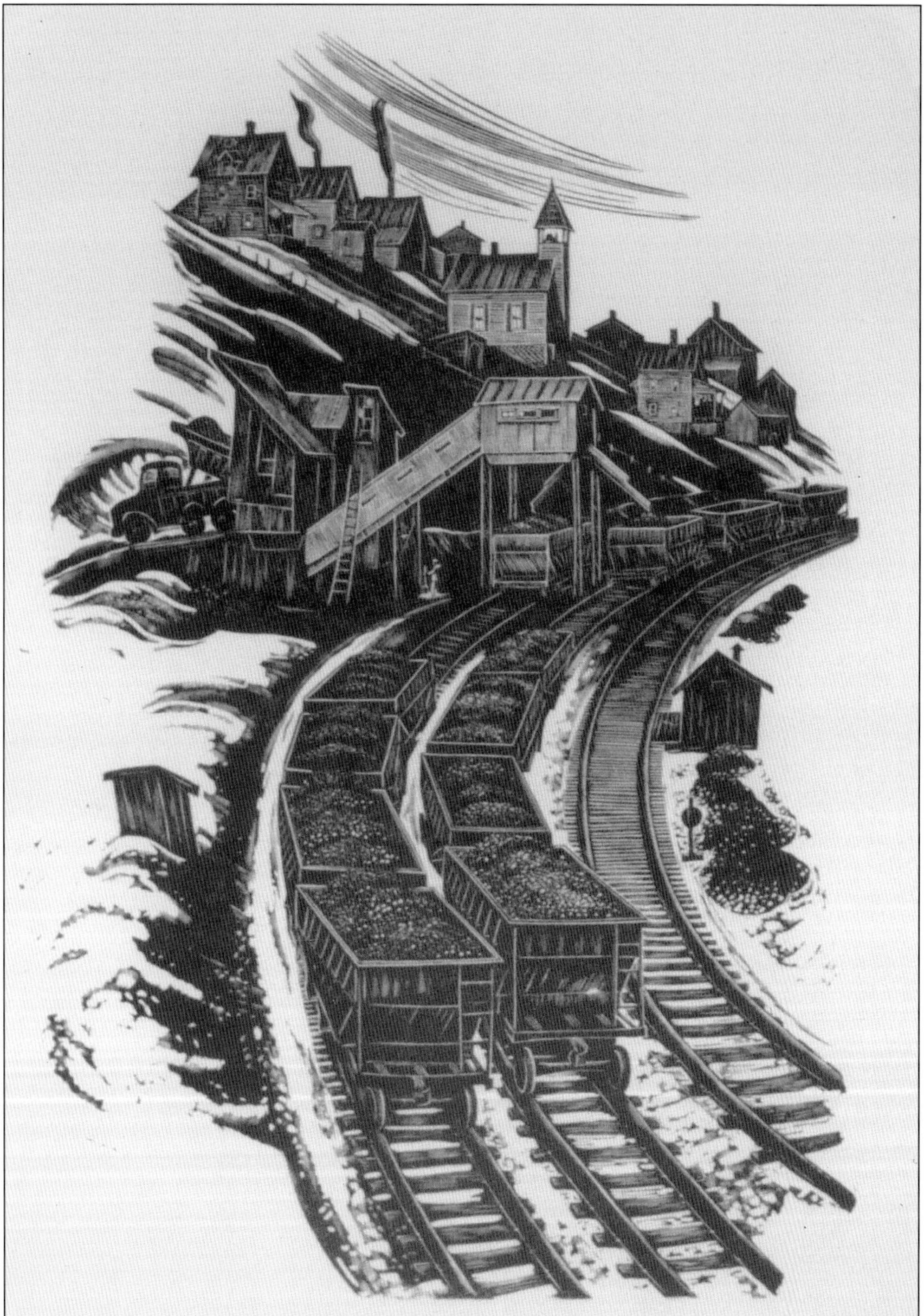

Herbert Waters, for many years Professor of Art at Alderson-Broaddus College, created this engraving called "Appalachian Mining Village." It clearly represents much of Barbour County, West Virginia. (Courtesy Leonard LoBello.)

Introduction

The only change in the map of the United States as a result of the Civil War was the creation of West Virginia by Abraham Lincoln in 1863. It is the only state which is located totally within Appalachia. Barbour County, a rural area, is located in north central West Virginia, right in the heart of Appalachia. To the immediate east are the Allegheny Mountains. To the west rolling hills lead to the Ohio River. The Tygart River and its tributaries run north through the county to the Monongahela and, eventually, Ohio Rivers. The Tygart forms the first major valley west of the Alleghenies. Before the establishment of the new state, this region was part of Augusta County, Virginia, which ran from the Shenandoah Valley all the way to the Mississippi River. The county seat was in Staunton.

Well into the 18th century, the area was a trackless forest used by Native Americans as hunting grounds during three seasons. A few of their villages were established in Cove Run and possibly elsewhere in the county. The first white people entered the area as hunters and trappers in the late 1700s. Settlers followed in the 1760s and 1770s, and by 1792 all the free land had been claimed, and acreage was selling at $2 per acre. With homesteads located on both sides of the river before the turn of the century, a ferry was established by William Anglin, and it was his name which was originally given to the settlement—Anglin's Ford. The ferry became the property of Daniel Booth, and the name of the town changed to Booth's Ferry. In 1843 the Virginia legislature created a new county from pieces of Lewis, Harrison, and Randolph Counties and renamed the area to honor Philip Pendleton Barbour, philanthropist and member of the U.S. Supreme Court from Orange County, Virginia. Covering 360 square miles, magisterial districts included Cove, Elk, Glade, Philippi, Pleasant, Barker, Union, and Valley.

Philippi, identified as the county seat in 1844, has historically been the largest town in the county, with a population of 27 families by 1850 and a current population of approximately 3,300. The entire county includes some 15,000 people. It covers 345.41 square miles, and its highest point is 1,300 feet above sea level.

Natural resources have included timber, coal, oil, gas, and fertile soil. U.S. Highways 250 and 119 serve the county. Once primarily a farming area, the major modern industries have been coal mining and timber. Other primary employers have been the board of education, Broaddus Hospital, Alderson-Broaddus College, and various federal, state, and local agencies.

In addition to the county seat, communities in modern Barbour County include Belington, Junior, Union, Mt. Liberty, Kasson, Tacy, Chestnut Ridge, Brownton, Berryburg, Arden,

Moatsville, Cove Run, Galloway, Elk City, Nestorville, Century, Meadowville, Valley Furnace, and Volga.

The county has for many years been known as a health center for the region, but it is best known as the site of the first land battle of the Civil War. This confrontation occurred on June 3, 1861. Colonel George Porterfield was in charge of the Confederate troops who were camped on the eastern side of the Tygart River. Union troops under Colonel Ebenezer Dumont and Colonel Benjamin Kelley had advanced from the north to the top of what is now called Battle Hill, where Alderson-Broaddus College is now located. Records indicate that Mrs. Thomas Humphreys, who lived on a nearby farm, shot at a fox that was stalking her hen house, and the shot was mistaken as having been fired by military personnel. The Union troops charged on horseback and on foot down the face of Battle Hill, going through the covered bridge which spanned the Tygart River and taking the Confederate troops by surprise. The latter retreated toward Beverly. So little was gained by either side that the skirmish has been nicknamed "The Philippi Races." According to legend, Abraham Lincoln and Jefferson Davis once met inside the renowned double-barreled bridge to try to prevent The War Between the States.

Best known of Barbour County landmarks is the bridge, which was constructed in 1852 and served both Union and Confederate forces during the Civil War. Other noteworthy sites include the courthouse, the Adaland mansion, Audra State Park, Tygart Lake State Park, Teter Creek Lake, Alderson-Broaddus College, the Myers Clinic, Broaddus Hospital, the iron furnace at Valley Furnace, and many others.

The history of Barbour County abounds with stories which feature people of courage, determination, industry, loyalty, and faith. Some things never change!

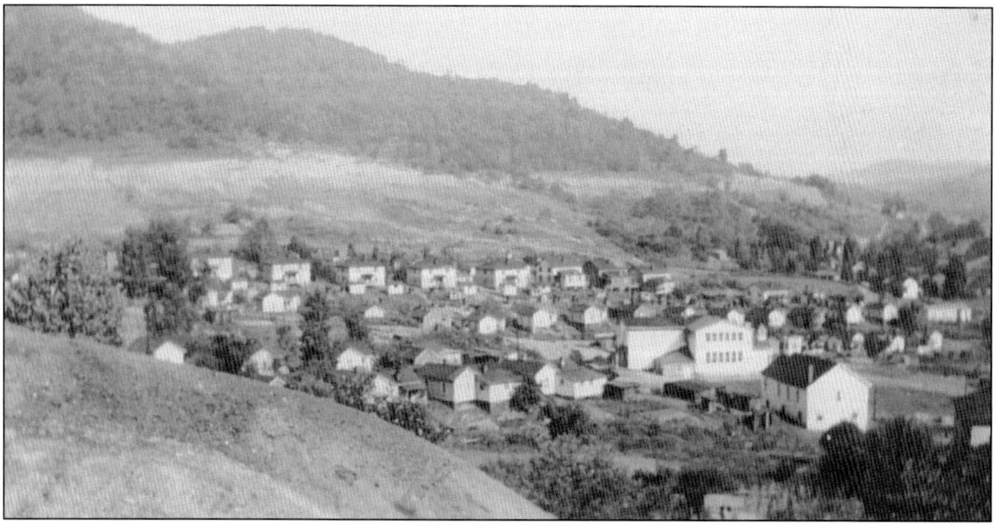

This photo, believed to be from the late 1930s, was taken on the hill near the mouth of the Galloway mine. The large buildings in the foreground are the Methodist church and the Galloway school. Residents of the time remember a cable with "buckets" running from the mine to the slag heap across the road. (Courtesy Alice "Bonnie" Rowan.)

One

Early On

Historic maps identify Barbour County as "the Western Waters," and the river is often called simply "the Valley river." Running through Randolph, Barbour, and Taylor Counties, the Tygart is fed by many tributaries. Well into the 19th century, each of these rivers or creeks was the site of a gristmill or a lumber mill or both. According to records, at least five of these existed even before 1795, their builders being Josiah Baker, Daniel Booth, Elias and William Barker, George Westfall, and John Hardin Jr. Even before that, a small fort, protection from Native American attacks, could be found at each settlement. Stories abound of massacres which occurred in the second half of the 18th century. Because of the violence and destruction that took place, the term "massacre" was applied no matter how few or how many deaths were involved. As late as 1822, survey maps name only three villages: Billsburg, Glady Creek Crossroads, and Maigsville. The first wagon road was built in 1800 at a cost of 75¢ per rod. It ran 7 miles from Anglin's Ferry (Philippi) to Billsburg.

Settlers raised their own food, including cows and pigs. Game was not as available as might be imagined, reportedly because the forest was so dense that there was little mast available. There is no doubt, however, that in addition to small game, hunters brought home deer, elk, and an occasional bear.

It was not until well into the 19th century that drawings and photos of the area were preserved.

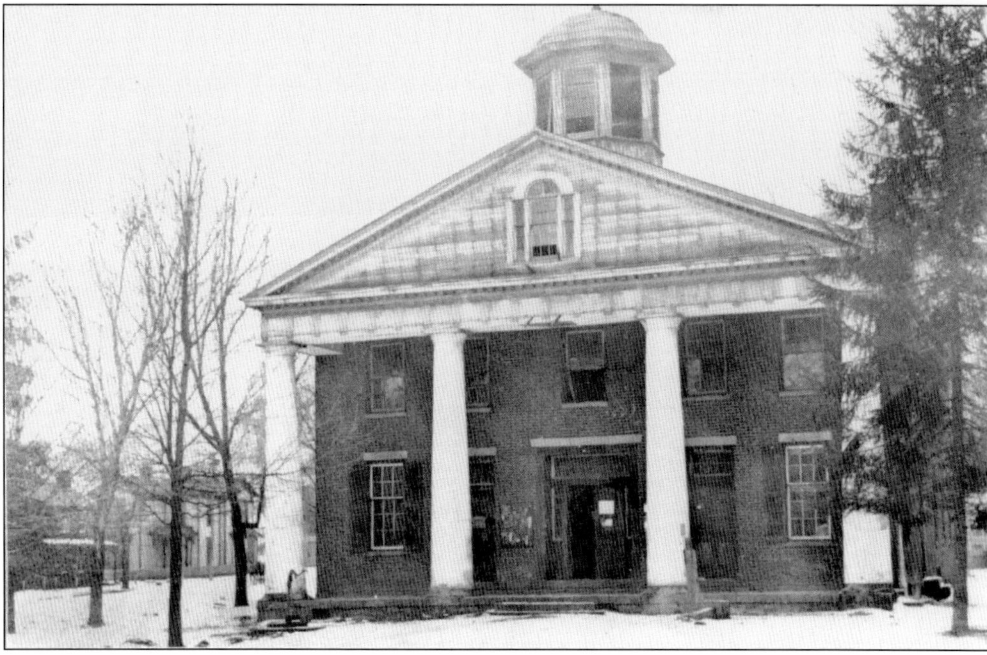

The first courthouse in Barbour County, built in 1845, carried the Georgian architecture of the South. Previously part of Augusta County, the new county was formed from sections of Lewis, Randolph, and Harrison Counties. The first flag to be flown from the tower of the new building was that of the Confederacy.

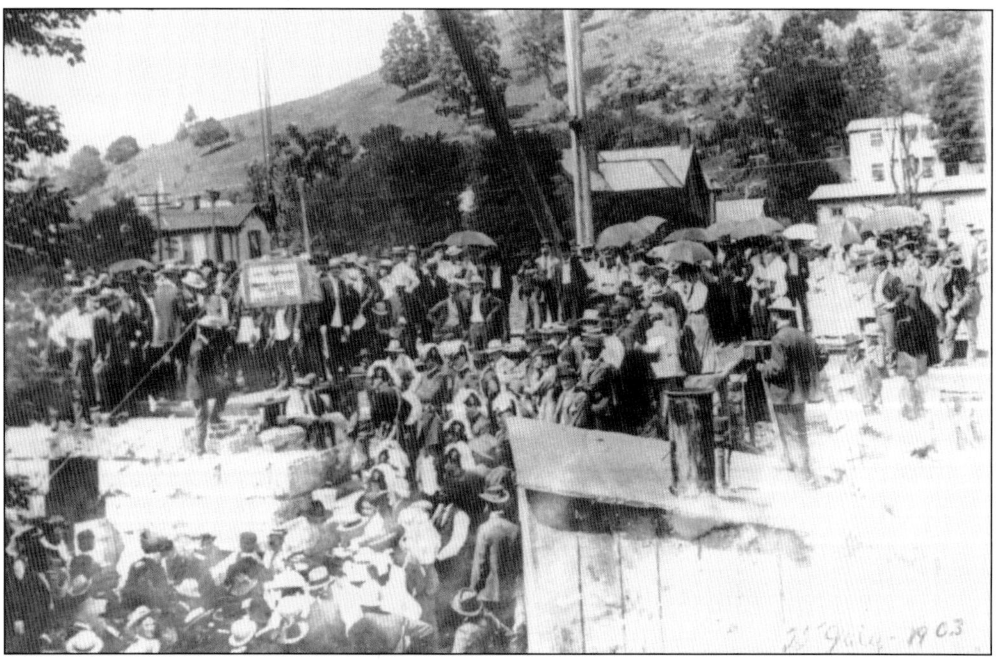

Great enough was the interest in the development of the new Virginia county that a large crowd gathered for the laying of the cornerstone of the new courthouse in 1903. The number of people actually living in Philippi at that time is uncertain, but in 1890 there were only 328, not including the outlying communities. (Courtesy Joe Mattaliano.)

The original Pringle Tree in Upshur County no longer stands, but offshoots still attract visitors. John and Samuel Pringle deserted the British Royal Army in 1761 or 1762. Having made their way south by hiring out as hunters and trappers, they lived for three years in a hollow tree at the mouth of Turkey Run. Samuel later guided many new settlers into what was to become Barbour County. (Photo Carl Briggs.)

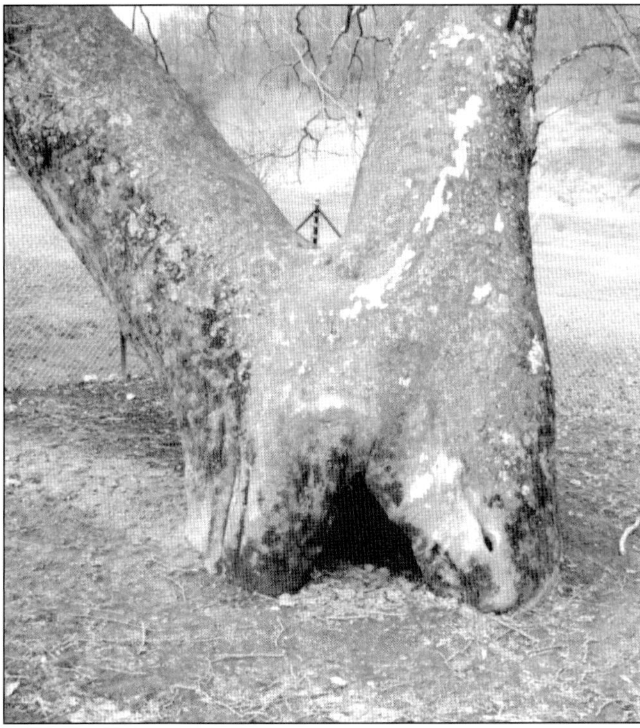

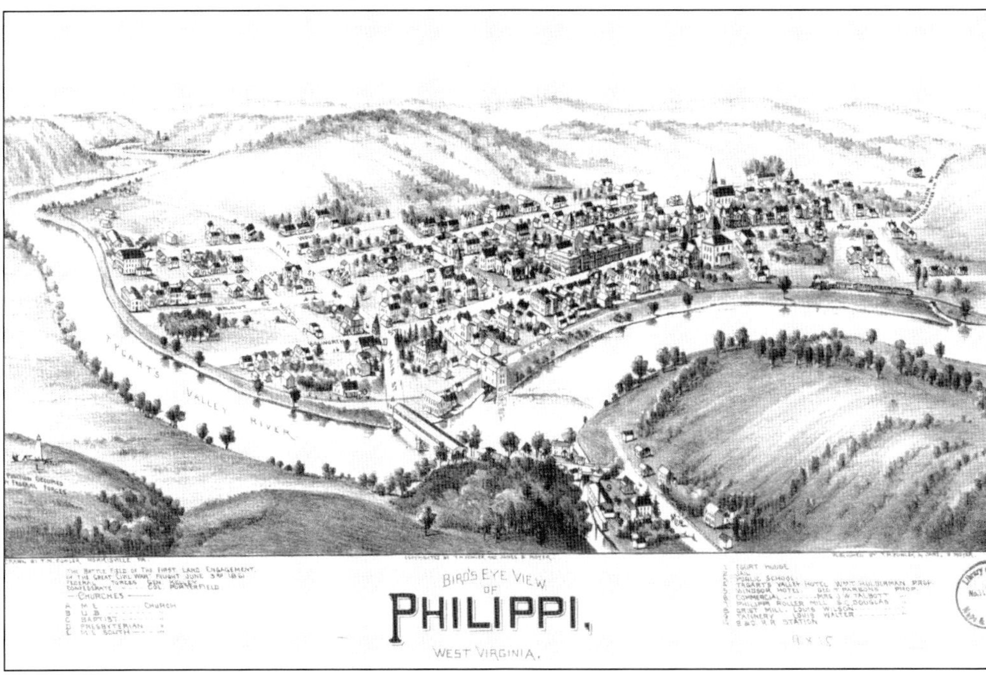

This "Bird's Eye View of Philippi," dated 1897, was executed by Pennsylvanian T.M. Fowler. At the bottom of the picture, Fowler identified five churches. Also identified are the courthouse, the jail, the public school, several hotels, Philippi Roller Mill, the gristmill, the tannery, and the B&O railroad station. On the lower left Fowler noted "position occupied by federal forces." (Courtesy Joe Mattaliano.)

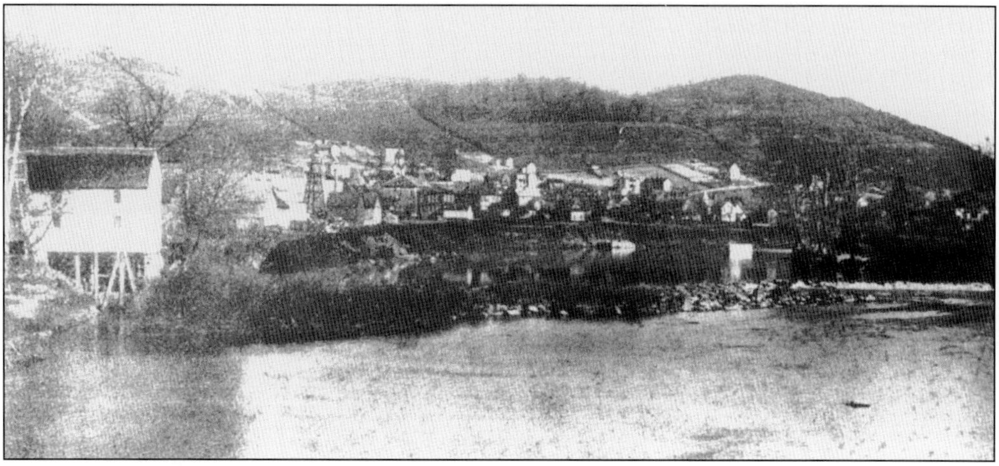

Grist- and sawmills were located on virtually every river and stream in Barbour County. This one on the left was located in Philippi. The last one in operation in the area was the Wilson Mill, built in 1857 and razed in 1917. (Courtesy Joe Mattaliano.)

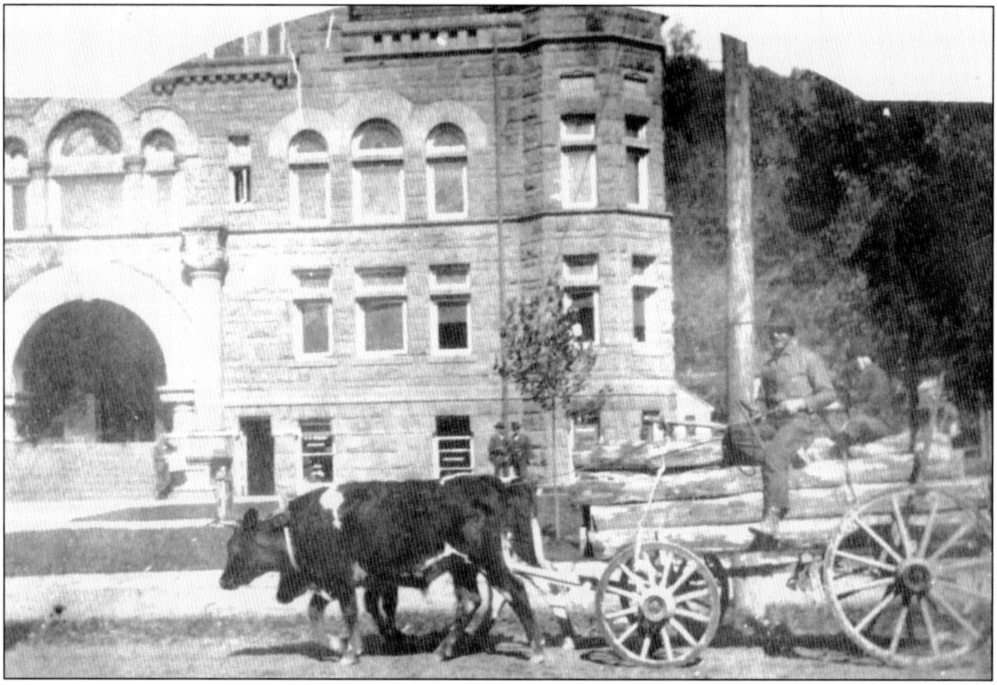

From the very start of the settlement, timber played an important role in the history of Barbour County. This industry was a mainstay of the economy until coal took over. Transport of the timber was accomplished by means of the rivers, the railroad, and wagons. (Courtesy Jane and Joe Mattaliano.)

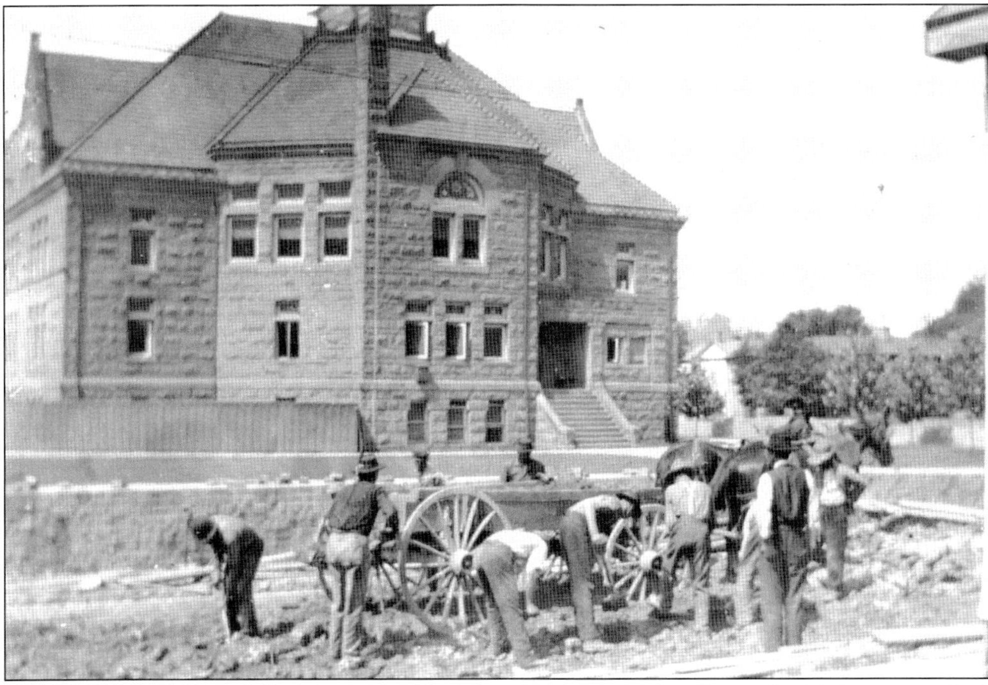

Horse- and ox-drawn wagons were used in Barbour County until well into the 20th century. Such conveyances were essential when streets were paved for the first time. The laying of the bricks proved to be an arduous undertaking for both laborers and horses. (Courtesy Joe Mattaliano.)

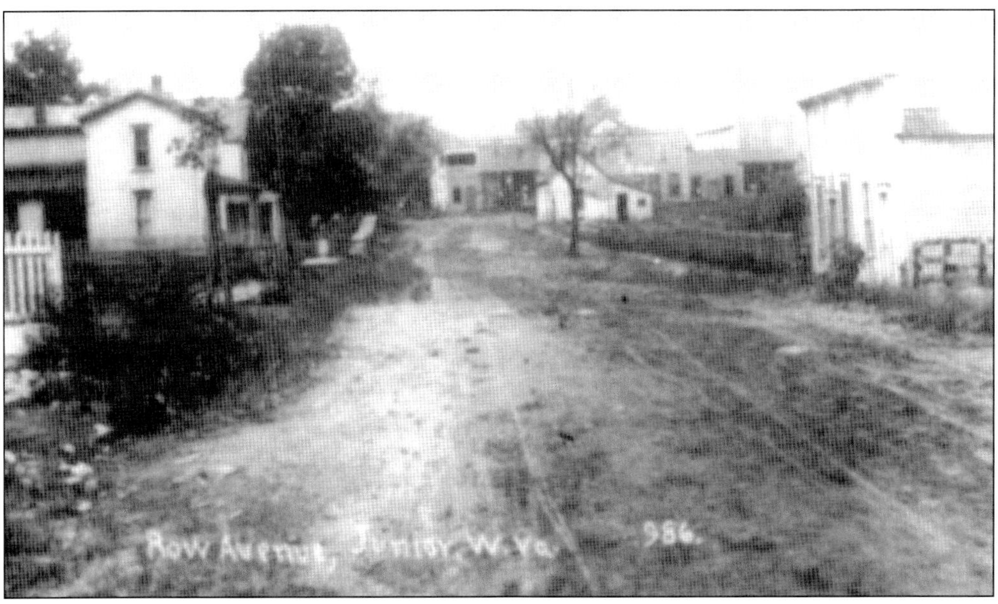

The community of Junior was originally called Row Town, and the main street, shown in this 1910 photo, was named Row Avenue. The largest industry ever enjoyed was the Junior Coal Company, organized in 1910 and operated by the Davises of Elkins. The mine, employing 100 men and 11 mules, produced some 500 tons of coal per day. The town was renamed in honor of Henry G. Davis Jr., who drowned at sea.

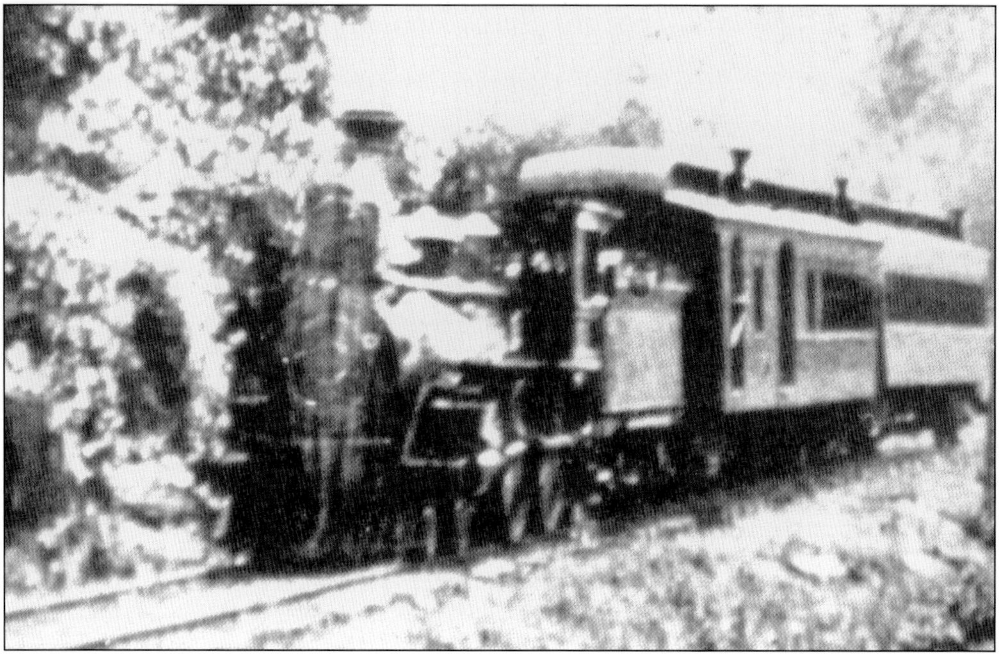

The railroad line which originated in Grafton reached Philippi in 1884 and Belington in 1887. In 1894, the Grafton to Belington line was taken over by the Baltimore and Ohio system. This first train into Philippi had a noteworthy crew: William Graham, engineer; Thomas S. Ball, fireman; Charles Bishop, brakeman; George Corder, baggage man; and George L. Woodford, mail clerk.

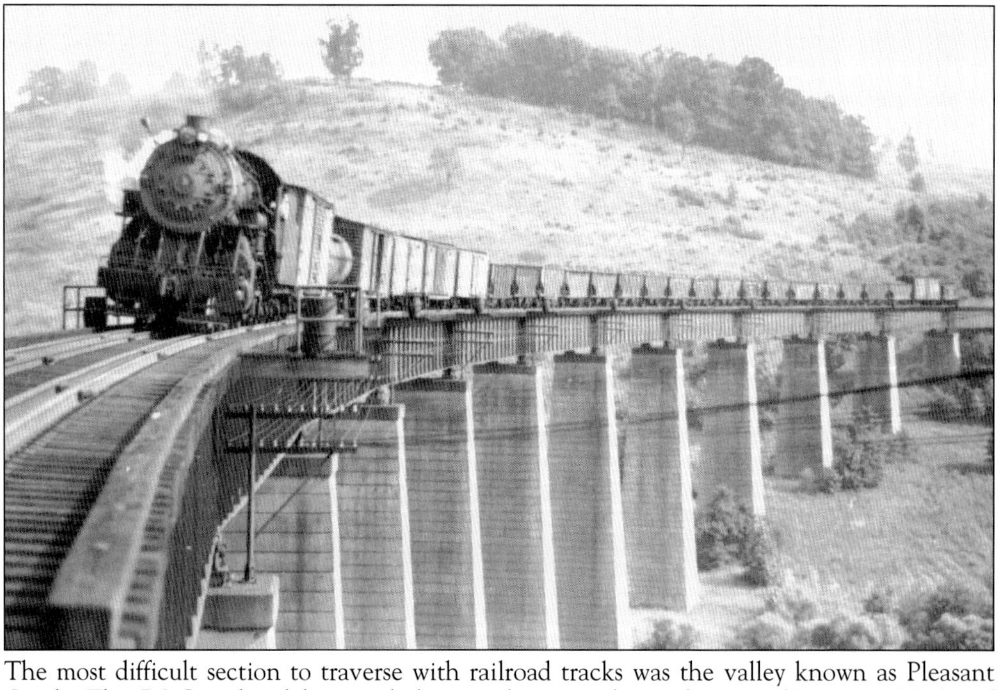

The most difficult section to traverse with railroad tracks was the valley known as Pleasant Creek. The B&O railroad has used this trestle since the mid-1880s. (Courtesy B&OHS/ Thompson/Barnard, Roberts and Co., Inc.)

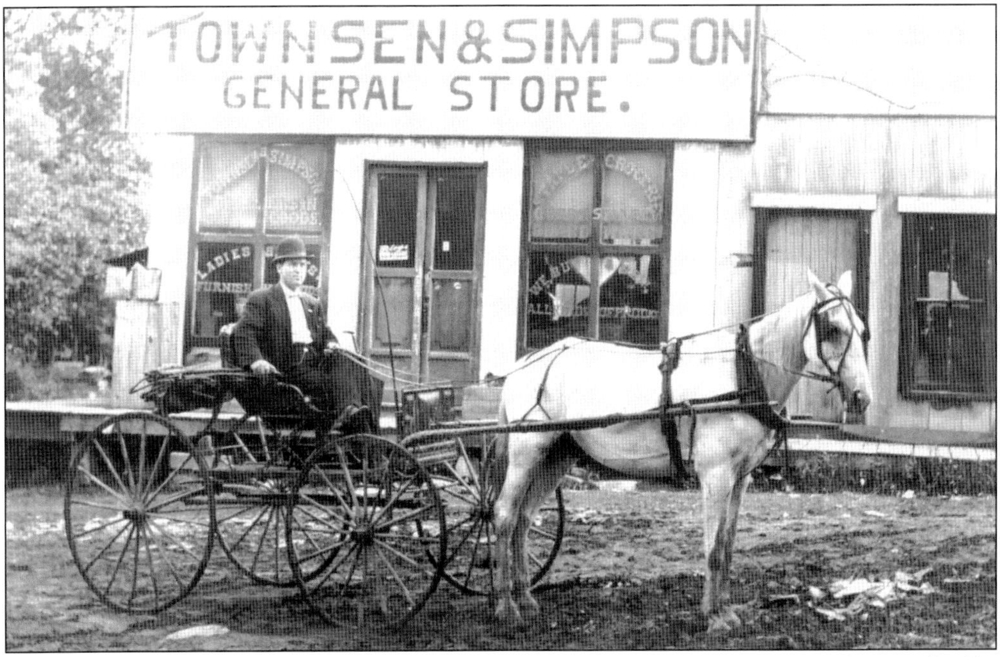

The first post office in Barbour County was established in 1825 and was located in Hoffsville, a community named for postmaster Hansen Hoff. At the time, Hoffsville was still a part of Harrison County. In this photo, A.C. Wilson, who lived in Nestorville, is delivering mail to the Boulder general store and post office. (Courtesy Amanza Nitz.)

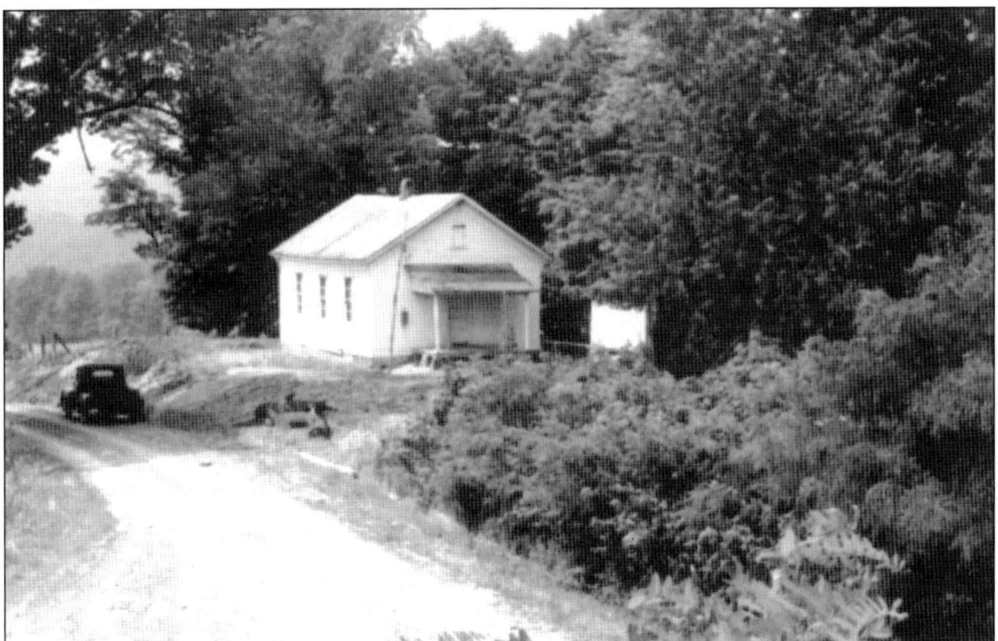

The Mt. Morris school was established in 1839, when students met in a log church. The schoolhouse was erected in 1869. Early pupils were enrolled on a subscription basis, patrons paying a "master." Records indicate that one such early Barbour County school met for a 65-day term with 4 patrons and 14 pupils. (Courtesy Peggy Robinson.)

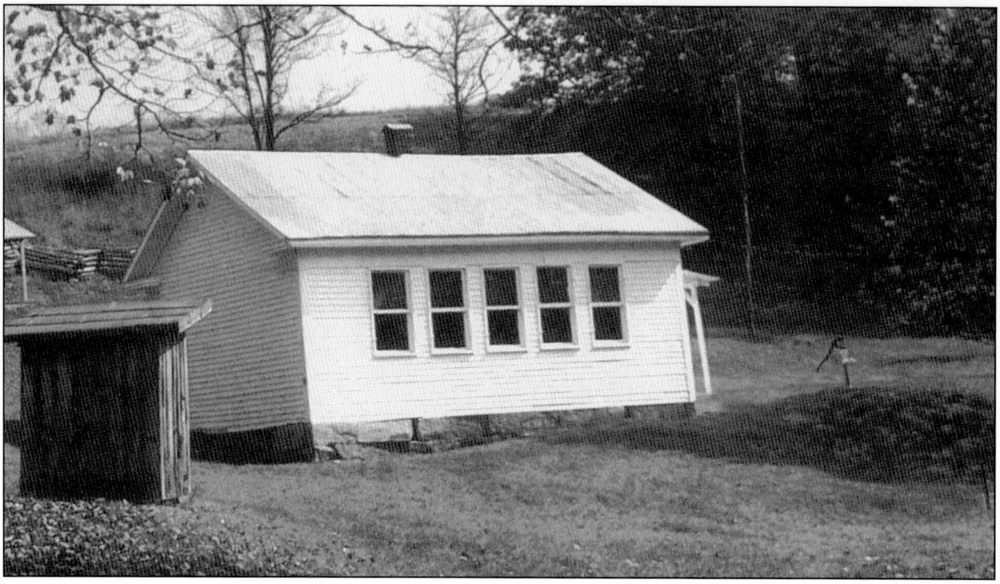

The first free (non-subscription) school in Barbour County was organized as the Campbell School near the present site of Audra State Park. The building was moved in 1881 to the Mitchell farm, then to the Campbell farm. In 1974 Elza and Nola Wilson undertook restoration of the building and had it moved in 1992 to the campus of Alderson-Broaddus College. Mr. Wilson attended the Campbell School. (Courtesy Arnout Hyde.)

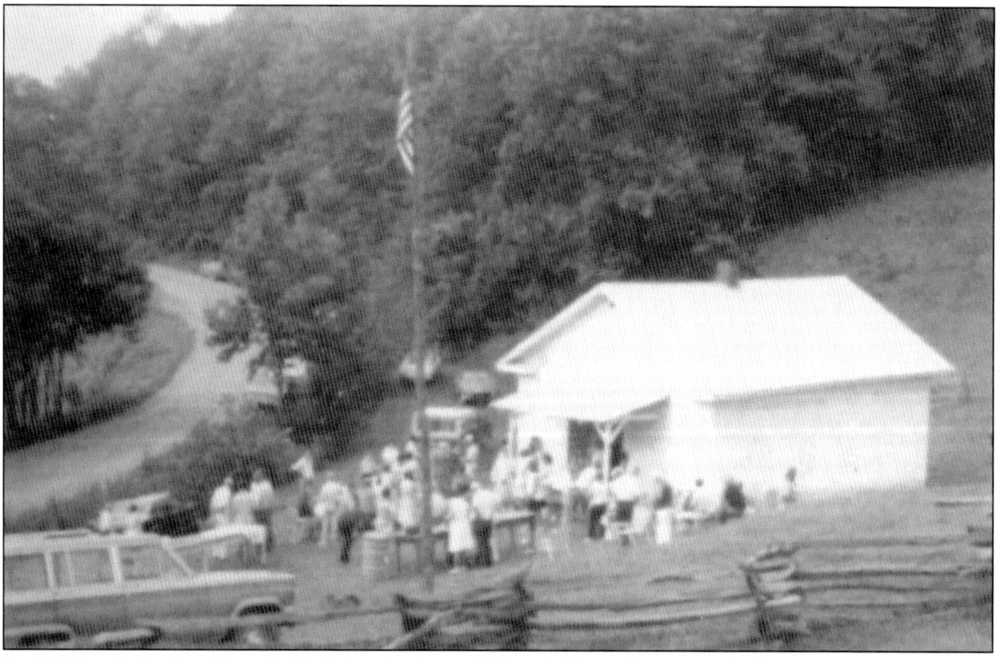

In 1977, while the Campbell School was still located on the Campbell farm, a homecoming was held. Many of the former students attended. The present building still holds a Burnside stove with an inscription indicating that it was made at a foundry in Philippi. Also located in the school is the first radio to appear in the Arden area. Nearby residents came to the school to listen to the inauguration of Herbert Hoover in 1929.

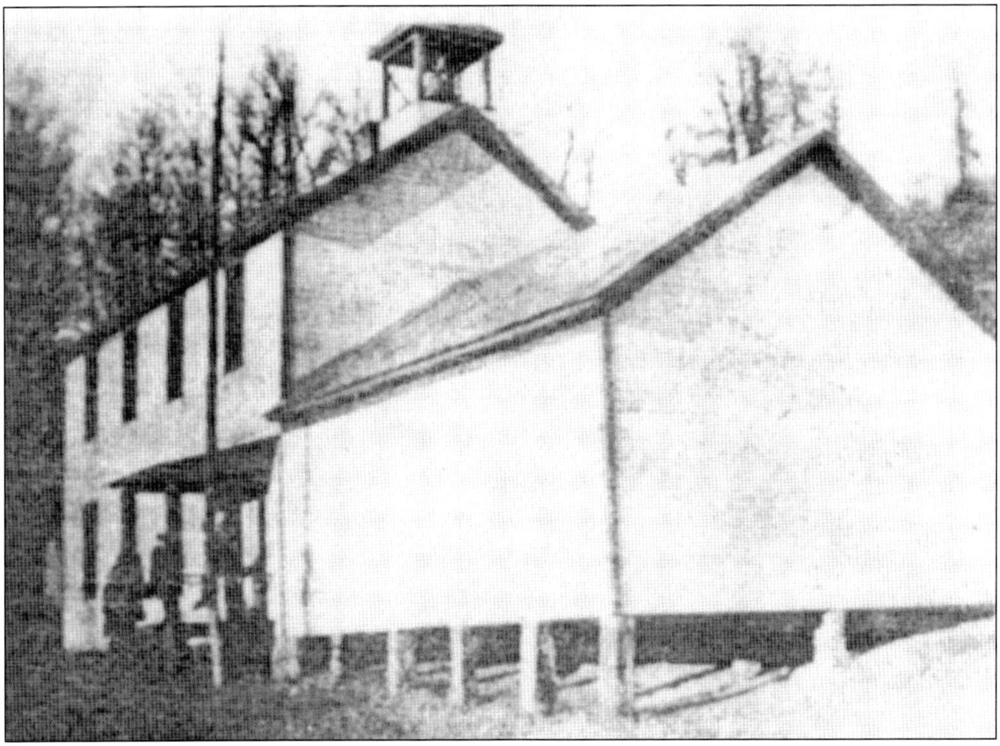

Typical of schools in most coal towns, the company-owned Century School was the starting point for many individuals who eventually entered professions such as medicine, law, and education. (Courtesy Nancy Streets.)

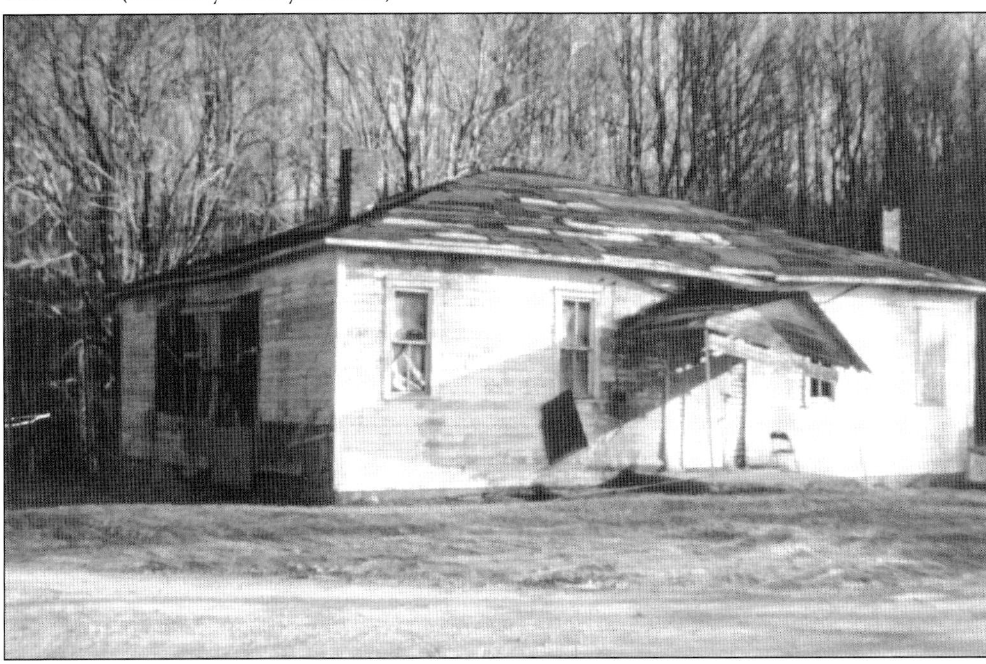

Nothing remains of the Clemtown School, which many residents of Barbour County once attended. (Courtesy Patty Marsh.)

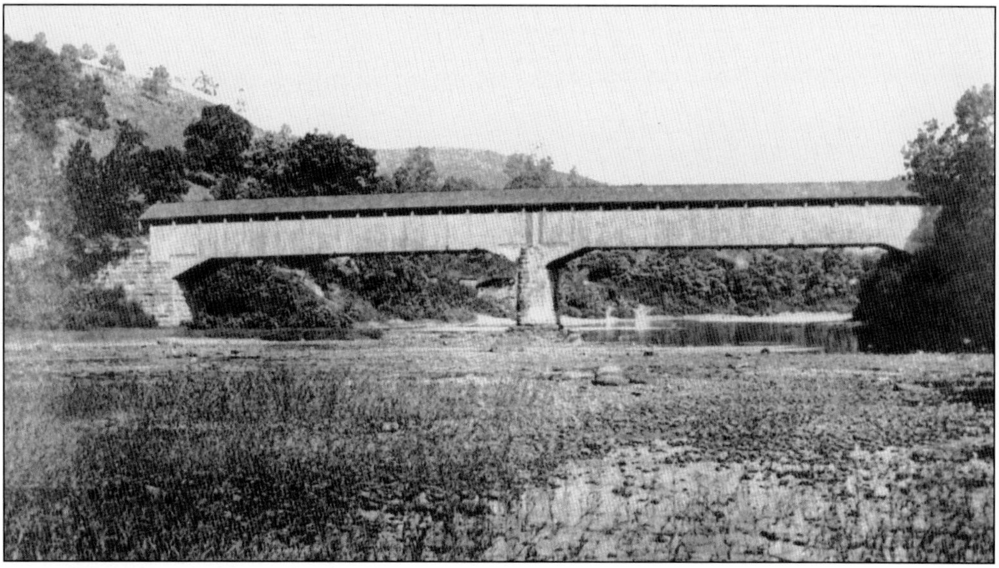

One of the most significant landmarks in all of northcentral West Virginia is the covered bridge in Philippi. Designed and built by Lemuel Chenoweth, it was completed in 1852 and for many years has been the only covered bridge still serving as a state highway. The bridge did not originally have an outside walkway, so pedestrians had to walk through the bridge itself. This photo was taken sometime before 1908. (Courtesy Joe Mattaliano.)

For every horse and rider	10c
For every led or driven horse	05c
For all 2 or 4 wheeled wagons drawn by 1 horse	20c
For carry-alls or Jersey Wagons without springs, drawn by 2 horses	25c
For all carriages or wagons with springs, drawn by 2 horses	35c
For every stage drawn by 2 or 3 horses	45c
For every stage drawn by 4 horses	50c
For empty cart drawn by 1 animal	05c
For cart with lading and every empty wagon	10c
For wagon with lading	25c
For animal drawing such cart or wagon	05c
For every head of cattle	01½c
For score of sheep	05c
For score of hogs	10c

A tollgate was placed at the east end of the covered bridge, and tolls, as indicated in this list, were collected as late as 1906. (Courtesy Joe Mattaliano.)

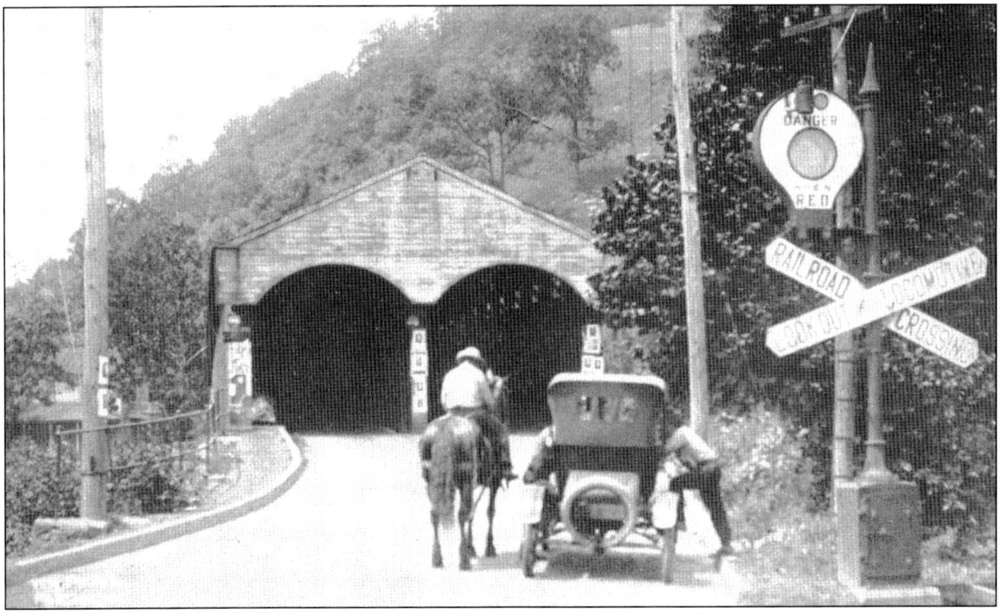

The covered bridge has witnessed many types of transportation from pedestrians to horses to buggies to Model-Ts to motorcycles and commercial trucks—provided that the trucks were not more than 12 feet in height. After the rebuilding of the bridge following a 1989 fire, large trucks were precluded and have had to use the bridge downstream. (Courtesy Joe Mattaliano.)

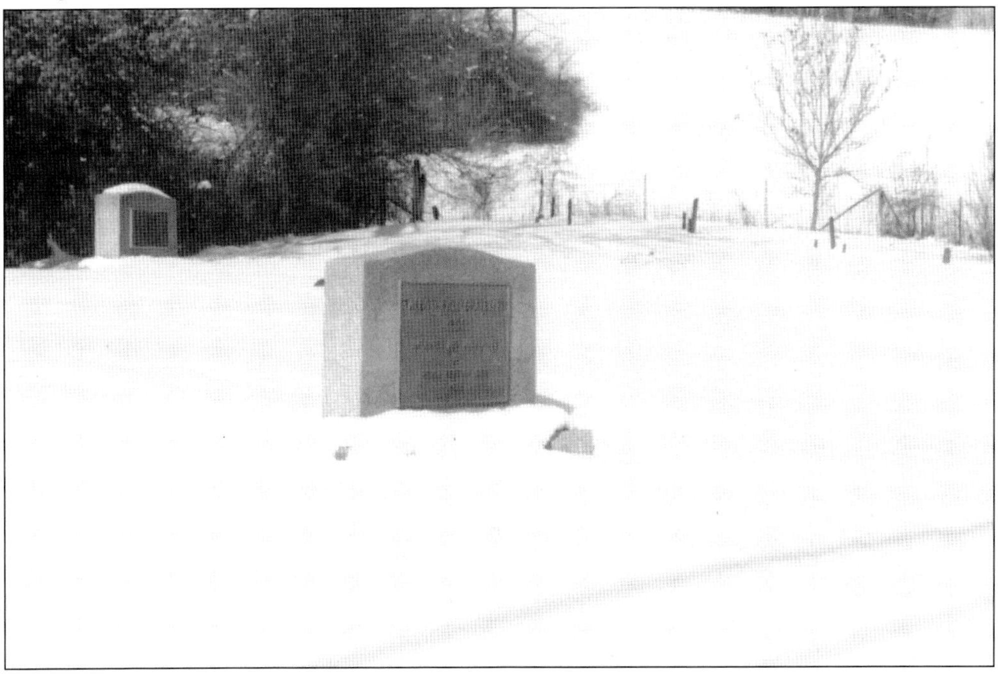

Near Volga on Route 119 is the Talbott-Hall Graveyard, established in 1880 when Cotteral Talbott was buried there. One of the first settlers in Barbour County, he married Elizabeth Reger and established a home on the Buckhannon River. He drowned while trying to retrieve a deer he had shot from the river. The modern monument was placed and the cemetery is maintained by the Volga Ruritan Club. (Photo Carl Briggs.)

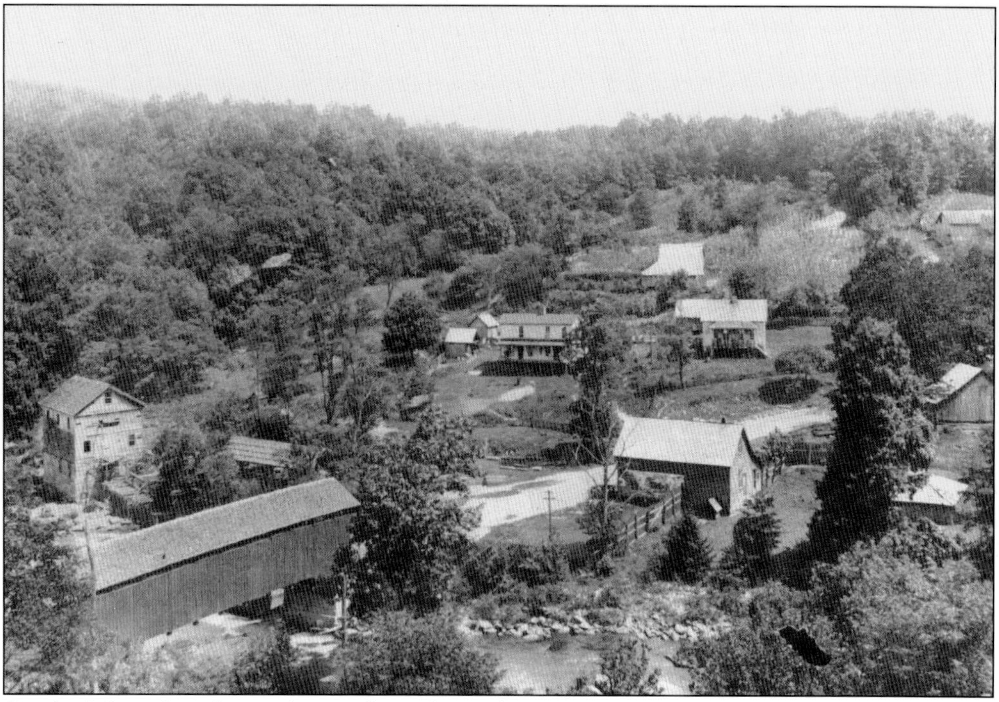

On the left in this photo taken early in the 20th century are a grain mill and a sawmill on the Middle Fork River in what is now Audra State Park. On the right beyond the covered bridge, which washed away in the 1940s, is the general store. In 1892 the land at the top of the photo was sold by the Jacob Hall family to the Joe Sandridge family. (Courtesy Elza Wilson.)

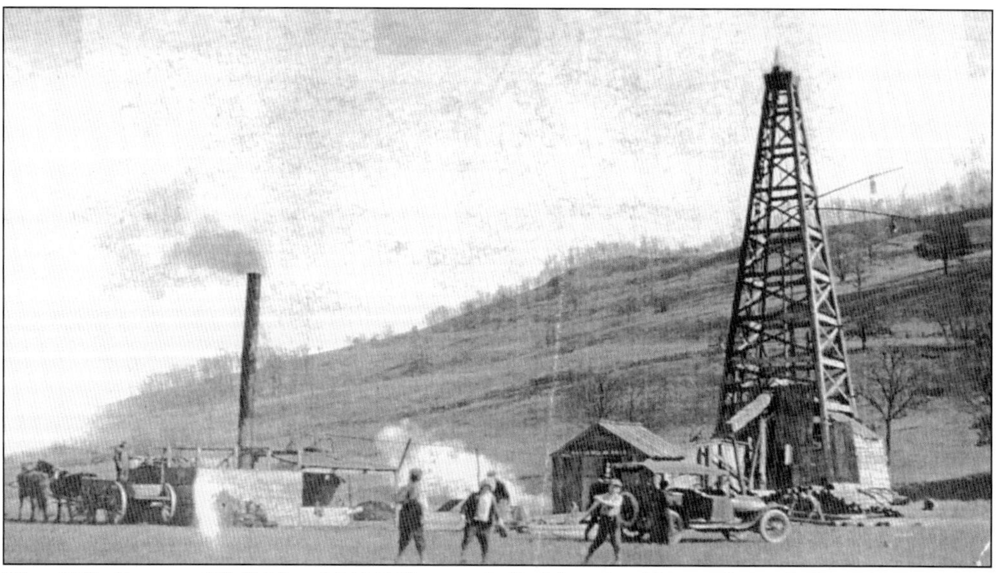

The J.W. Benson Well No. 3612(10) was drilled by the Hope Natural Gas Company at Overfield. In this 1915 photo, the derrick is being manned by Junior Davis, Forest Stuart, Charlie Stewart, and John Benson. Unloading coal from the wagon is Doris Hickman. At 4,570 feet, it was probably the deepest gas well in West Virginia at the time. Producing for 68 years, the well was plugged in 1983. (Courtesy Elizabeth Benson Talbot.)

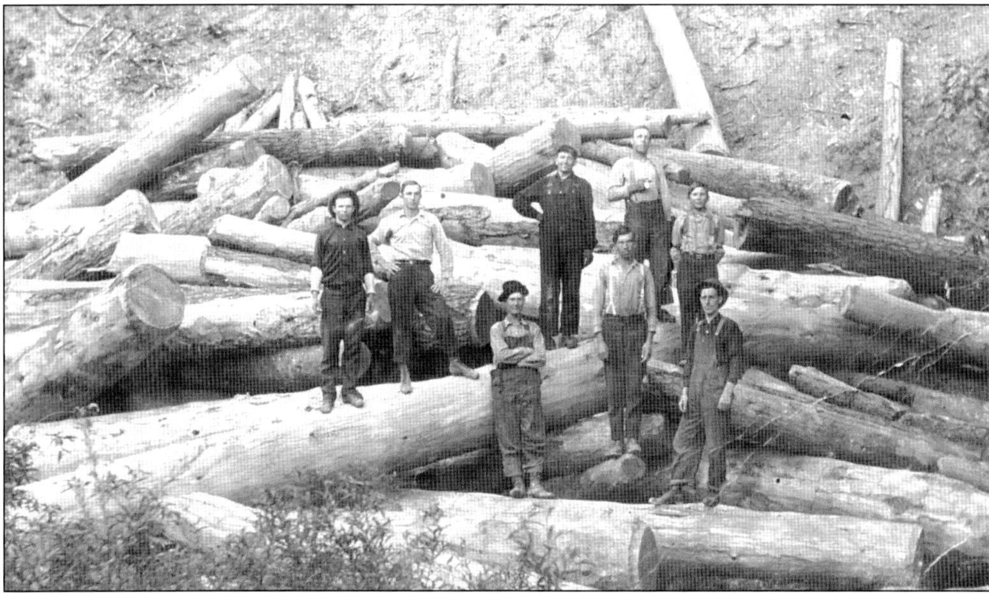

Timber was plentiful in Barbour County, and the logs were sizable and straight, as evidenced in this early-20th-century photo. Generally, the logs were transported out of the forest and to the river by means of grappling hooks and skids. (Courtesy H.A. "Red" Payne.)

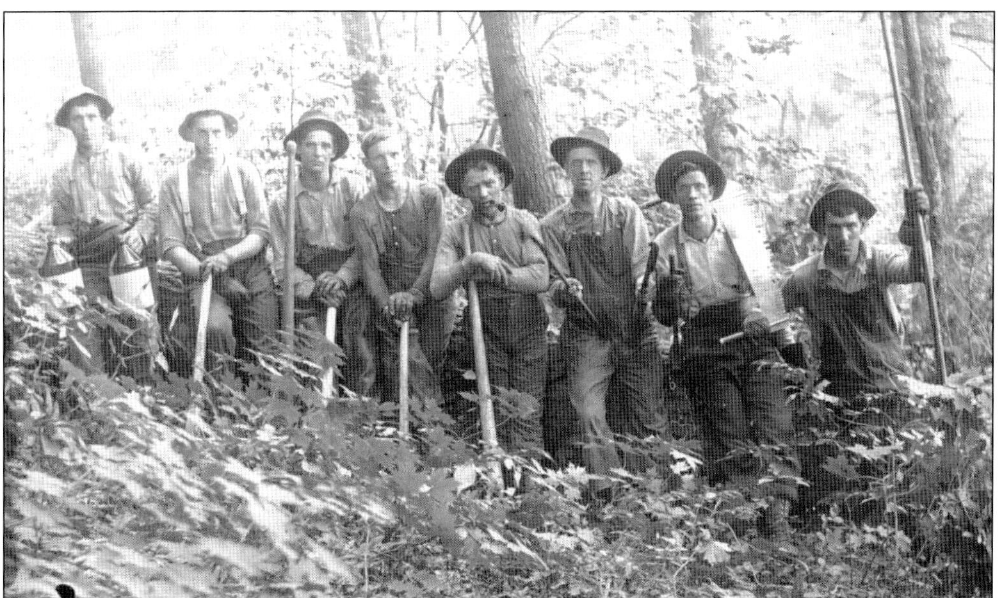

This photo of a timber crew, taken soon after the turn of the century, includes Charley Ervin, father-in-law of current Belington resident H.A. "Red" Payne. Note the jugs in the hands of the man on the far left. (Courtesy H.A. "Red" Payne.)

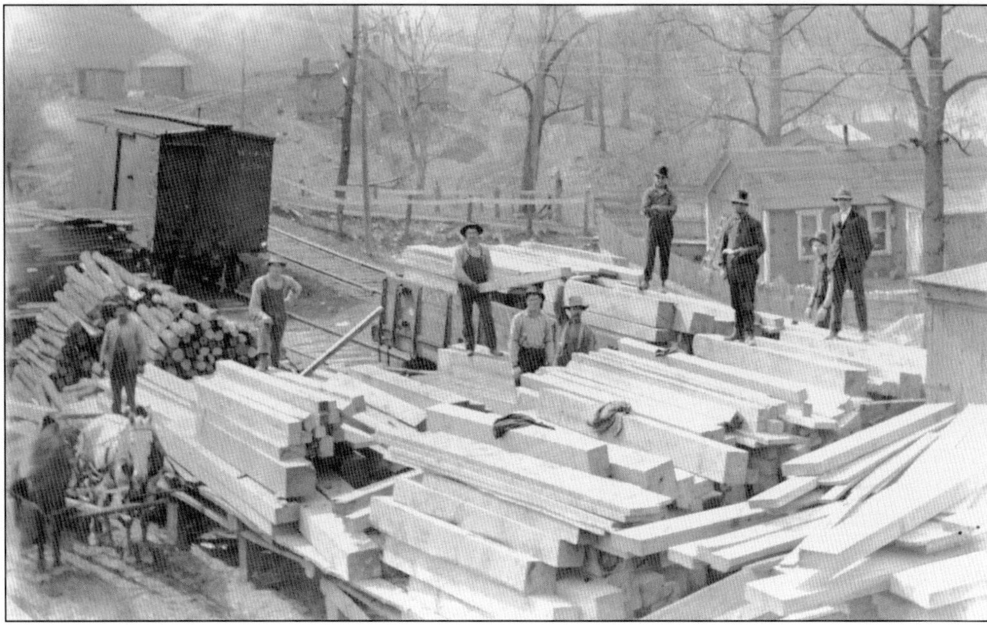

One of the very successful businesses in early Boulder was the lumber mill, the product of which is pictured here. Area farmers came by cart and horseback along bridle paths to trade and make purchases. (Courtesy Amanza Nitz.)

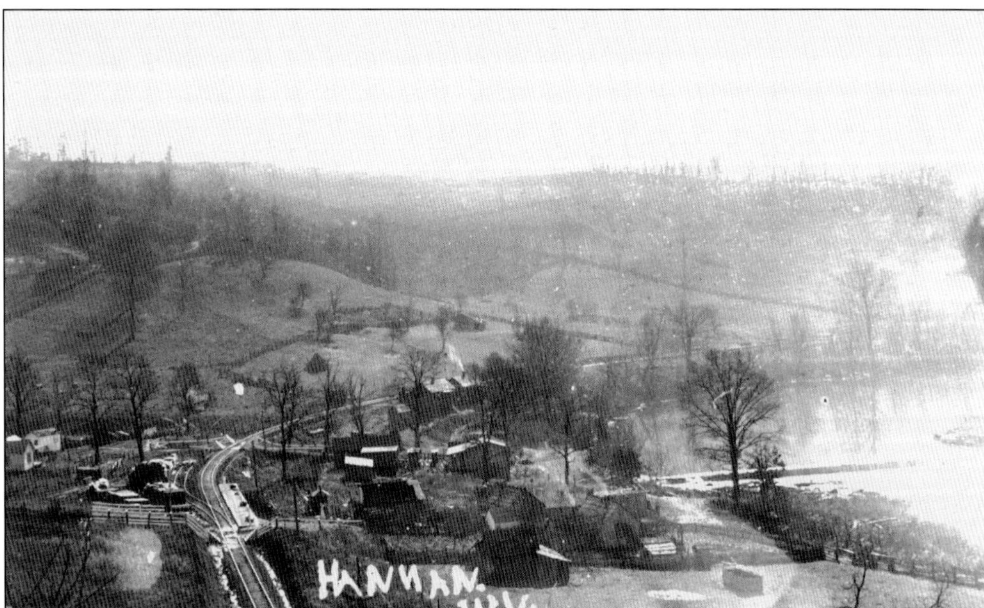

Before being named Boulder and before the bridge was built in 1904, the community was called Thorn and then Hanna or Hannah. Even now the community carries two names—Boulder and Rangoon. (Courtesy Amanza Nitz.)

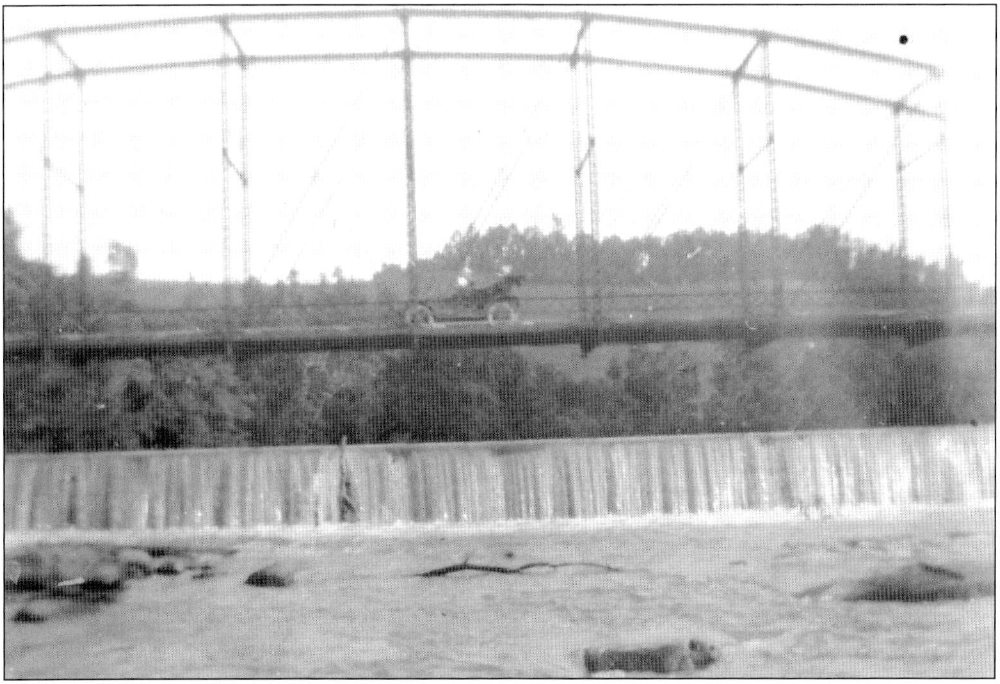

Under the bridge which spanned the Buckhannon River at Boulder was a small dam. It supplied energy for the grain mill built by the area's first settler, John Bozarth, who brought his family by horseback from Virginia before 1795. (Courtesy Amanza Nitz.)

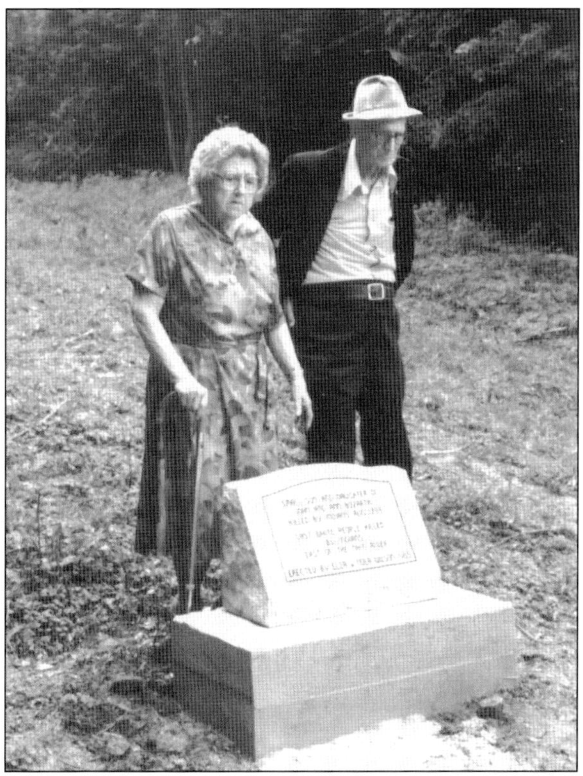

This photo of Leona and Howard Cool was taken in 1985 on their property near the Buckhannon River and the Boulder bridge. Elza and Nola Wilson donated the monument, which honors the two children of John Bozarth who were killed by Native Americans at this location in 1795. (Courtesy Elza Wilson.)

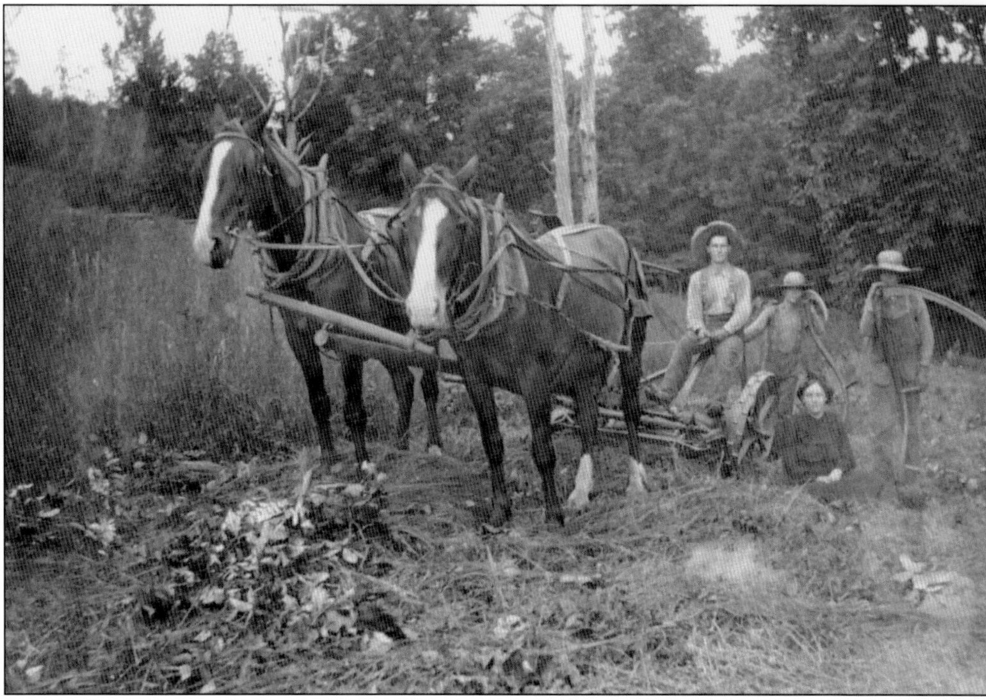

Moatsville was named after the Moats family, some of whom are pictured here. With the team of horses that belonged to their father are Burke, Eula, Arthur, and Martin. The young people seem to have been cutting "filth." (Courtesy Peggy Robinson.)

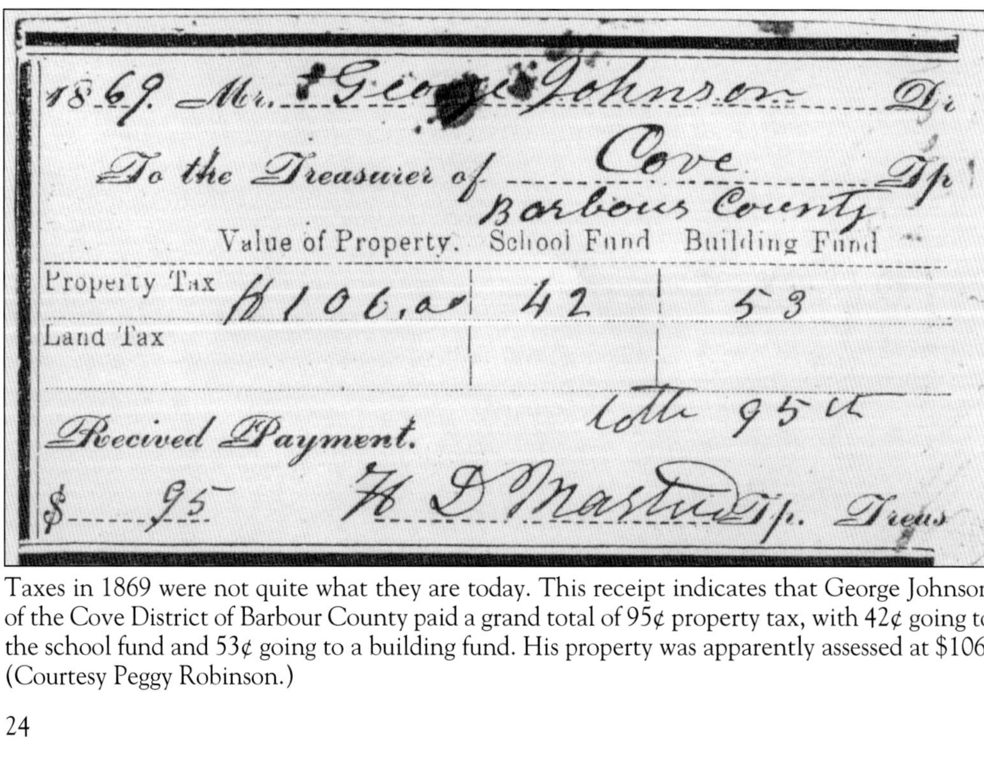

1869 Mr. George Johnson Dr

To the Treasurer of Cove Tp

Barbour County

	Value of Property.	School Fund	Building Fund
Property Tax	$106.00	42	53
Land Tax			

Received Payment. total 95 ct

$ 95 H D Martin Tp. Treas

Taxes in 1869 were not quite what they are today. This receipt indicates that George Johnson of the Cove District of Barbour County paid a grand total of 95¢ property tax, with 42¢ going to the school fund and 53¢ going to a building fund. His property was apparently assessed at $106. (Courtesy Peggy Robinson.)

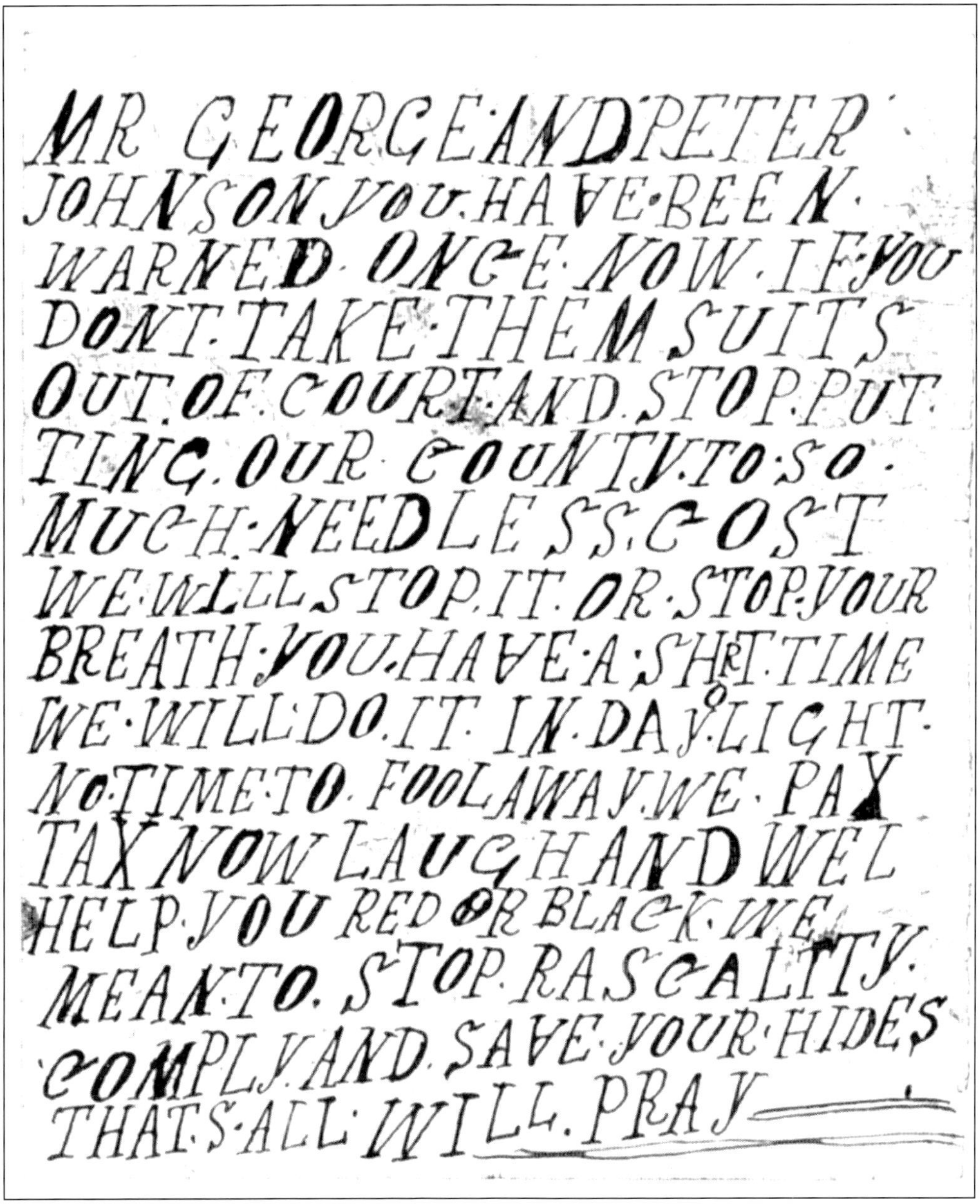

MR GEORGE AND PETER
JOHNSON YOU HAVE BEEN
WARNED ONCE NOW IF YOU
DONT TAKE THEM SUITS
OUT OF COURT AND STOP PUT
TING OUR COUNTY TO SO
MUCH NEEDLESS COST
WE WILL STOP IT OR STOP YOUR
BREATH YOU HAVE A SHRT TIME
WE WILL DO IT IN DAYLIGHT
NO TIME TO FOOL AWAY WE PAY
TAX NOW LAUGH AND WEL
HELP YOU RED OR BLACK WE
MEAN TO STOP RASCALITY
COMPLY AND SAVE YOUR HIDES
THATS ALL WILL PRAY

The exact nature of the problem resulting in this handwritten threat is not known, but it appears that George Johnson was suing one of his neighbors. The entire note reads, "MR. GEORGE AND PETER JOHNSON YOU HAVE BEEN WARNED ONCE NOW IF YOU DON'T TAKE THEM SUITS OUT OF COURT AND STOP PUTTING OUR COUNTY TO SO MUCH NEEDLESS COST WE WILL STOP IT OR STOP YOUR BREATH YOU HAVE A SHORT TIME WE WILL DO IT IN DAYLIGHT NO TIME TO FOOL AWAY WE PAY TAX NOW LAUGH AND WEL HELP YOU RED OR BLACK WE MEAN TO STOP RASCALITY COMPLY AND SAVE YOUR HIDES THATS ALL WILL PRAY OLD MOATS LOOK OUT WE MEAN YOU TOO U HOG THIEF FIX FOR DEATH." (Courtesy Peggy Robinson.)

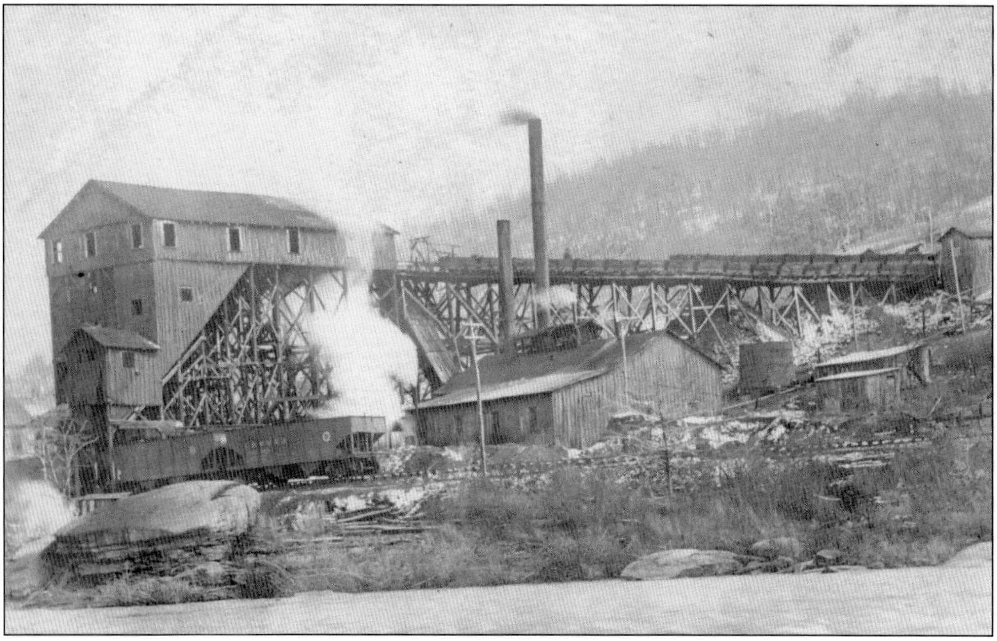

In the early part of the 20th century there were seven mines operating in the Arden-Moatsville area. This 1910 photo indicates the considerable size of one of the operations. (Courtesy Patty Marsh.)

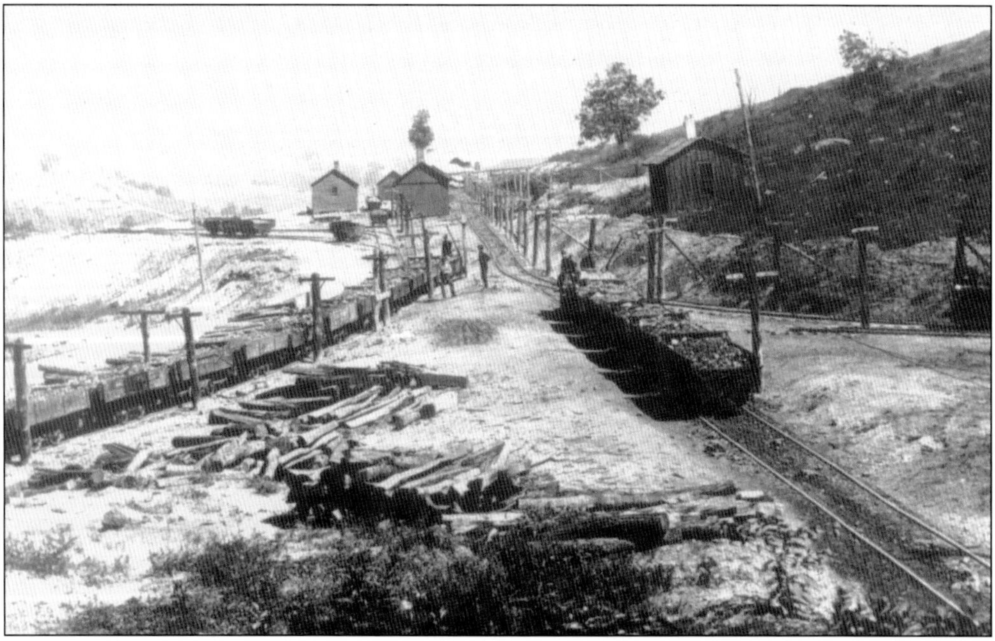

The Abbott Mines also functioned early in the century in the Belington-Junior area. Mine timbers are stacked in the foreground of this photo. (Courtesy Stephen Rautner.)

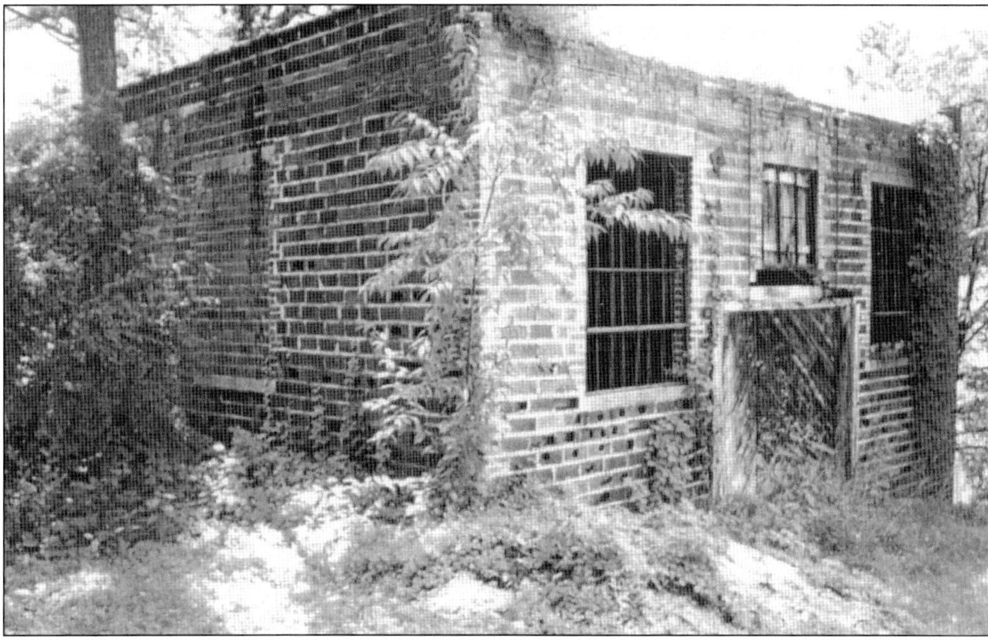

In many coal towns or "camps" the companies constructed and equipped "show buildings." This structure in Century housed a movie theater, a dance hall, a pool room, a store, and space for meetings. (Courtesy Nancy Streets.)

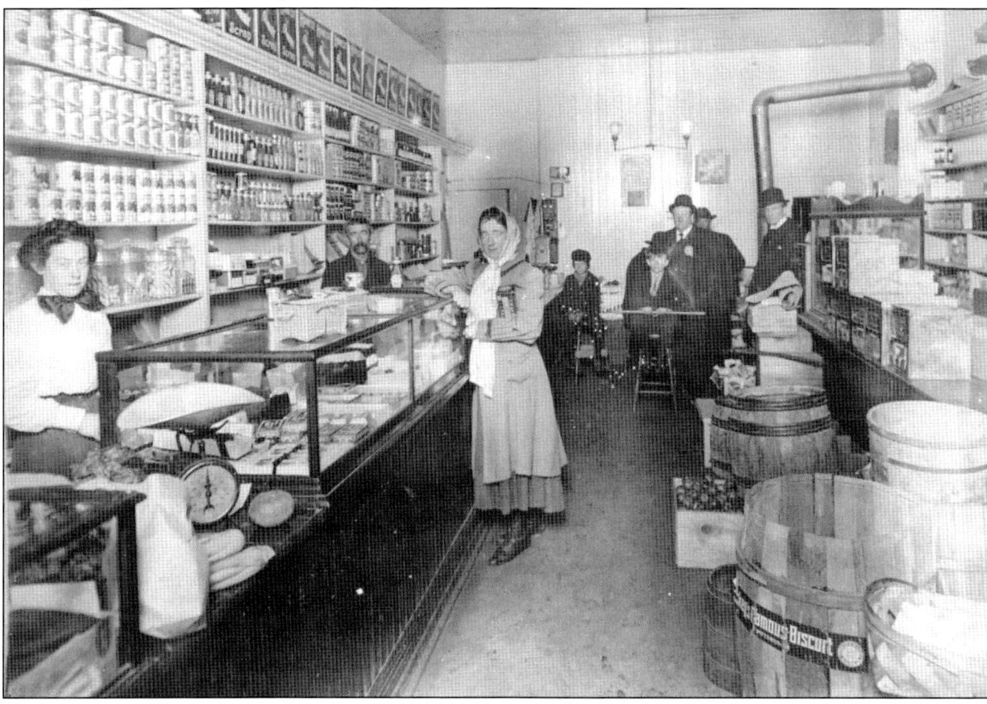

This picture of Scotts' Grocery in Philippi, a thriving business at the time, was taken in 1910. Other businesses in Barbour County included brick plants in both Belington and Philippi, a livery stable run by Walter Criss, a soda bottling plant, four or more blacksmith shops, and at least one pottery. (Courtesy Joe Mattaliano.)

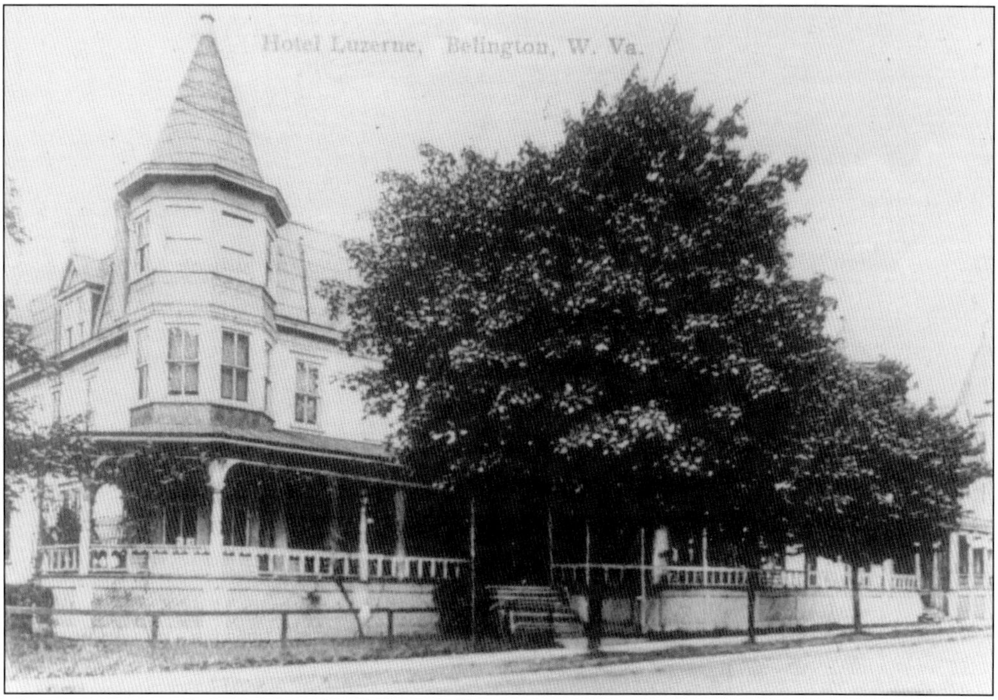

The Lucerne Hotel, once owned and operated by the Brandon family in Belington, was a showplace and a favorite meeting place for residents and travelers alike. (Courtesy Stephen Rautner.)

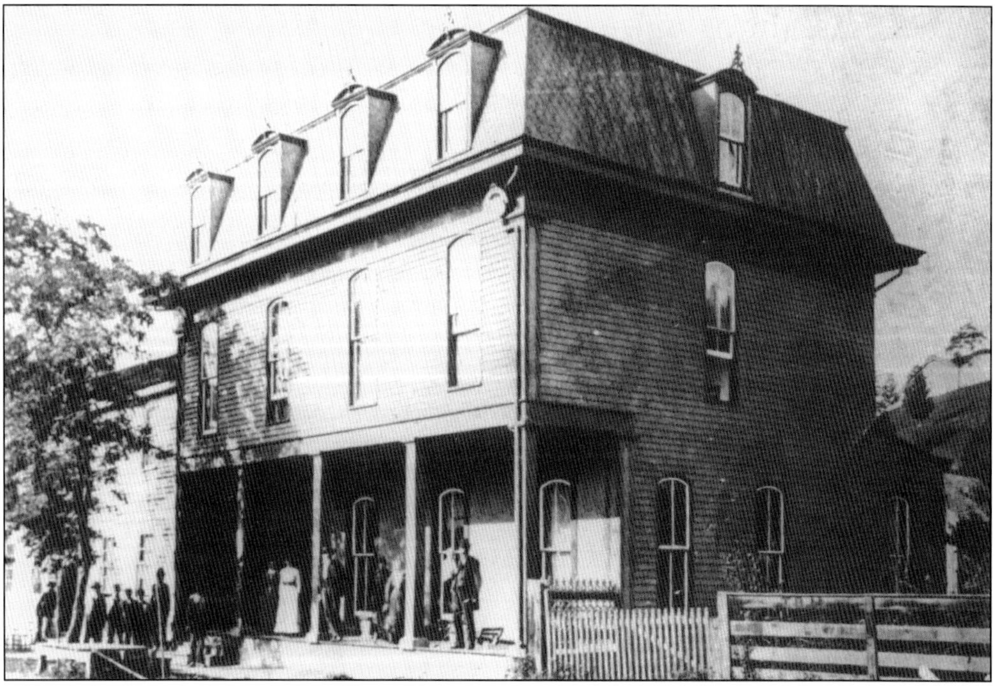
The Valley Hotel or Tygart's Valley Hotel, victim of fire in 1900, was the scene of numerous celebrations and countless business deals in the early days of Barbour County.

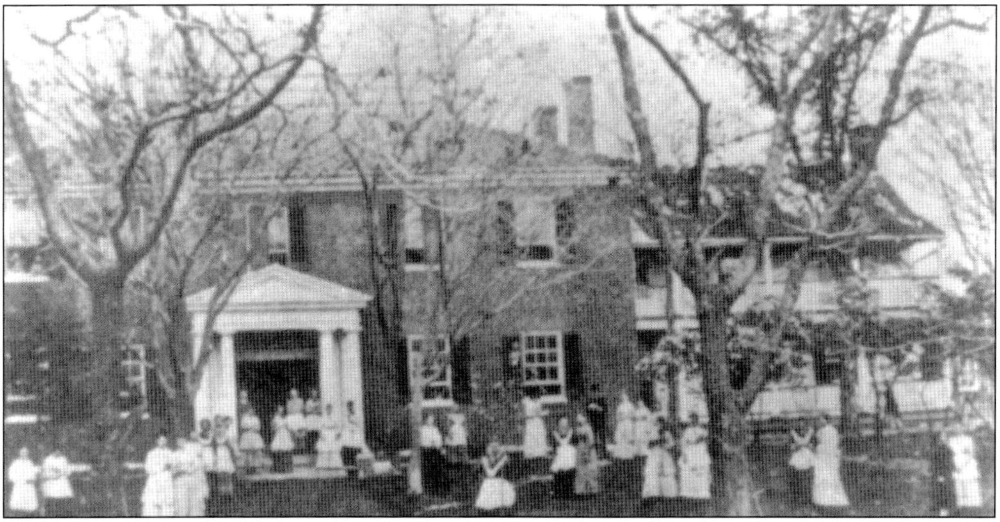

Broaddus Female College originated in Winchester, Virginia, under the leadership of E.J. Willis. Constructed in 1834 by Peter Louck, this building was named Sensery Mansion in honor of Jacob Sensery, its second owner. From 1873 to 1876 it housed Broaddus Female College. The building later became Hill Crest Nursing Home. Most recently, it serves as a rehabilitation center and is called Edgewood.

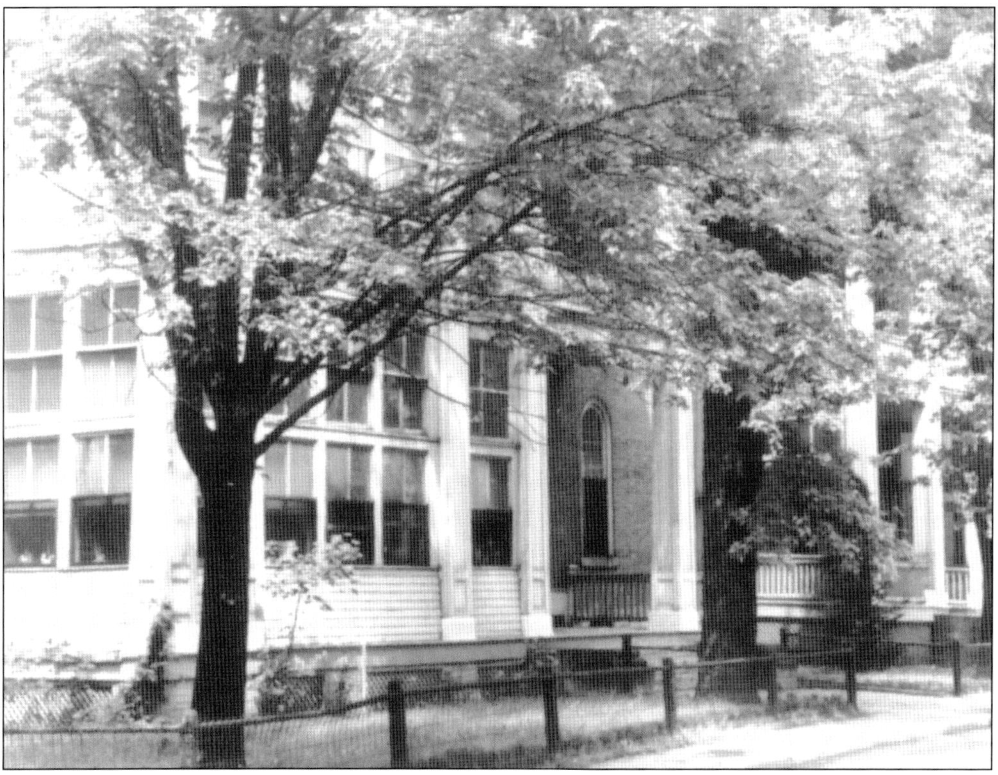

In 1876 Broaddus Female College moved to the Bartlett Hotel, also known as the National Hotel, in Clarksburg. The college stayed in that location, occupying the hotel and several other buildings until moving to Philippi in 1908.

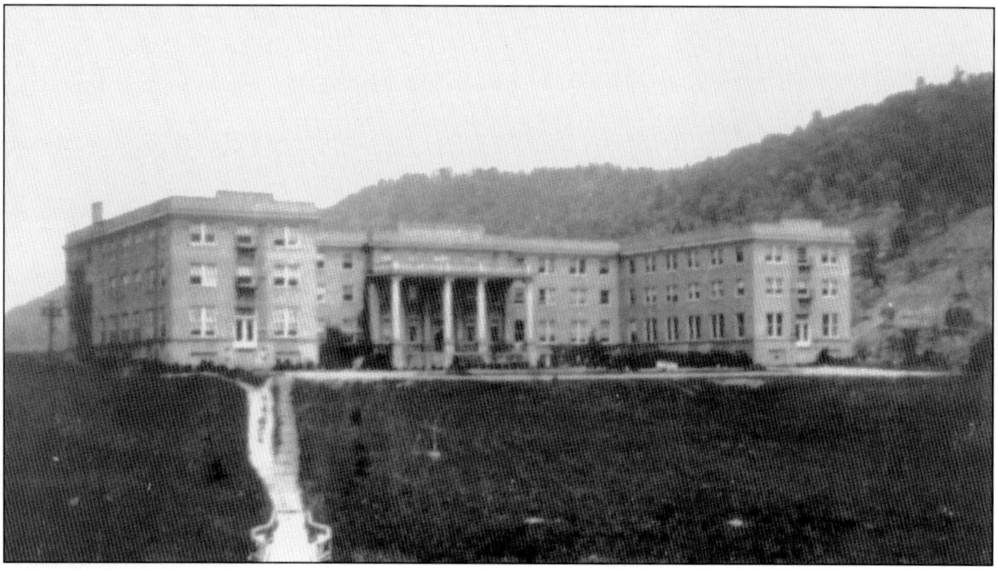

Broaddus Female College was one of two predecessors of Alderson-Broaddus College. The other was Alderson Junior College, founded in 1901 in Alderson, West Virginia. The entrance to the college, with its massive columns and broad portico, closely resembled the design used in the construction of Old Main Hall on the Philippi campus where Alderson and Broaddus combined operations in 1932.

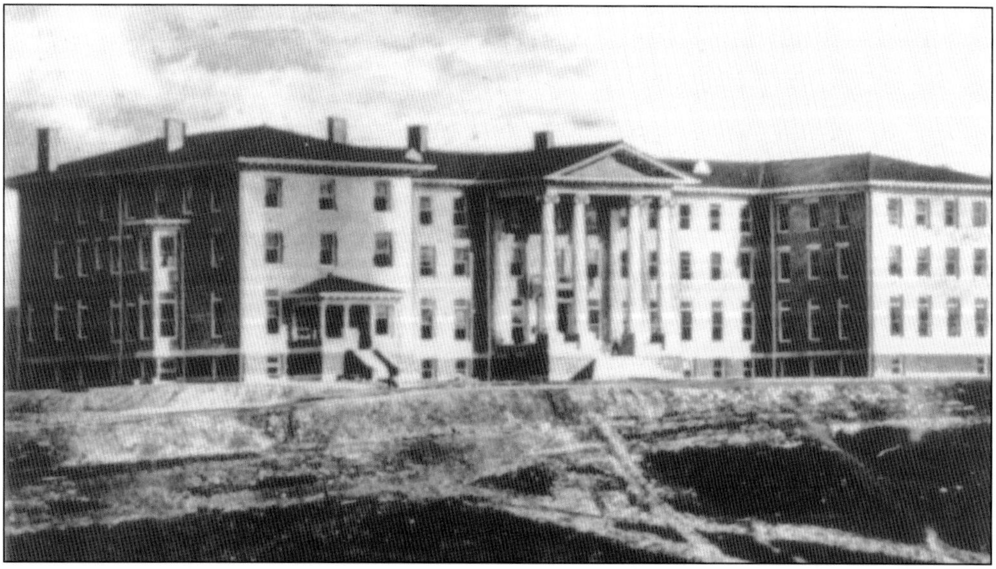

The first building constructed on the Philippi campus of what was to become Alderson-Broaddus College was Old Main in 1909. Outstanding features included stained-glass windows and a Y-shaped dark oak staircase from the lobby to the second floor. The building was in use from 1932 to 1977, when it burned.

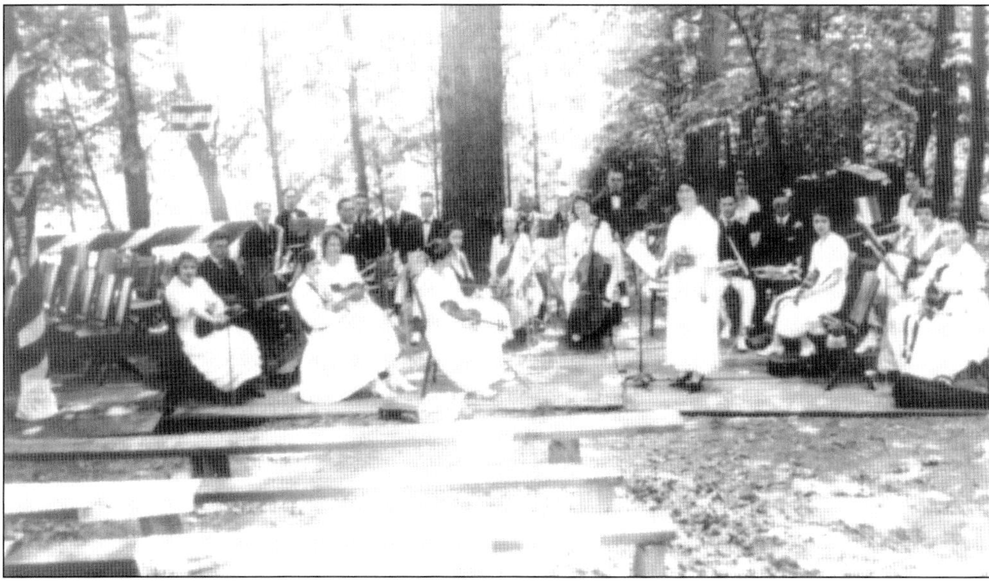

Before the building of Broaddus Hospital, the site was used as an amphitheater. This was the location of many college and community cultural events.

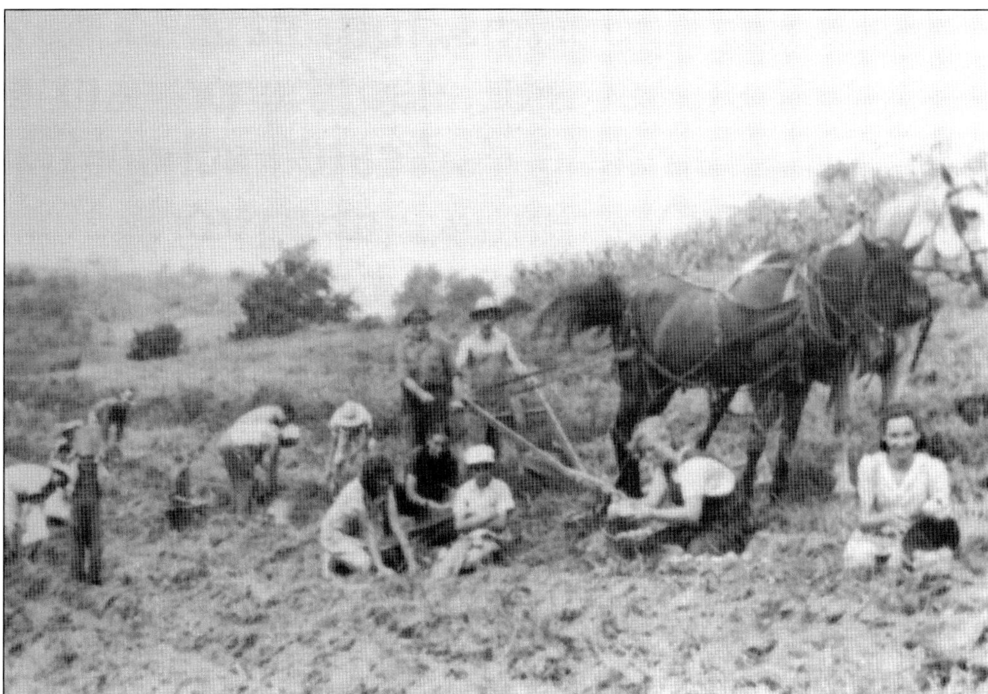

Members of the Shiloh Church, in addition to worshiping together, have worked on "The Lord's Acre." Established near Kasson in 1845, the congregation ordains its own ministers and has built and maintained and remodeled the church building.

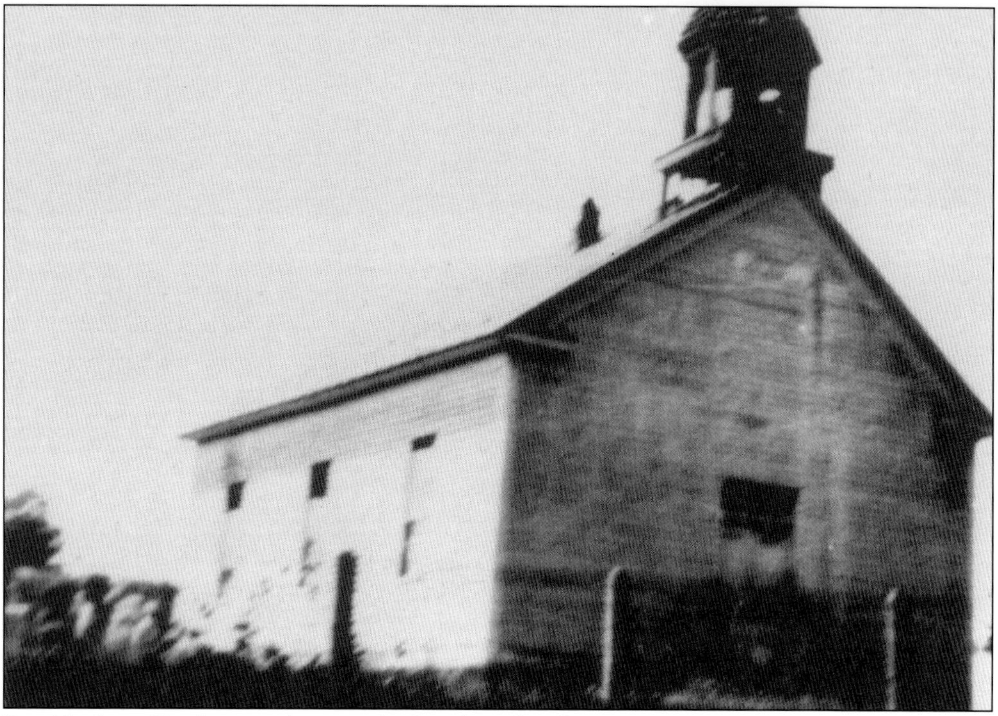

Dr. Abraham Hershman, who preached at the schoolhouse in Tacy for a number of years, was a physician. In 1873 people of the community used local lumber and wooden pegs to build a frame structure on land donated by Andrew and Rachel Stalnaker. The new building was named the Cross Roads Church. The congregation soon identified itself as United Methodist. A red brick building replaced the frame structure in 1953.

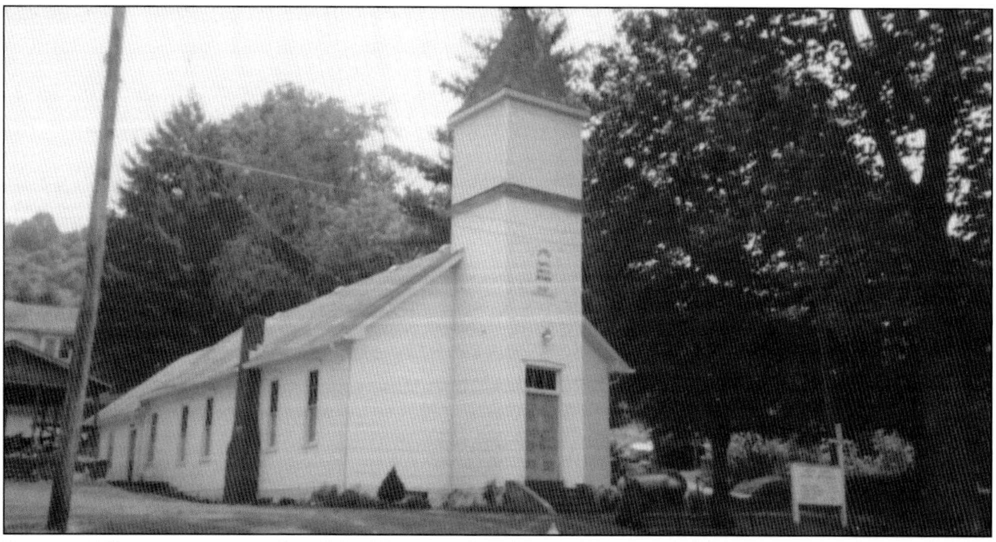

For two full centuries, people of the Pleasant Creek area have attended services at the Methodist church. Jedediah Sayre donated the land in 1800, and a log building was constructed, and served until 1822. In 1900 John Chenoweth was authorized to design and build the fourth and current structure. Gravestones in the adjoining cemetery date back to the mid-1800s. (Courtesy Patty Marsh.)

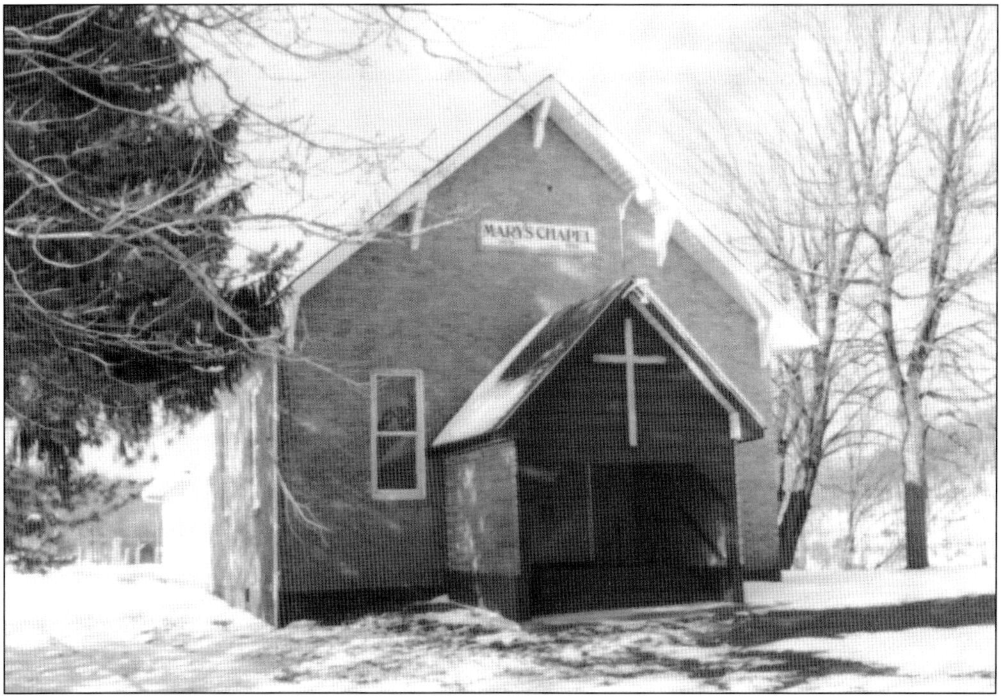

Old churches still in the United Methodist charge include Mary's Chapel. It is believed that when the Tygart Dam was constructed, cemeteries at Stonehouse and lower Pleasant Creek were moved to the grounds of the Pleasant Creek church and Mary's Chapel. (Courtesy Patty Marsh.)

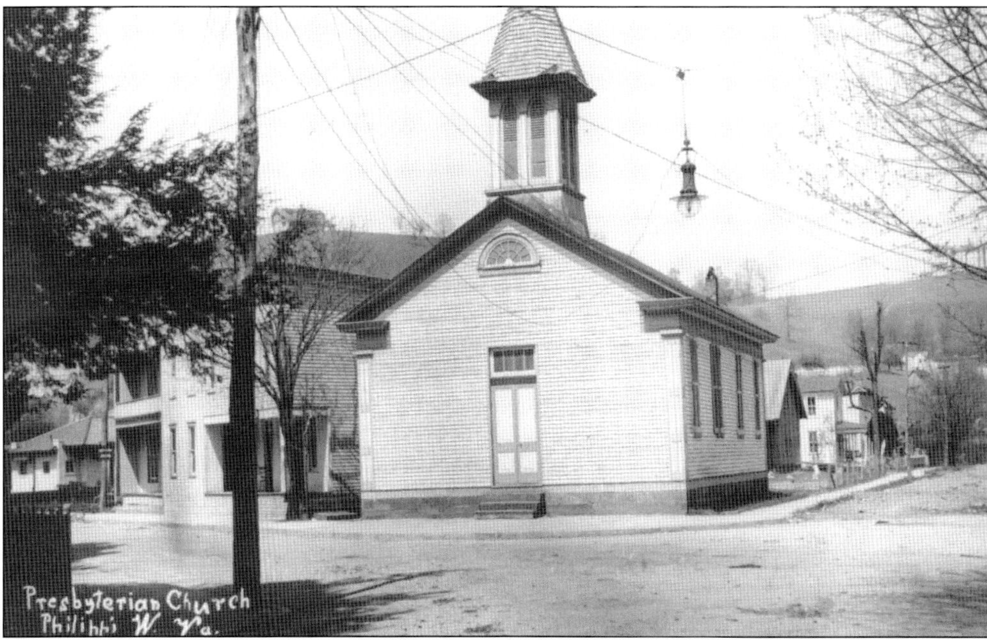

Remodeled in recent years, the Presbyterian church is the oldest church building in Philippi. The logs used were hewn by some of the same laborers who worked on the covered bridge. Construction began in 1873 and was completed in 1876.

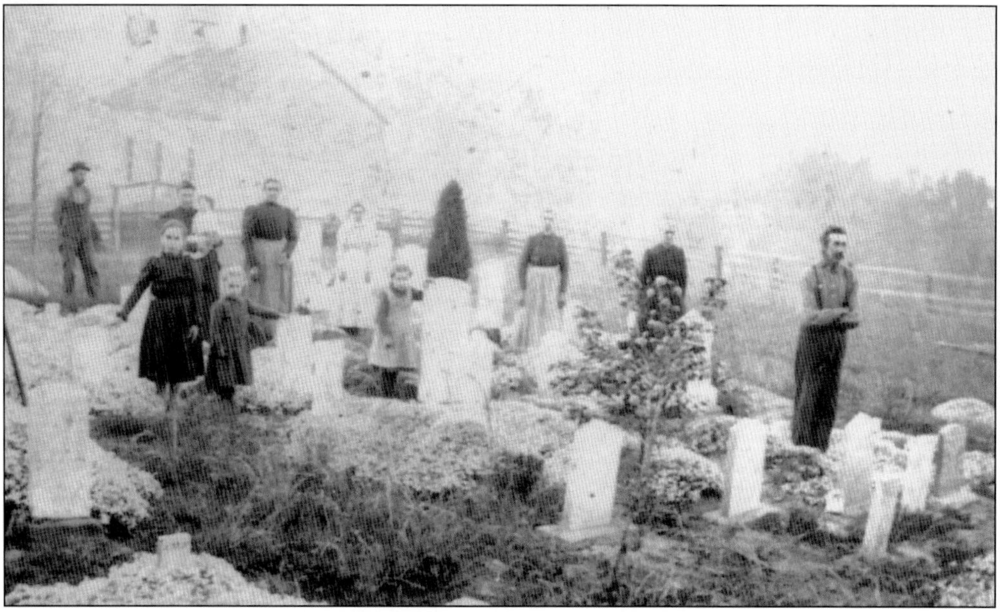

St. Johns' Evangelical United Brethren Church, still functional, is located high on a hill near Bootjack, beyond Tacy. Gravestones date back to the early 19th century. (Courtesy Peggy Robinson.)

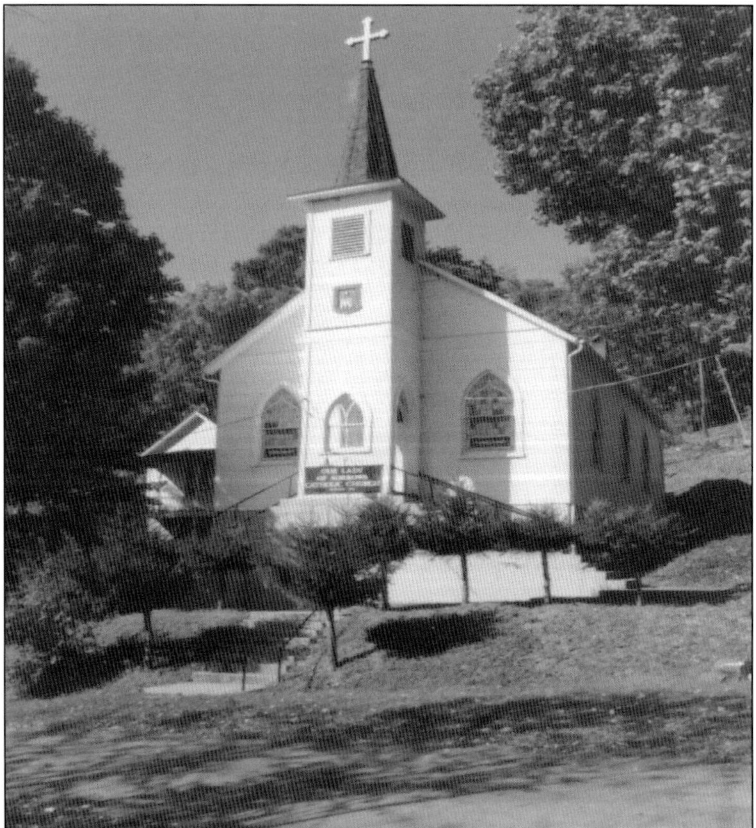

Unlike other coal town churches, which were built and owned by the companies, Our Lady of Sorrows, the first church constructed in Century (1902), was built and owned by its members. Although services are no longer held in the building, it is being restored and is considered a historic landmark. This photo was taken in 1982. (Courtesy Nancy Streets.)

Two

What Has Happened

Most residents of Barbour County would claim that the most significant event to occur in this area was the first land battle of the Civil War on June 3, 1861. The massacres of the 17th century and the later withdrawal of the Native Americans, the "packing in" of the settlers by Sam Pringle and others around 1770, the establishment of the railroad in the 1880s, the development of roads, particularly the one which would become U.S. Route 250, the moving of Broaddus Institute and Alderson Junior College from Clarksburg and Alderson, WV, to Philippi, the building of the Myers Clinic and Broaddus Hospital, the periodic major floods, particularly that of 1985, the tornados of 1944 and 1948, the major fires of the 1970s and 1980s, the building of a highway to by-pass the covered bridge have been among the other major events to occur here.

One can only imagine the excitement caused by the installation of the first telephone lines, the opening of the first post office, the incredible advances brought about by the building of roads and railroad tracks, or the importance of clearing land, planting crops, and building schoolhouses.

Most important have been and continue to be the routine but stabilizing activities of everyday life. What seems significant at a given moment may be forgotten over time, or it may become a notable historic event. Only a few can ever be recorded adequately.

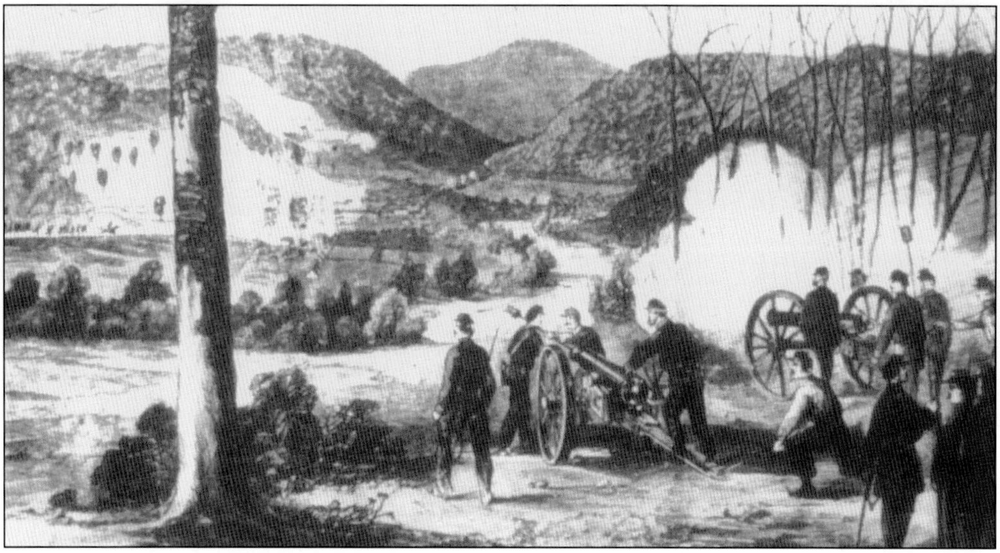

Hardly a matter of sophisticated military strategy, the first land battle of the Civil War reportedly began when Mrs. Thomas Humphreys fired a pistol at a fox in her chicken yard. Union troops that were camped on what was later called Battle Hill assumed that the war had begun and opened fire on Confederate troops camped in the valley. The Confederates retreated toward Beverly. A second encounter occurred in Philippi on March 20, 1862.

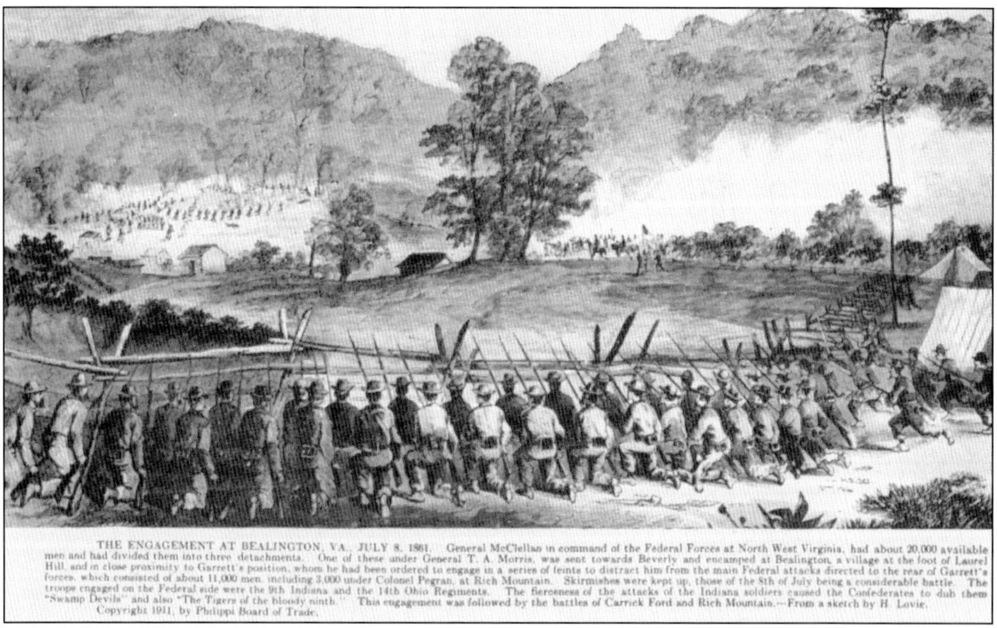

"The Engagement at Bealington, Va" took place on July 8, 1861. Union forces under McClellan took on Confederate forces headed by Garrett. Reportedly, the fierceness of the Indiana and Ohio soldiers caused Confederates to label the northerners "Swamp Devils" or "The Tigers of the Bloody Ninth." The battle of Rich Mountain soon followed this confrontation. (Courtesy Stephen Rautner.)

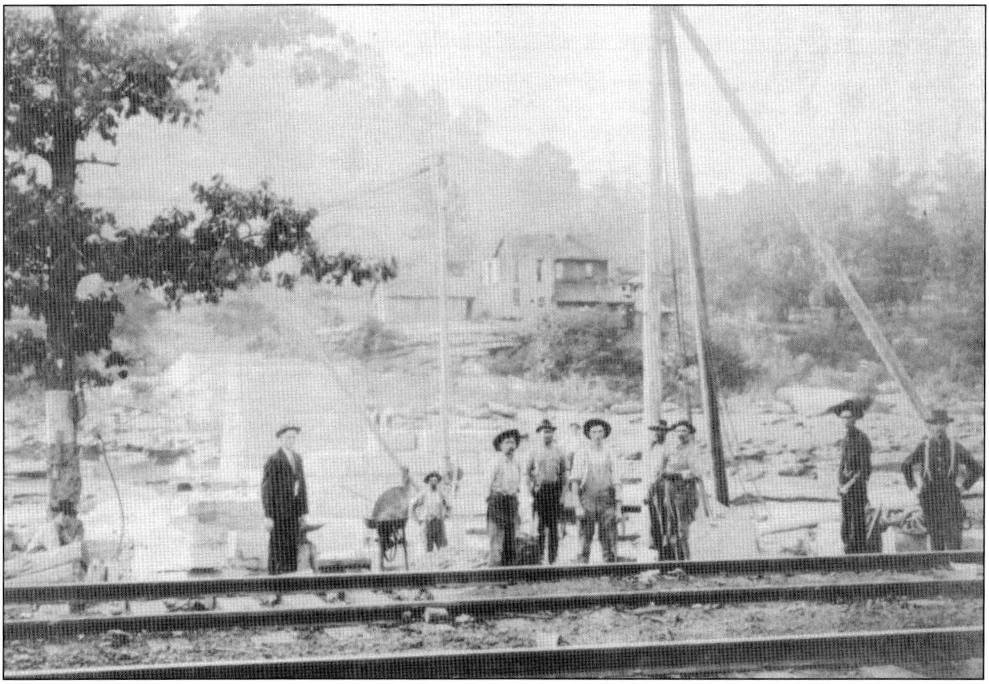

One of the most significant events in the history of any river community is the building of the first bridge. Until that occurs, individuals needing to cross the stream must travel to whatever bridge exists. This photo was taken in 1903 in Arden, some 7 miles from the Philippi bridge. (Courtesy Patty Marsh.)

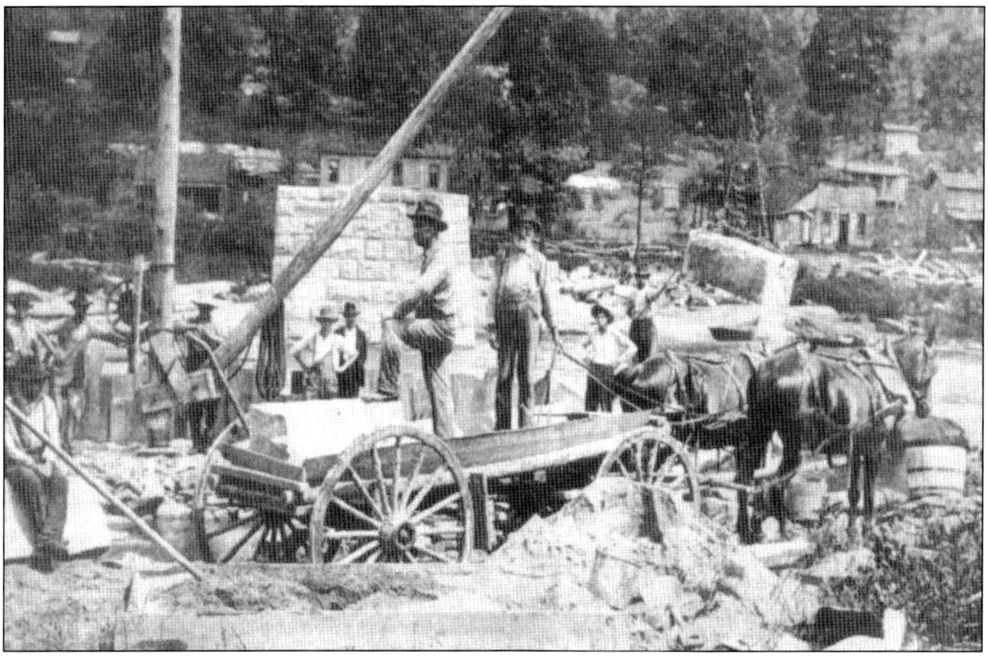

Crossing the Tygart River, the Arden bridge remains in constant use. The stone, hauled by horse or oxen and wagon, was locally quarried, and any wood involved was local timber. (Courtesy Peggy Robinson.)

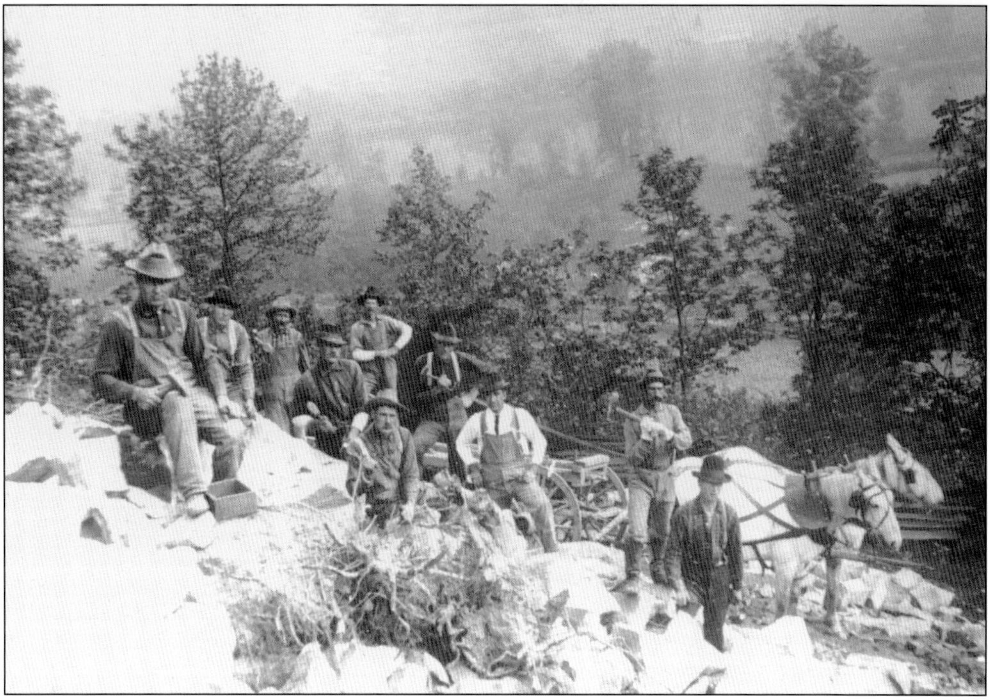

The group working at this Barbour County quarry included C.H. Poling, A.W. Poling, John Poling, Grant Wildman, Jim Cross, and Columbus Poling. The photo was taken sometime between 1900 and 1910. (Courtesy Newton Poling via Jane Mattaliano.)

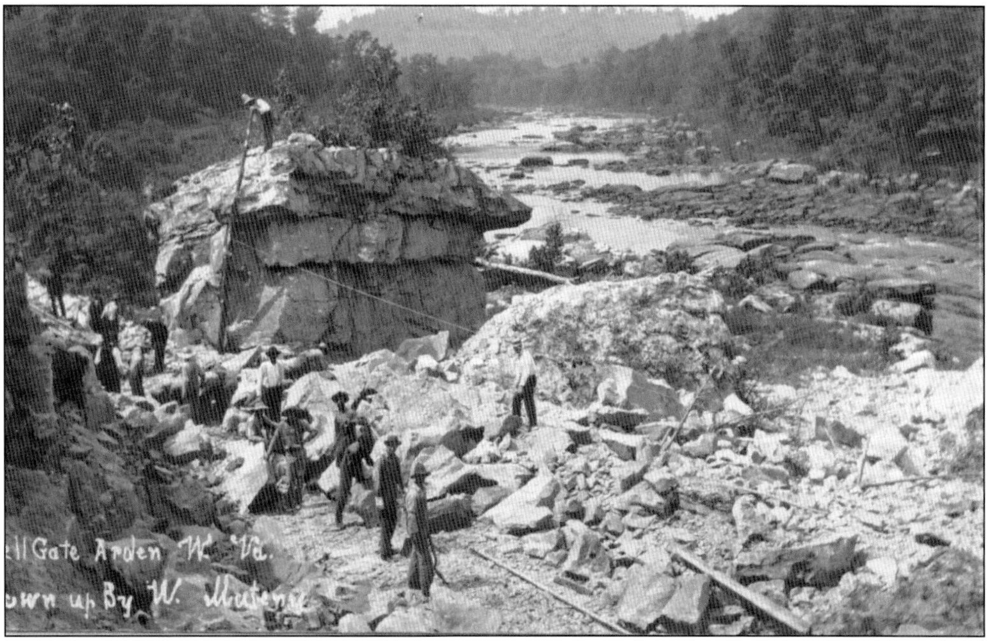

When the Grafton to Belington railroad tracks were laid along the river near Arden, a site called Hell's Gate had to be dynamited. Given credit for that feat was a man identified as W. Mutery. (Courtesy Peggy Robinson.)

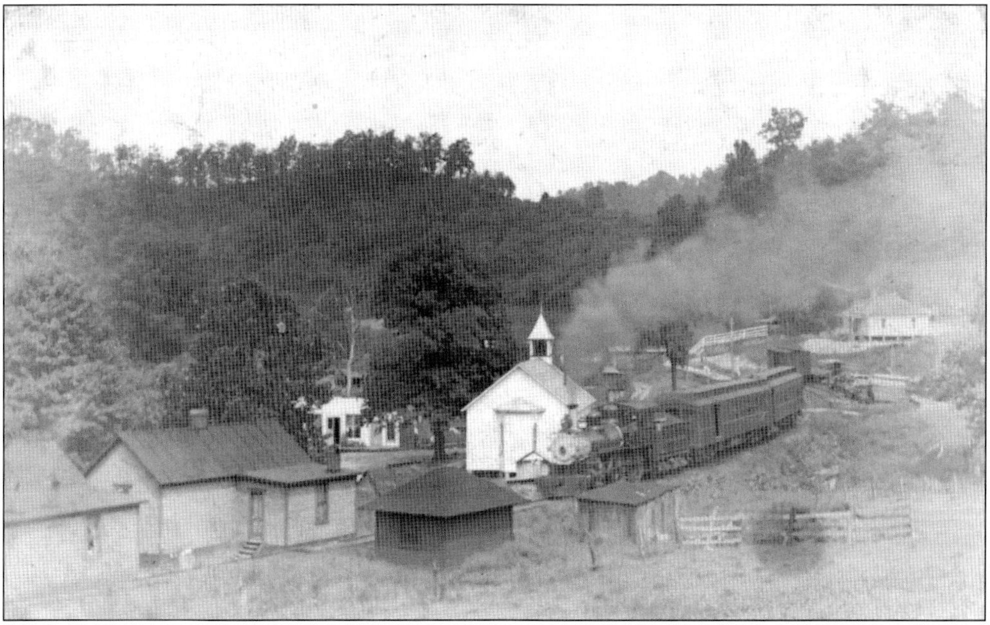

The railroad came to Boulder in 1903, the tracks being extended from Tygarts Junction to Buckhannon. In the background in this photo are the Methodist church and the Townsen & Simpson store. Heavy smoke was emitted by the engines of these early trains. (Courtesy Amanza Nitz.)

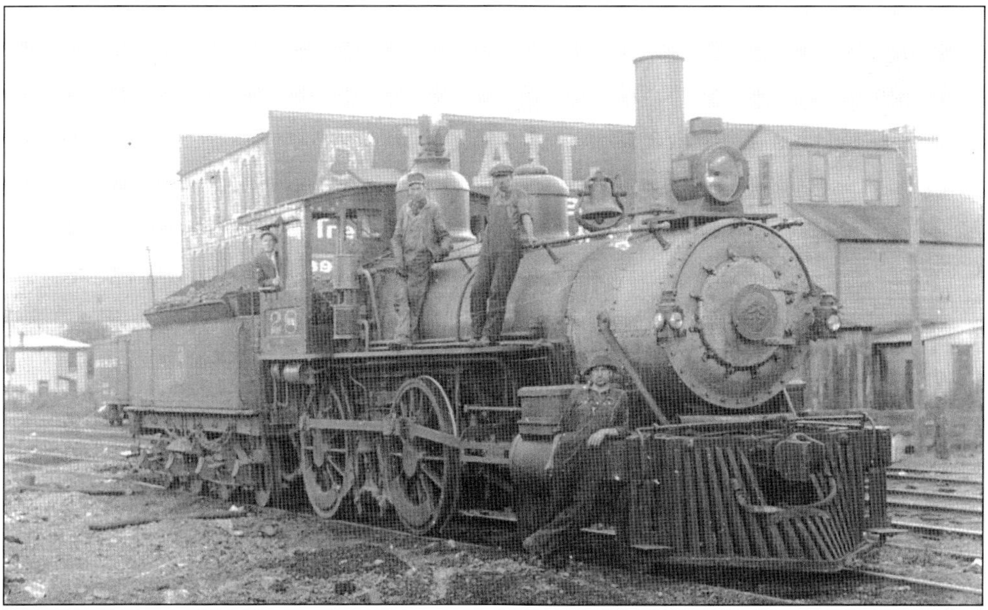

This train engine, sidetracked behind the Valley Grocery Store, which later became the Golden Rule Store, demonstrates the importance of Belington as a railroad center. The depot and tracks and the train itself have been restored as a tourist attraction. (Courtesy H.A. "Red" Payne.)

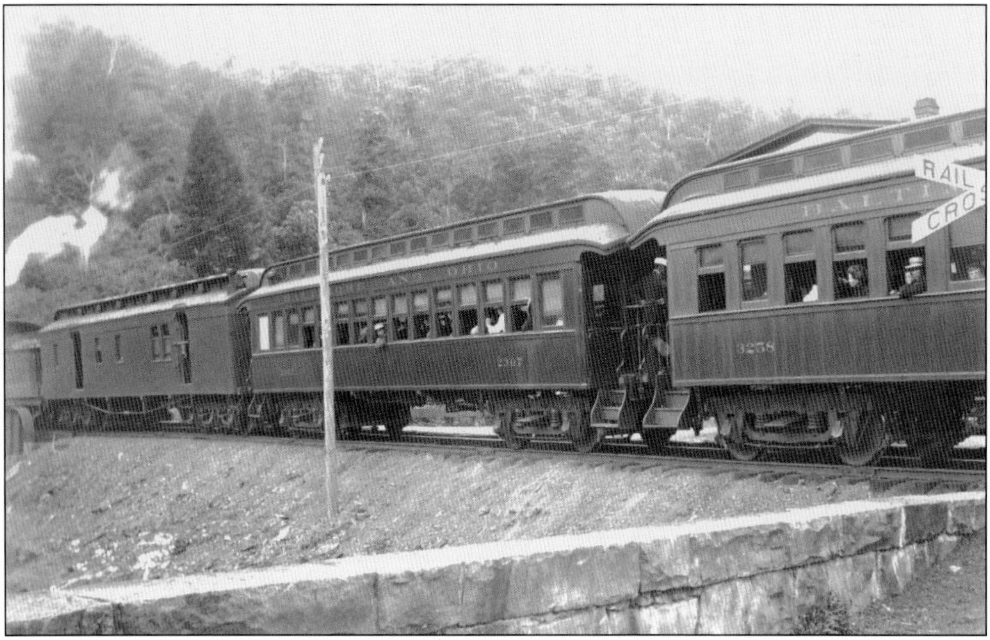

The Baltimore and Ohio passenger train which served Moatsville and Arden was called the *Doodlebug*. It ran from Grafton to Buckhannon and was the only mechanized means of transportation for most people of the area. (Courtesy Peggy Robinson.)

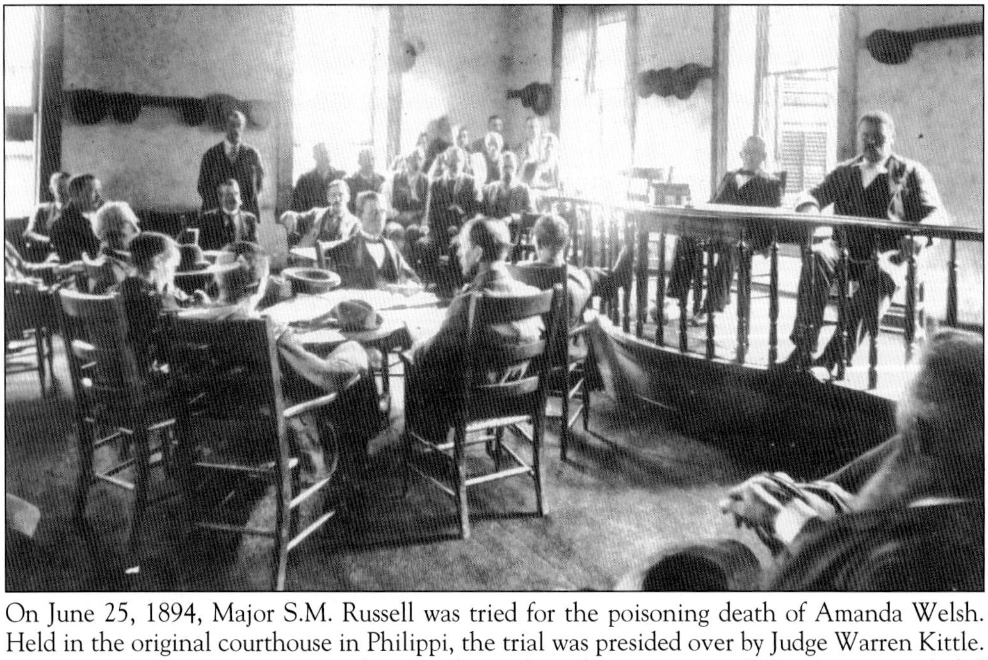

On June 25, 1894, Major S.M. Russell was tried for the poisoning death of Amanda Welsh. Held in the original courthouse in Philippi, the trial was presided over by Judge Warren Kittle. Representing the state were M. Peck, Samuel Woods, and C.F. Teter. Defense attorneys included A.G. Dayton, W.B. Kittle, and J.F. Woods. The accused was declared not guilty. (Courtesy Marie Kittle via Joe Mattaliano.)

Telephone service came to Barbour County when Dr. J.W. Myers had this switchboard installed in the home of the grandfather of Opal Holsberry, whose grandmother was obliged to answer calls even in the middle of the night. Opal Holsberry, Ruby Poling, and a few other women were the daytime operators. The annual fee for telephone service was $3. (Courtesy Jane Mattaliano.)

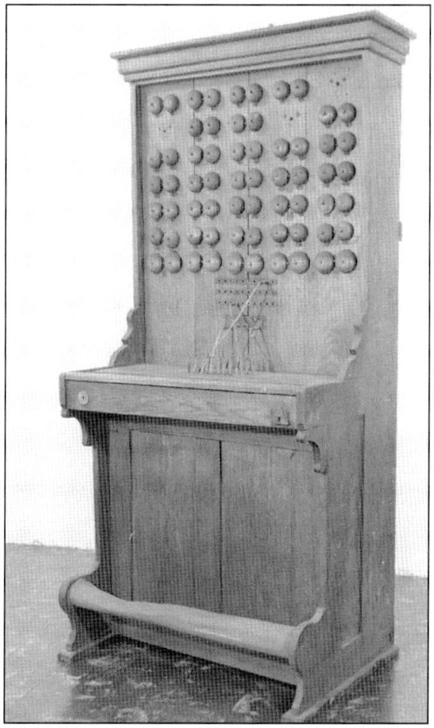

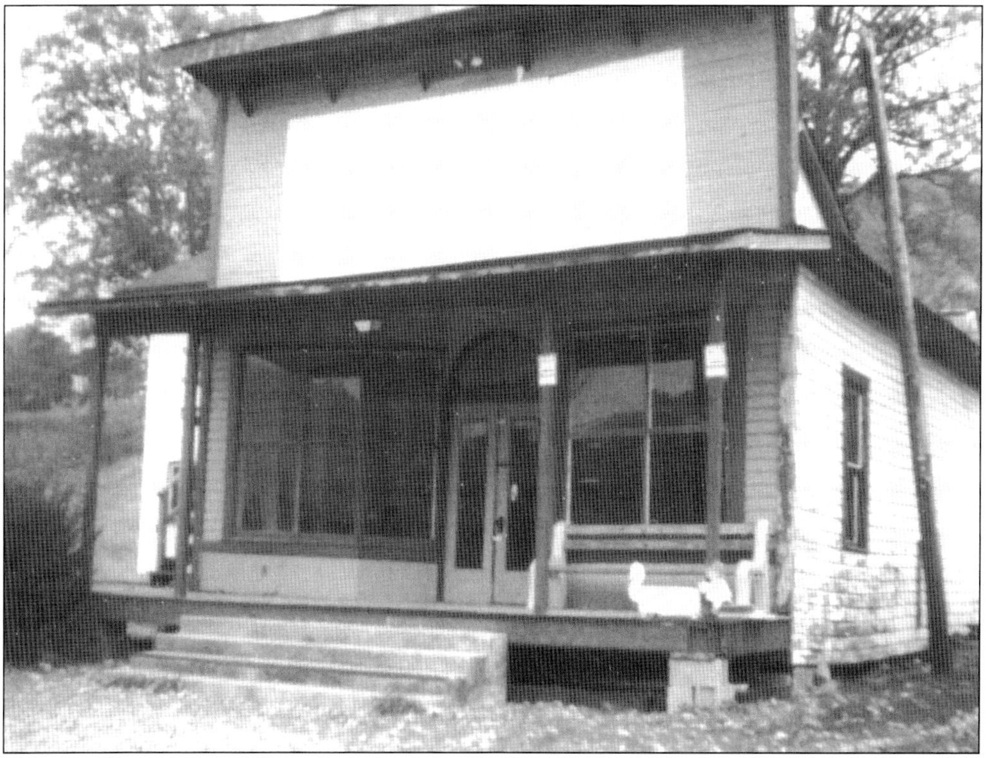

One of the earliest buildings in Arden was the Shahan store. This photo was taken in 1992 before the appearance of the facade was changed. (Courtesy Patty Marsh.)

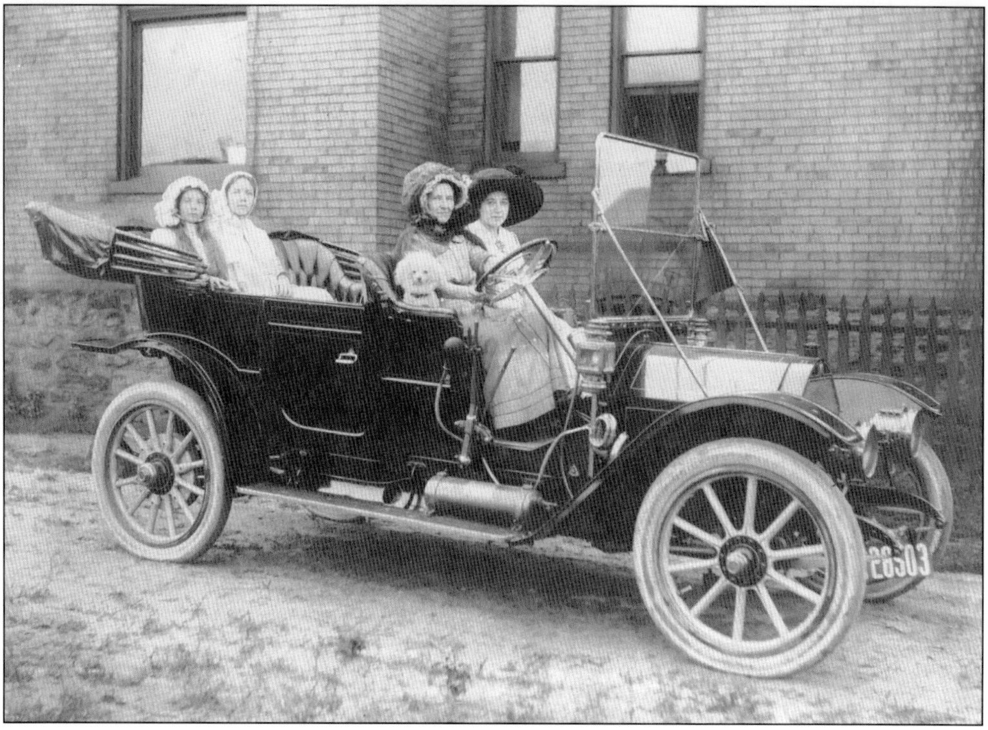

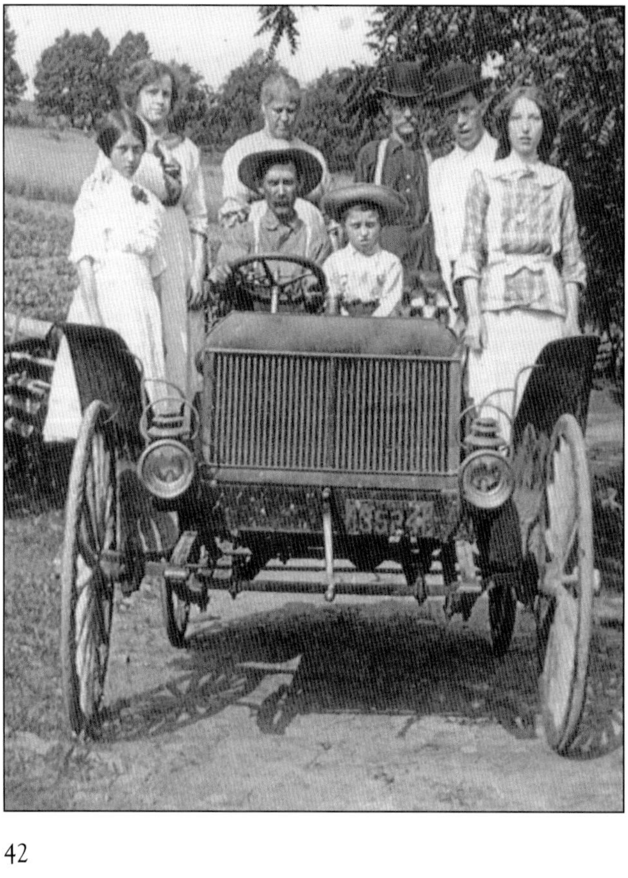

These unidentified women posed proudly in one of the first automobiles to arrive in Barbour County. It is unlikely that the women were actually allowed to drive the car, and they certainly needed help starting it. (Courtesy Joe Mattaliano.)

Posing proudly on Laurel Run Road, this family boasted another of the first cars in Barbour County. (Courtesy Peggy Robinson.)

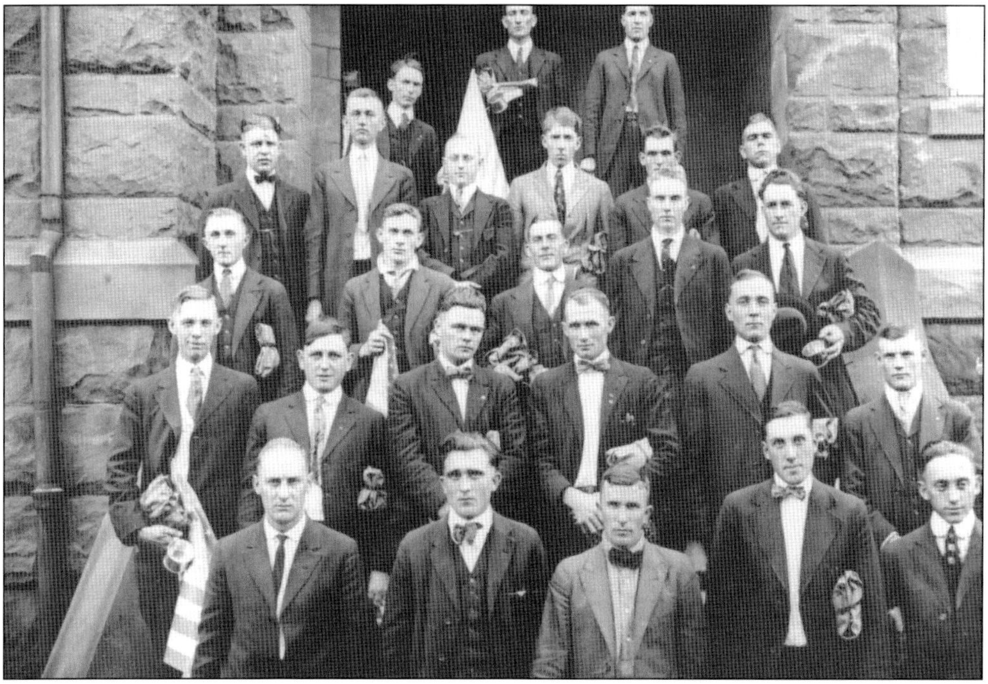

Every community in the United States was affected by World War I. Barbour County was no exception. Recruits were treated as heroes, with crowds witnessing their induction and their departure by train. This group of inductees posed in front of the county courthouse.

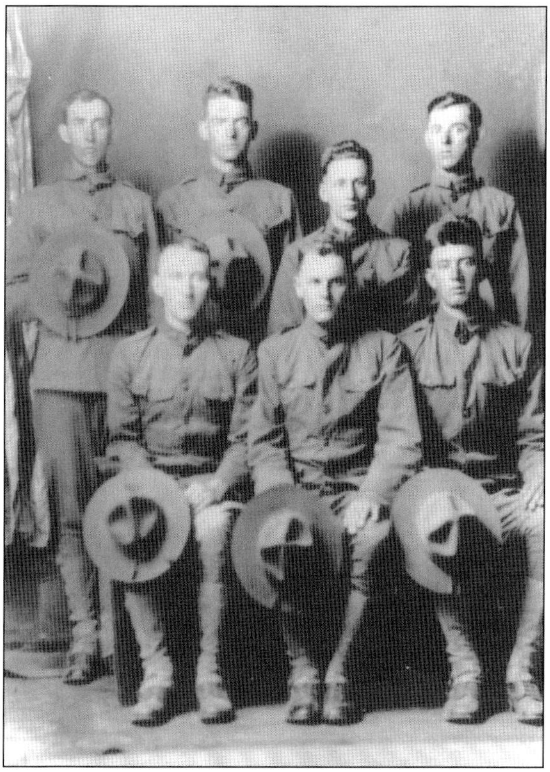

Clearly proud of their uniforms and their calling, these World War I soldiers were ready for action. (Courtesy Stephen Rautner.)

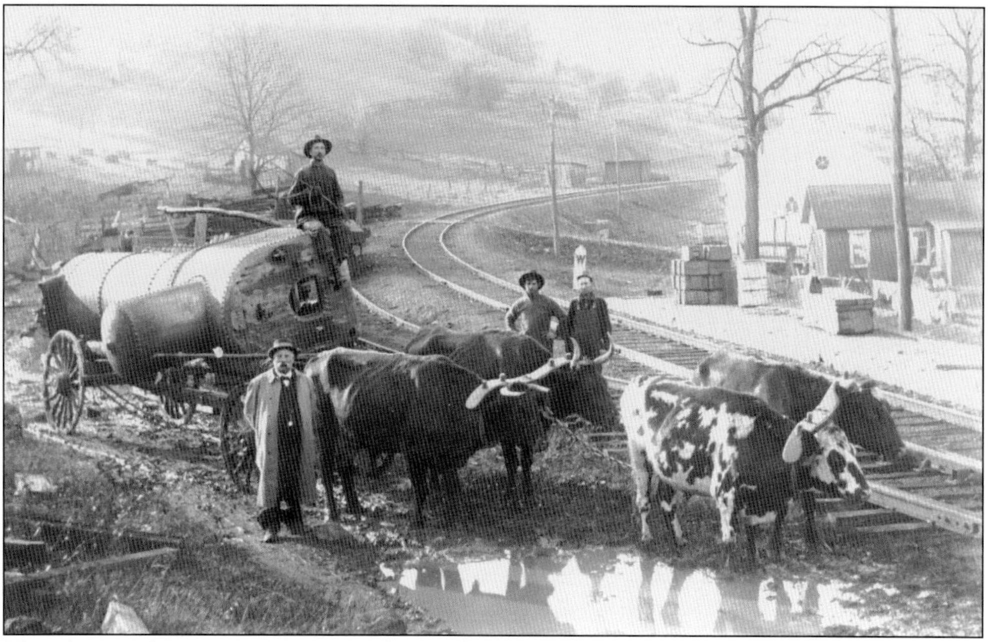

This photo, taken in 1915, gives graphic evidence of the difficulty of travel and transport before roads were paved. The four handsome oxen in this picture were hauling equipment for an oil drill. (Courtesy Amanza Nitz.)

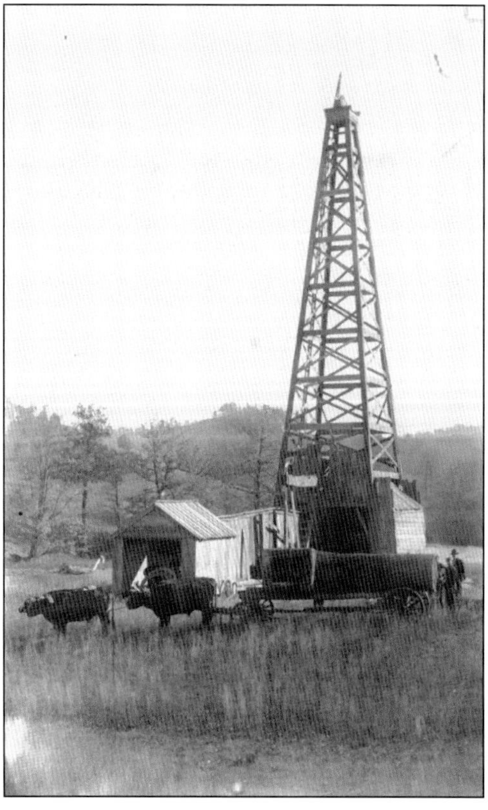

Even while wildcatters such as Michael Late Benedum were striking it rich elsewhere, hopes were high for an oil strike in the Boulder area. Unfortunately, this derrick never produced much. (Courtesy Amanza Nitz.)

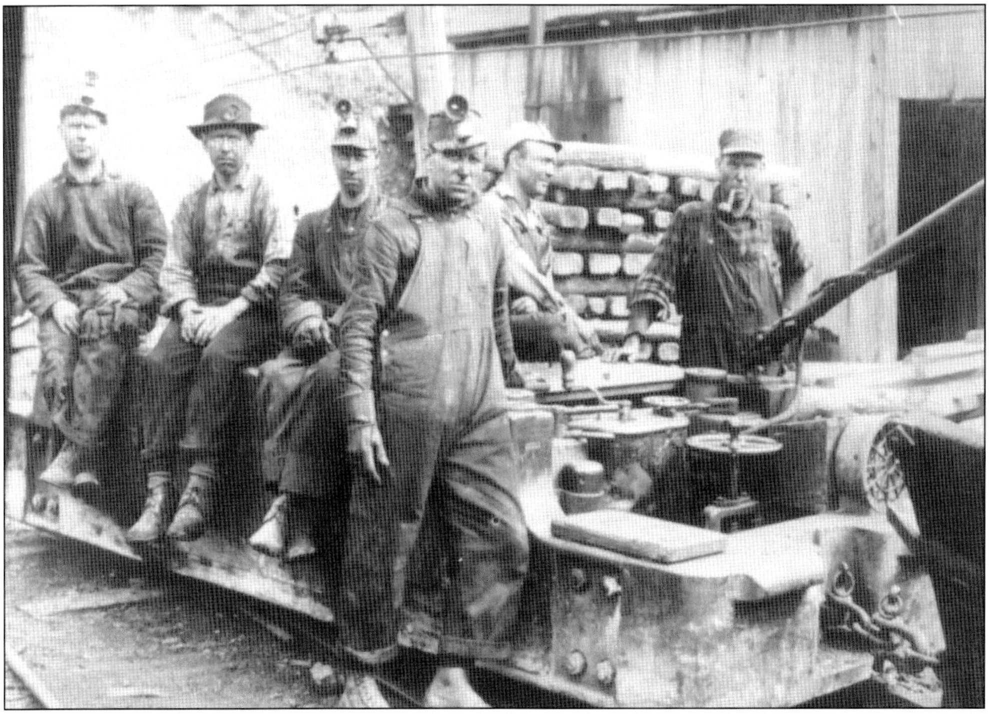

Miners in the Arden-Moatsville area included Elihu and Walter Mitchell, Noble Marsh, Andy Carpenter, Andy Shanabarger, and Andy "Farmer" Reed. (Courtesy Patty Marsh.)

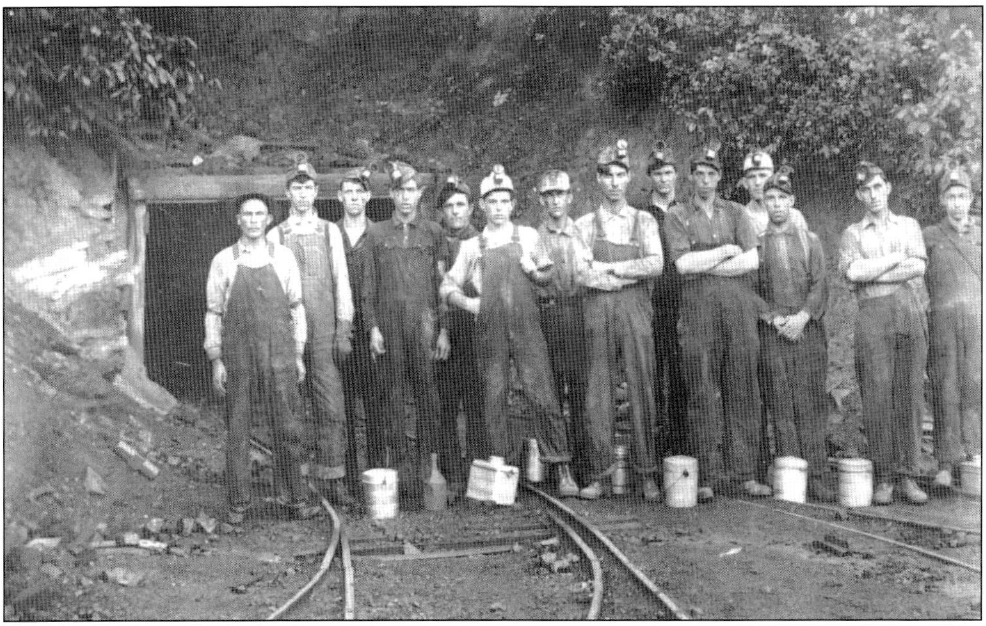

Pictured here is another group of miners who, judging from their cleanliness, were about to start a shift. (Courtesy Jane Mattaliano.)

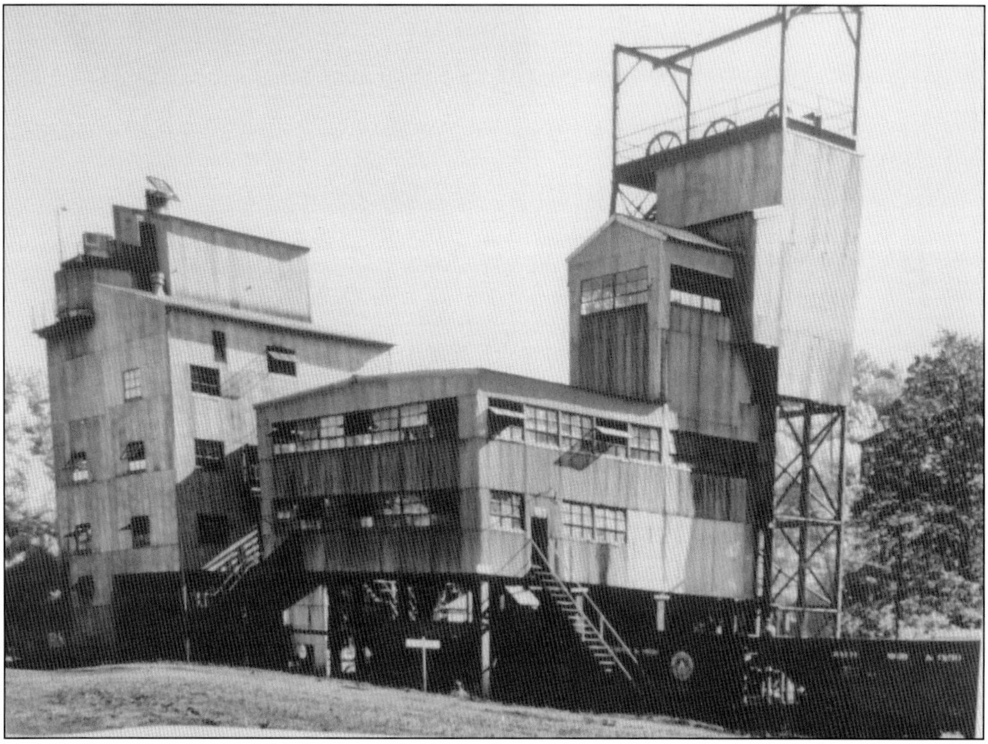

Once a major coal-mining community, Century boasted a processing plant which included this wash house, shut down in 1960. It was owned by Bethlehem Steel Corporation. (Courtesy Nancy Streets.)

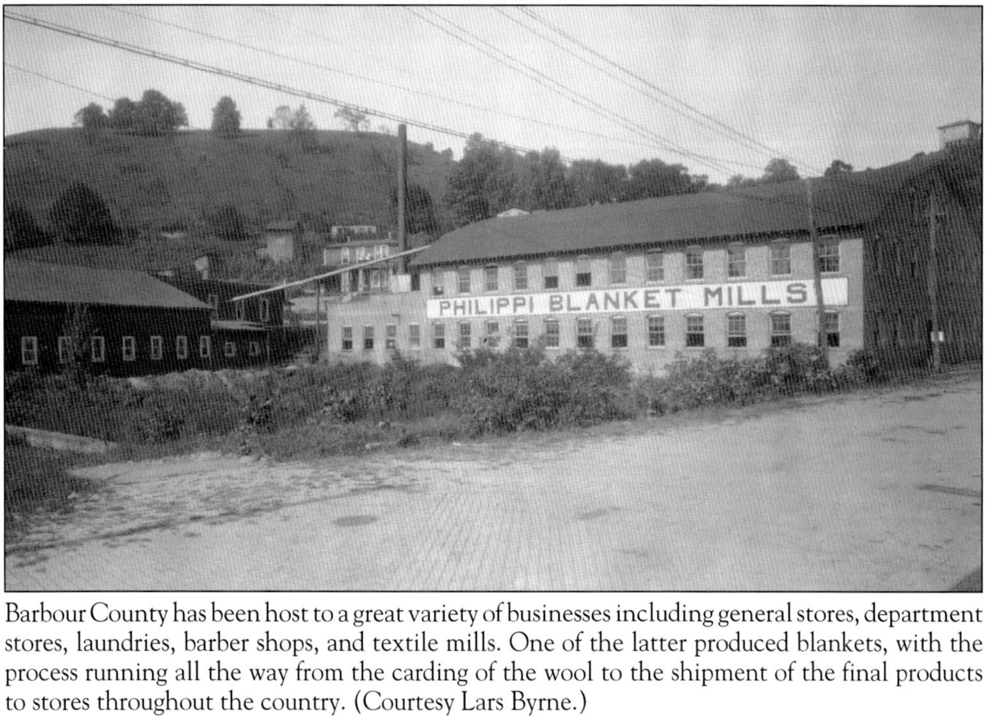

Barbour County has been host to a great variety of businesses including general stores, department stores, laundries, barber shops, and textile mills. One of the latter produced blankets, with the process running all the way from the carding of the wool to the shipment of the final products to stores throughout the country. (Courtesy Lars Byrne.)

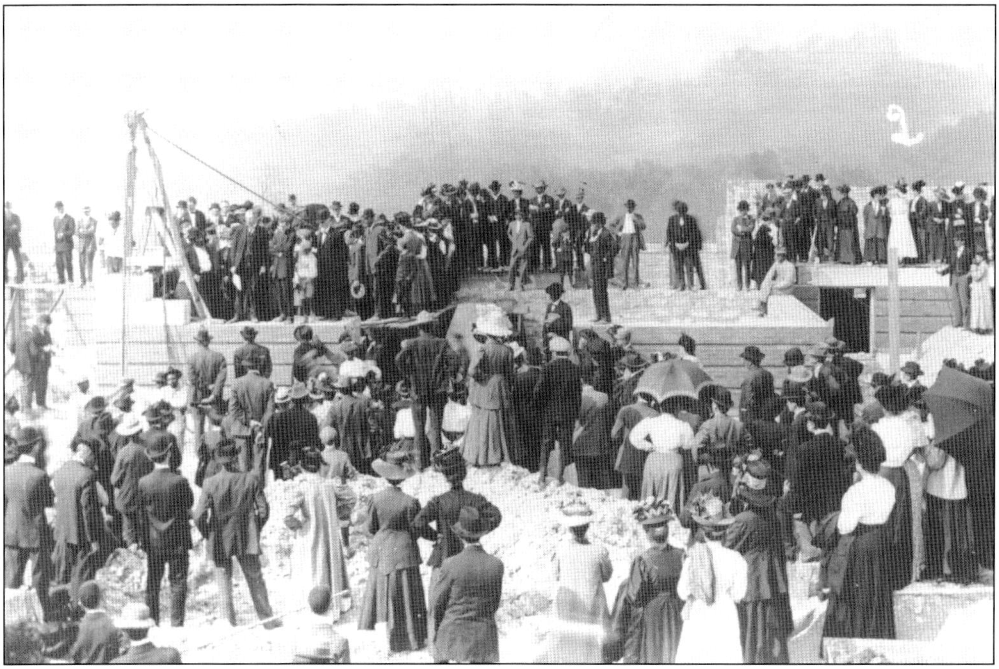

A truly historic occasion was the laying of the cornerstone for Broaddus Institute on October 21, 1908. The first school term began the following fall, as indicated on the accompanying advertisement. The building became known as Old Main. (Courtesy Joe Mattaliano.)

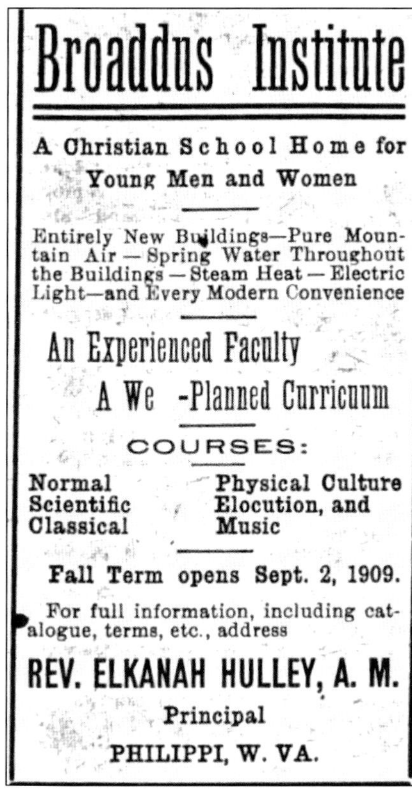

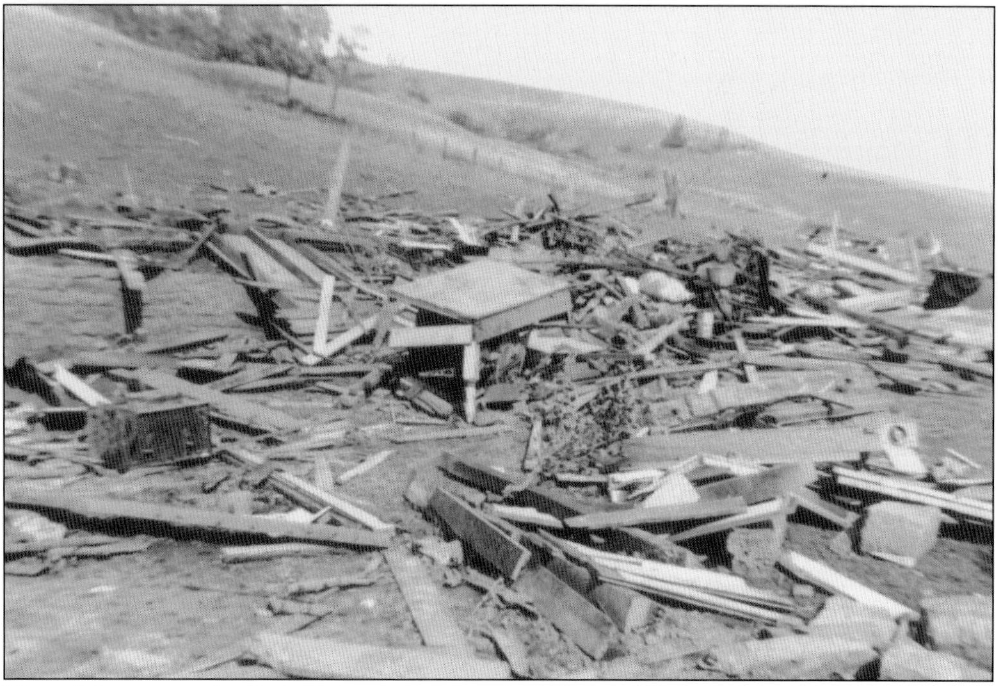

Natural disasters in the Barbour County area included a tornado on June 22, 1944, the results of which are graphically evidenced in these two photos of residences owned by the Hugh Mouser and Coy McDaniel families. (Courtesy Don Funk.)

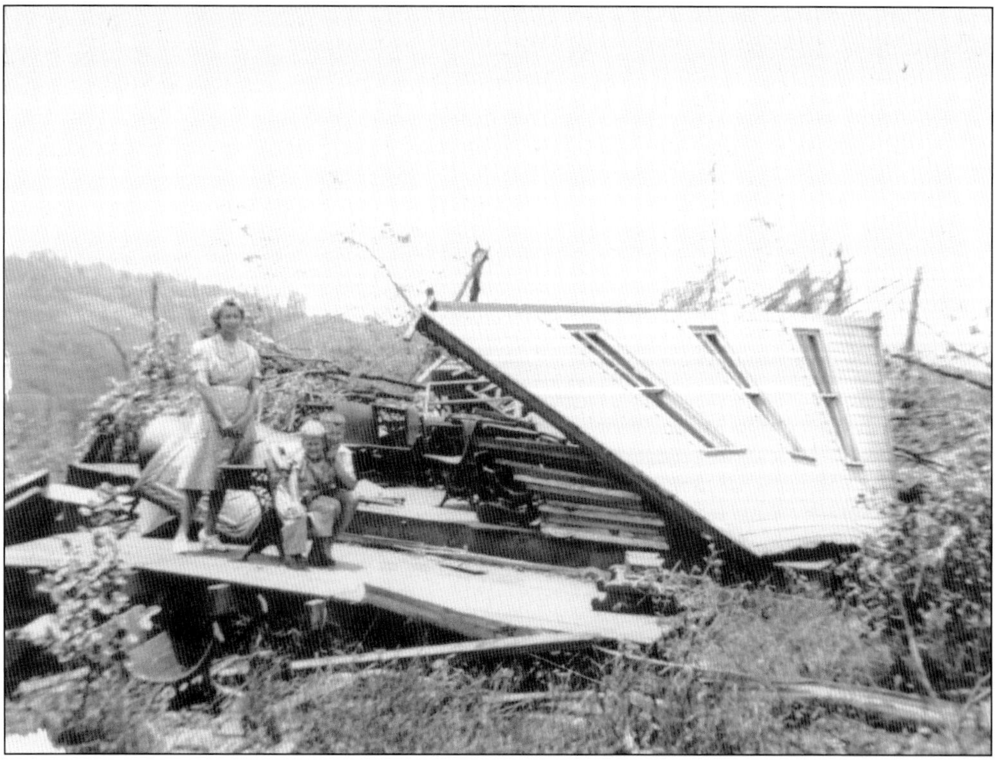

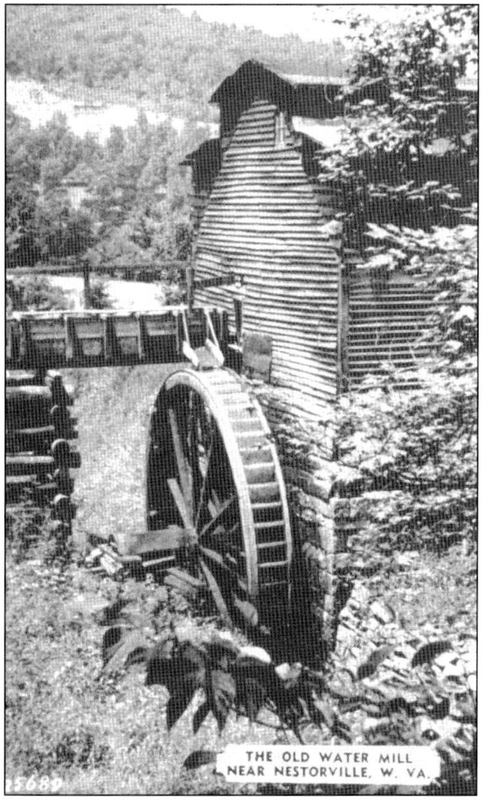

Before-and-after photos of Righman's Mill demonstrate the extent of damage caused by the tornado which struck the Nestorville area on May 3, 1948. The mill had been constructed around 1800 by early Righman settlers and remained in service until the middle of the 20th century. (Before-photo courtesy Peggy Robinson, after-photo courtesy Joe Mattaliano.)

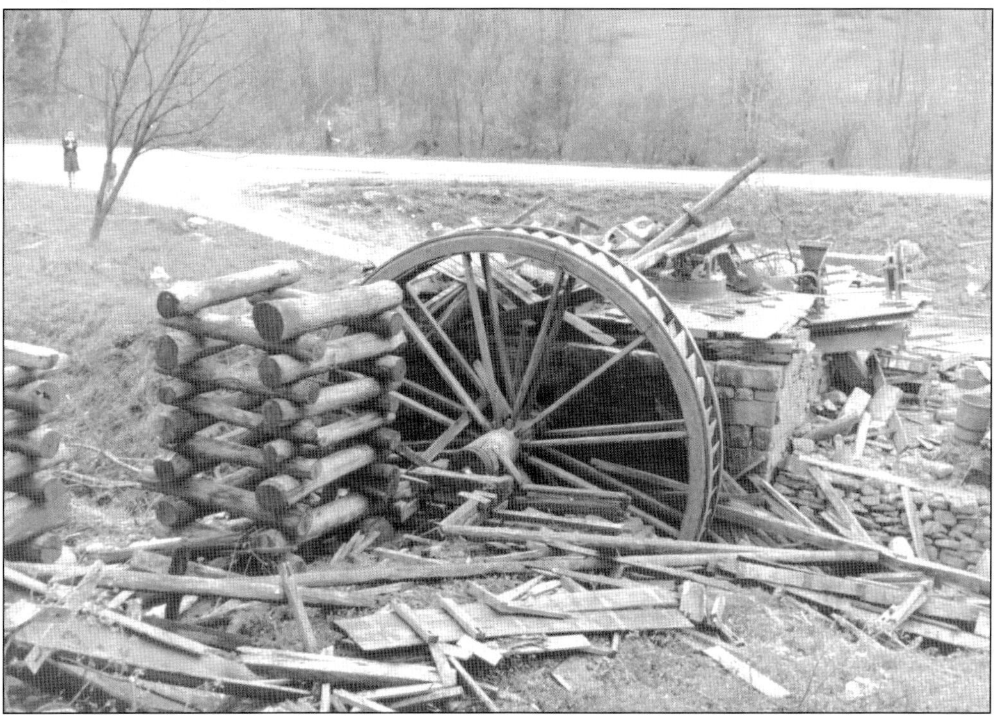

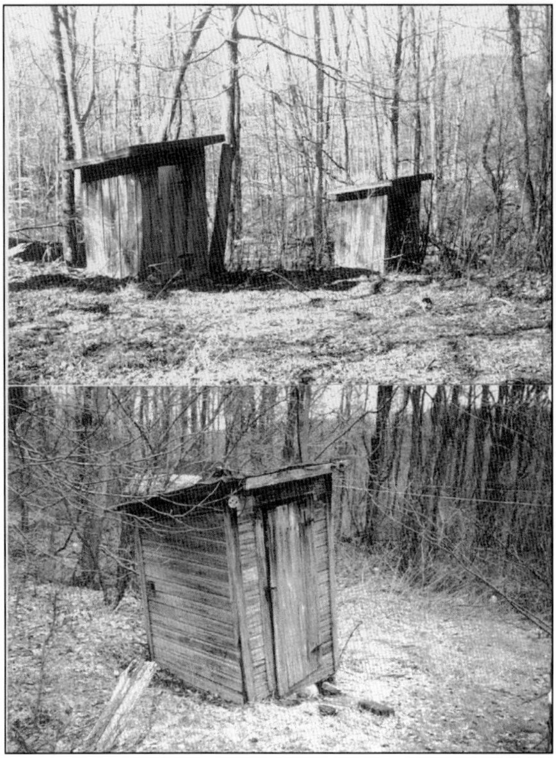

Many "Roosevelt Houses" were constructed—and used—during the presidency of Franklin Delano Roosevelt. The three pictured here are still intact—though no longer in use—in Clemtown and White Oak. (Courtesy Don Funk.)

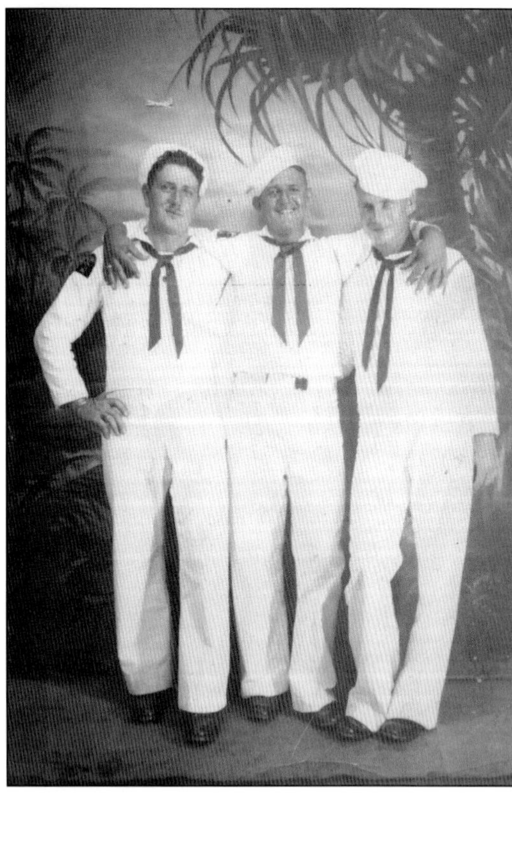

World War II, like World War I, affected all parts of the country, including Barbour County. This trio, posing while on duty with the U.S. Navy in Hawaii, called itself The Three Musketeers and included (left to right) Albert Gleza, who currently resides in Buckhannon, Alfin Zbosnik, and Charles Glendora. (Courtesy Helen and Albert Gleza.)

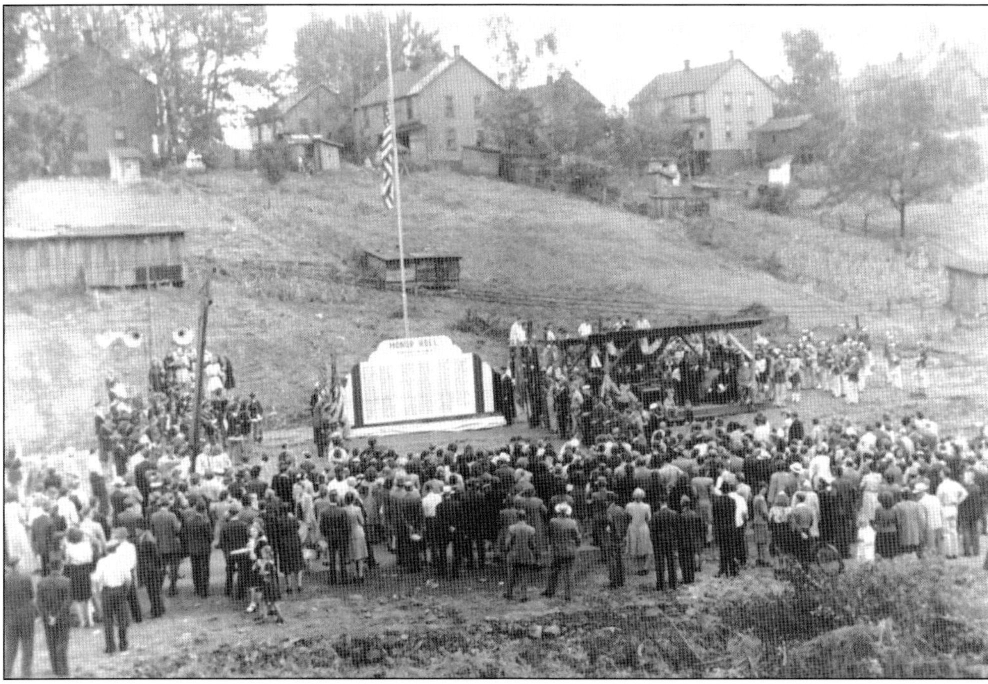

A major event in the history of the Century community was the construction and dedication of a monument on which are listed the names of all those from the community who served in the armed forces in World War II. (Courtesy Nancy Streets.)

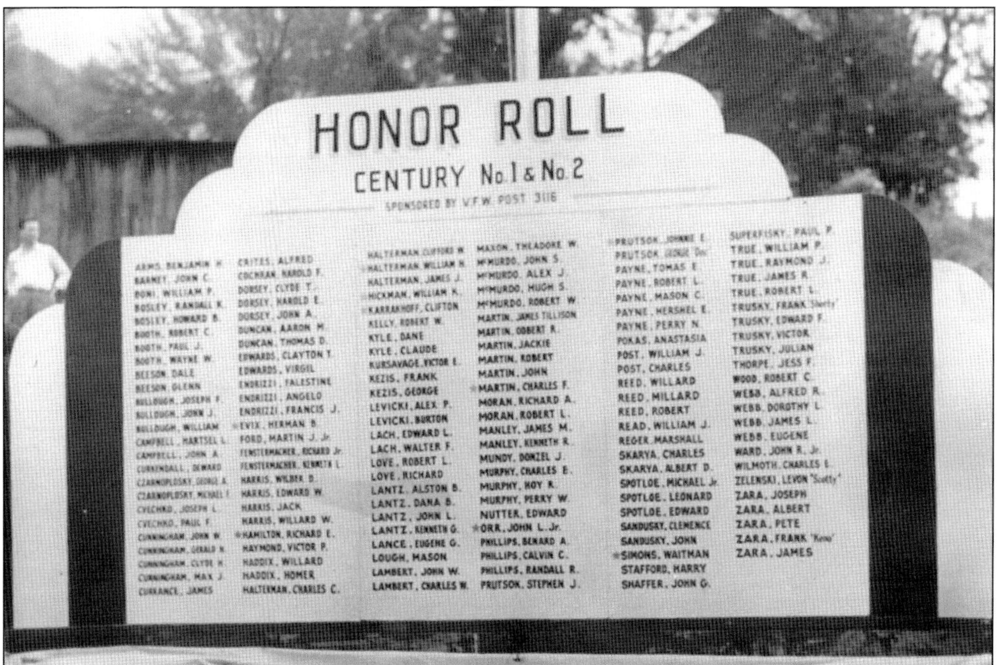

Many monuments of the type pictured here include the names of several members of the same family. This memorial is no exception. At least 40 Century families had more than one member in the services. (Courtesy Nancy Streets.)

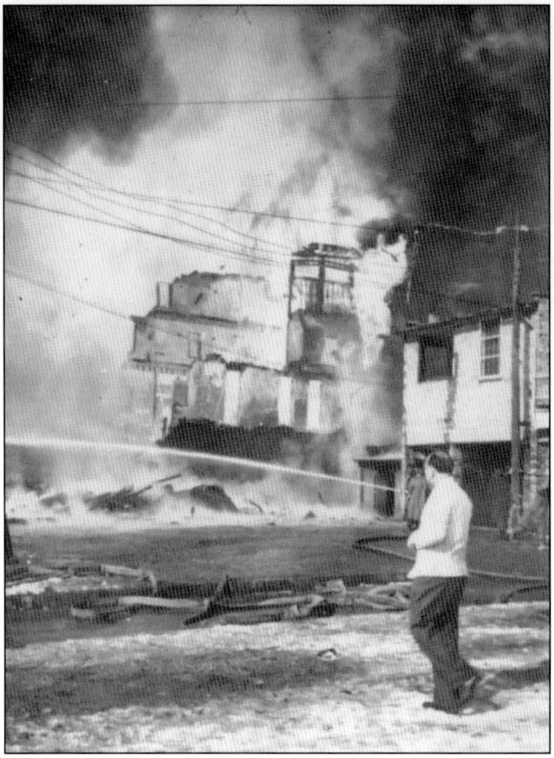

Major fires struck Main Street in Philippi in 1908 and 1942. These two photos suggest the extent of damage which occurred in 1942. (Courtesy H.A. "Red" Payne.)

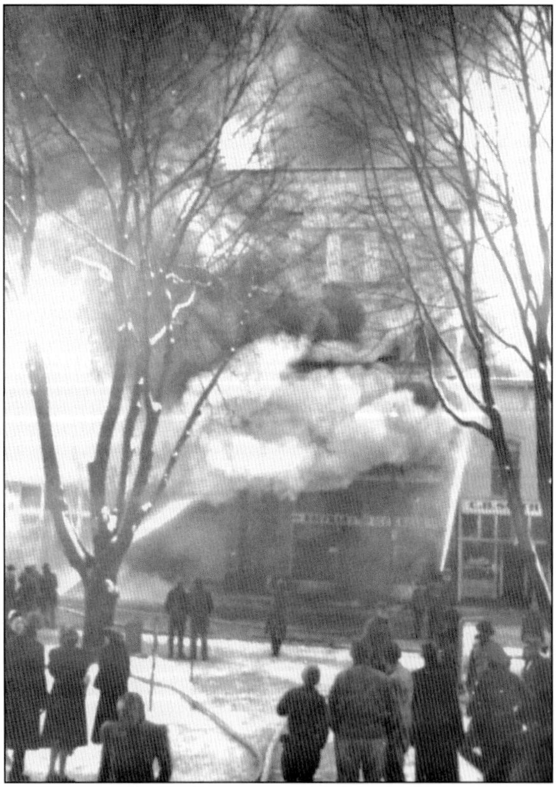

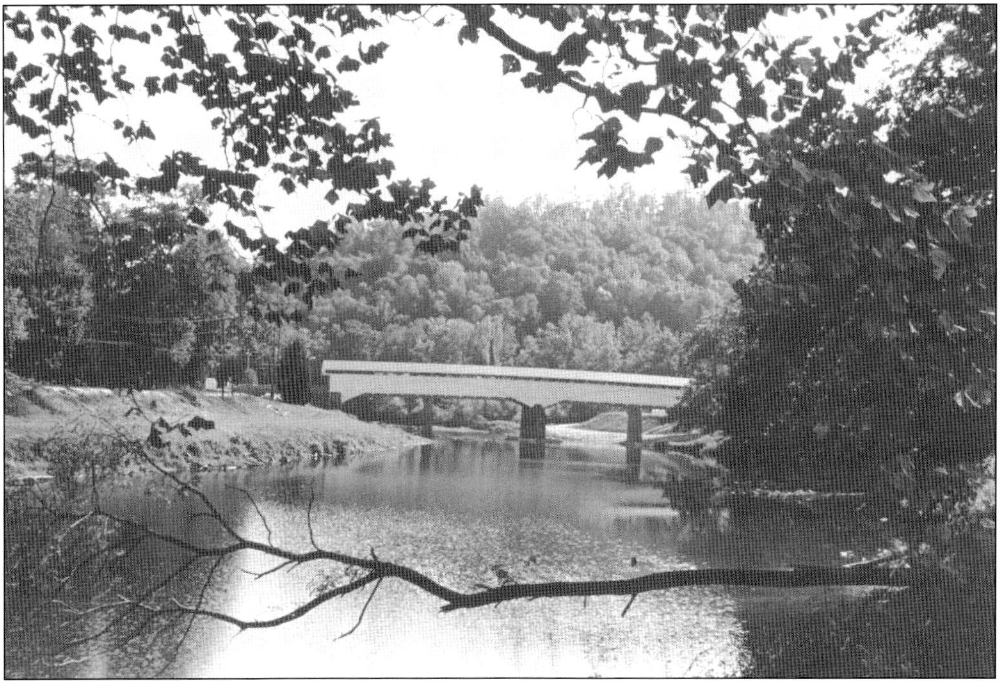

For almost 150 years, the covered bridge in Philippi remained solid and, with minor repairs and modifications, indefinitely durable. Hundreds of pictures such as this one testify to its beauty. (Courtesy Joe Mattaliano.)

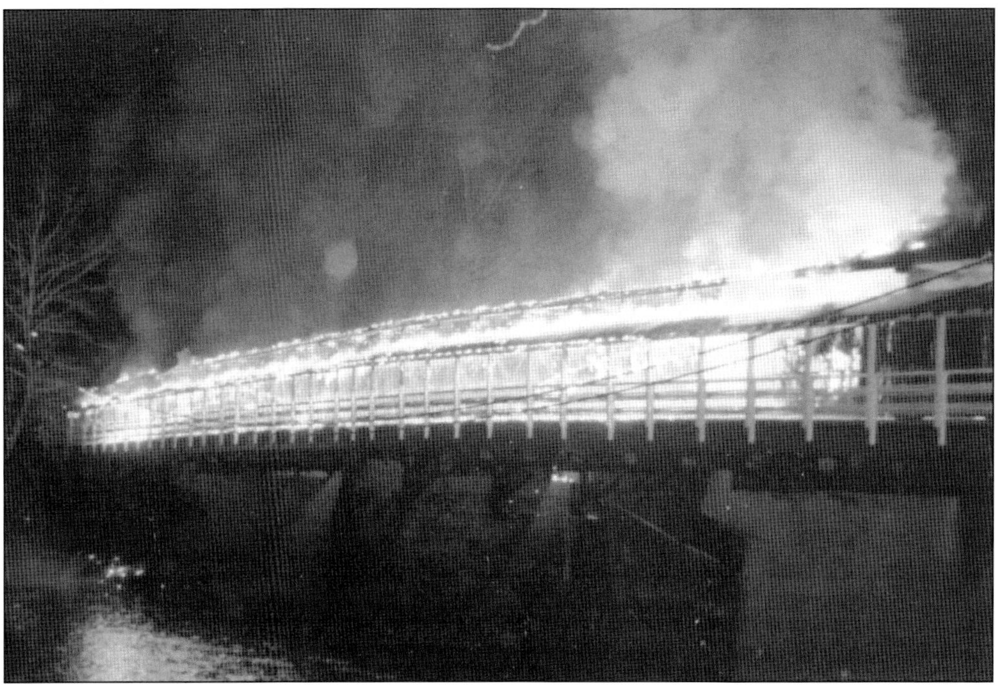

On February 2, 1989, a gasoline spill ignited by the catalytic converter on a passenger car virtually exploded into a massive fire which within less than an hour burned the exterior of the covered bridge. (Courtesy Rusty Freeman via Lars Byrne.)

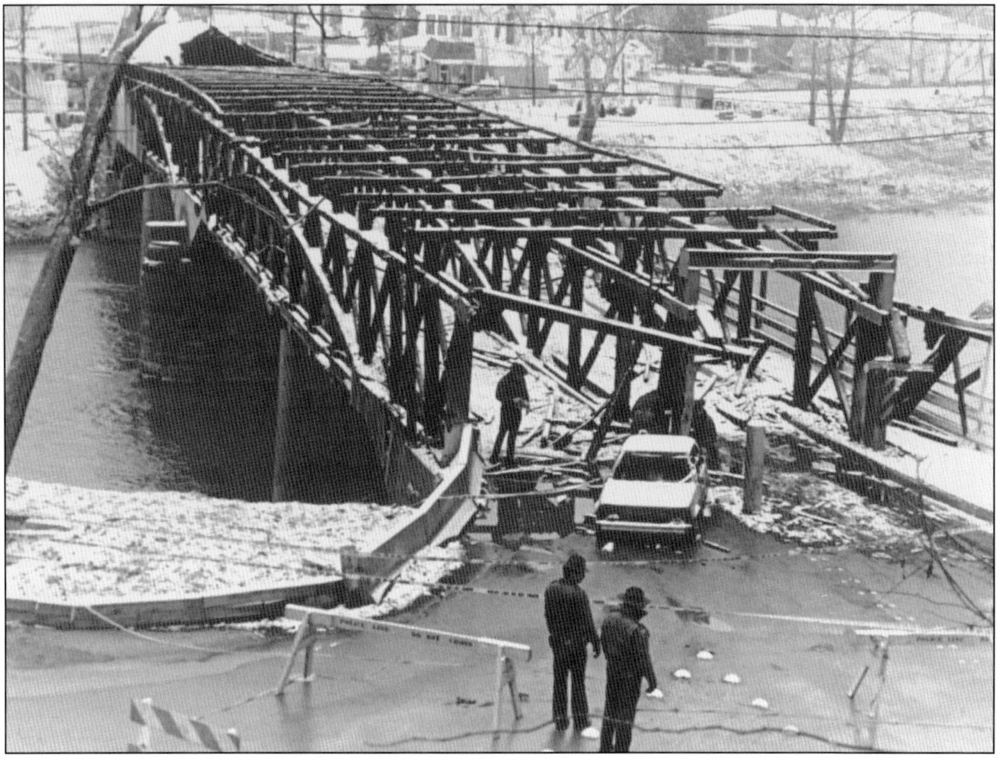

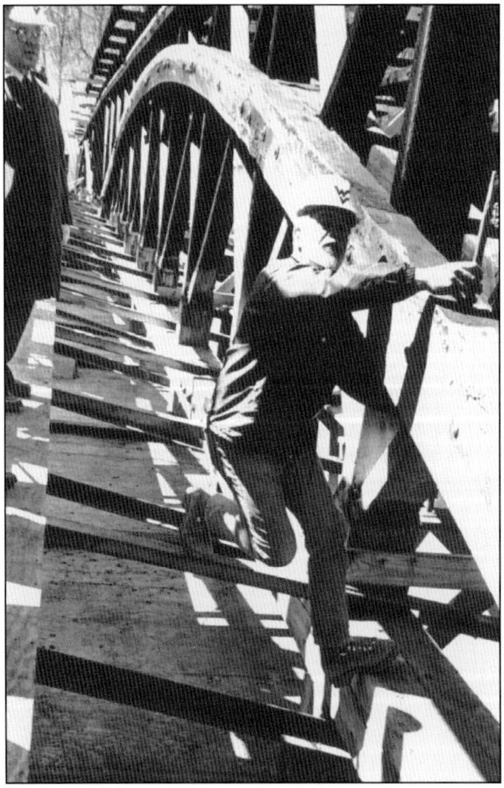

Although the outer shell of the covered bridge was completely destroyed, the original handhewn structural timbers were only charred. Efforts began immediately to restore this historic landmark. (Courtesy Joe Mattaliano.)

Once research was completed and funds were acquired, crews worked day and night on the reconstruction of the bridge. Charred beams were scoured, foundations were secured, and original specifications were imitated meticulously.

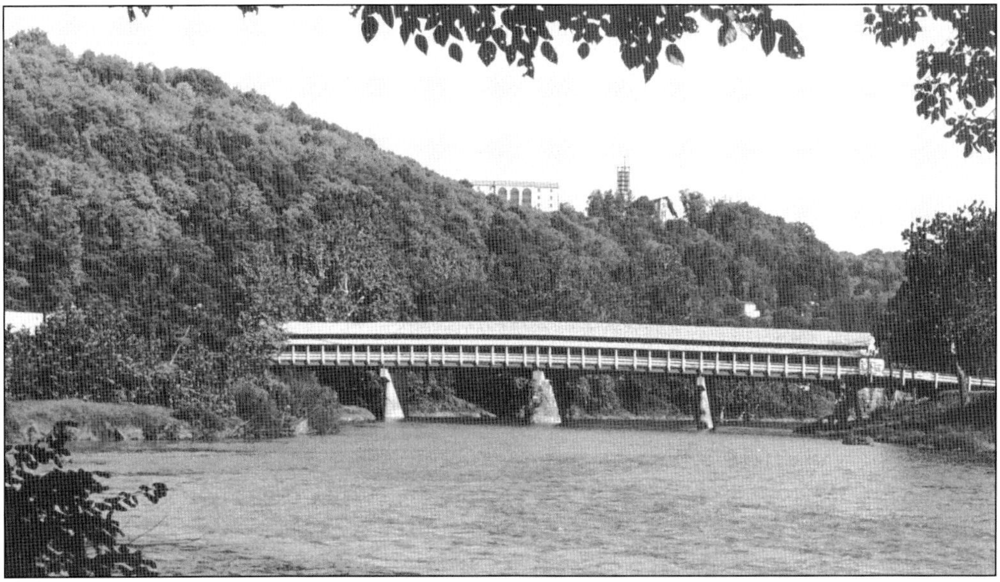

The cost of the original covered bridge came to $12,181.24. Total cost of reconstruction approximated $1.5 million. Experts in historic architecture were called in to assure that the reconstruction followed as closely as possible the original Chenoweth design and fabrication. (Courtesy Joe Mattaliano.)

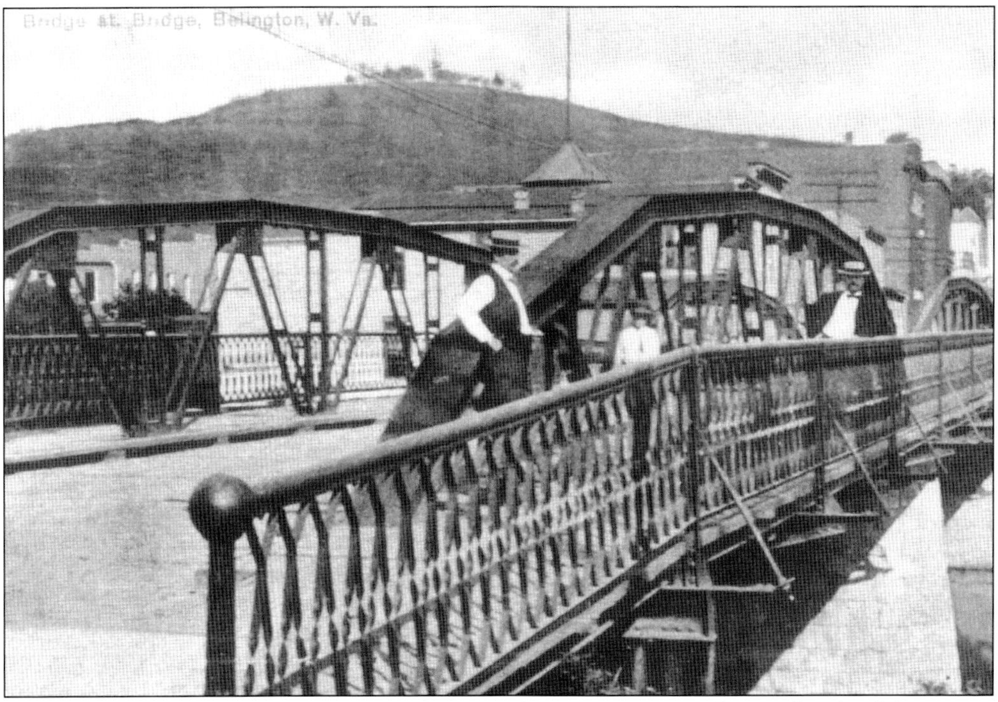

Until this bridge was built in 1886 in Belington, the community on the north side of the Tygart was known as the Barker district, the community on the south Austin. Once called Yeagers after George Yeagers, who arrived in 1785, the community was renamed for storekeeper Joe Beal. The bridge served the area until 1999, when it was replaced by a safer and more modern structure. (Courtesy Joe Mattaliano.)

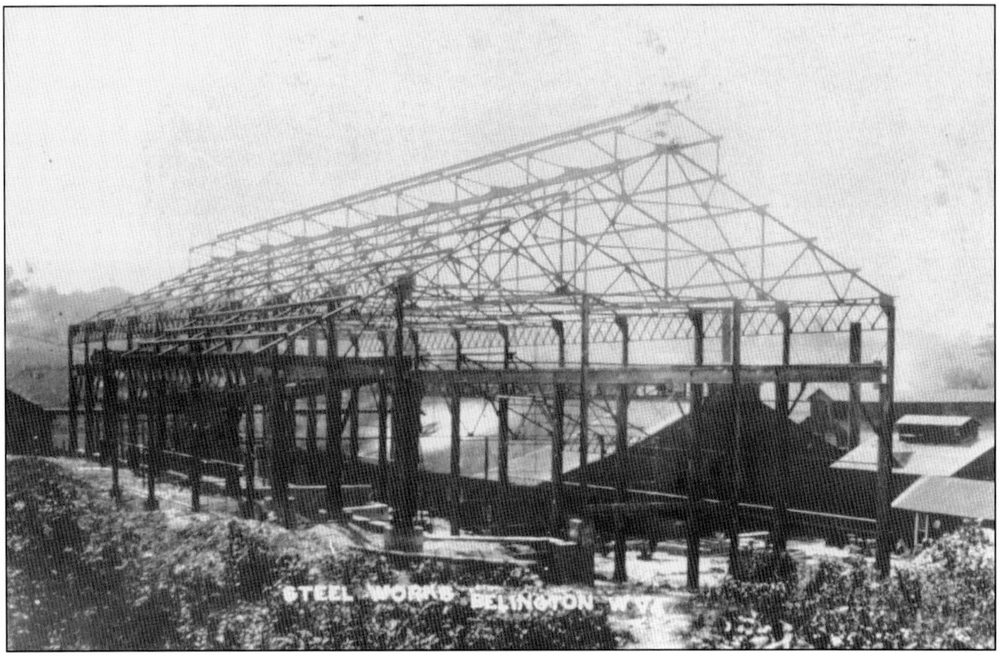

Little is known of the steel works of Belington, but this photo, identified only as "steel works in Belington," suggests a highly sophisticated operation. (Courtesy Joe Mattaliano.)

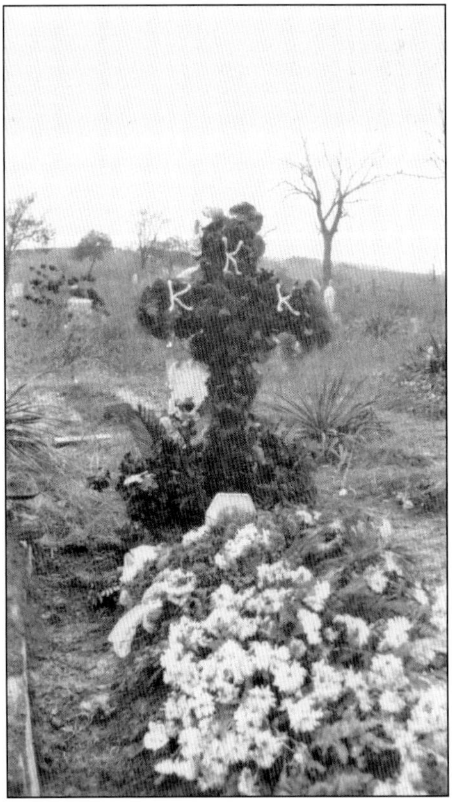

In the days when the Ku Klux Klan was far less controversial than in recent years, Artie Robinson was buried in a clearly marked grave near Clemtown. (Courtesy Peggy Robinson.)

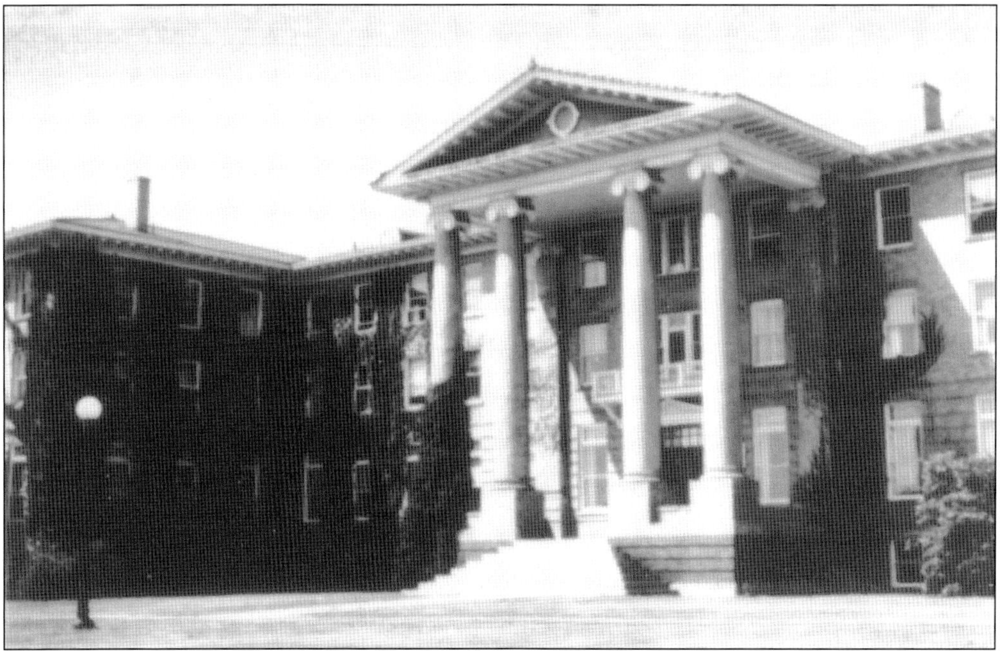

No photograph can ever record the full effect of a major fire, but these before-and-after pictures of the front of Old Main Hall on the Alderson-Broaddus campus give some indication of the extent of loss following such an event. The building had been emptied and renovations had just begun when the fire broke out in 1977.

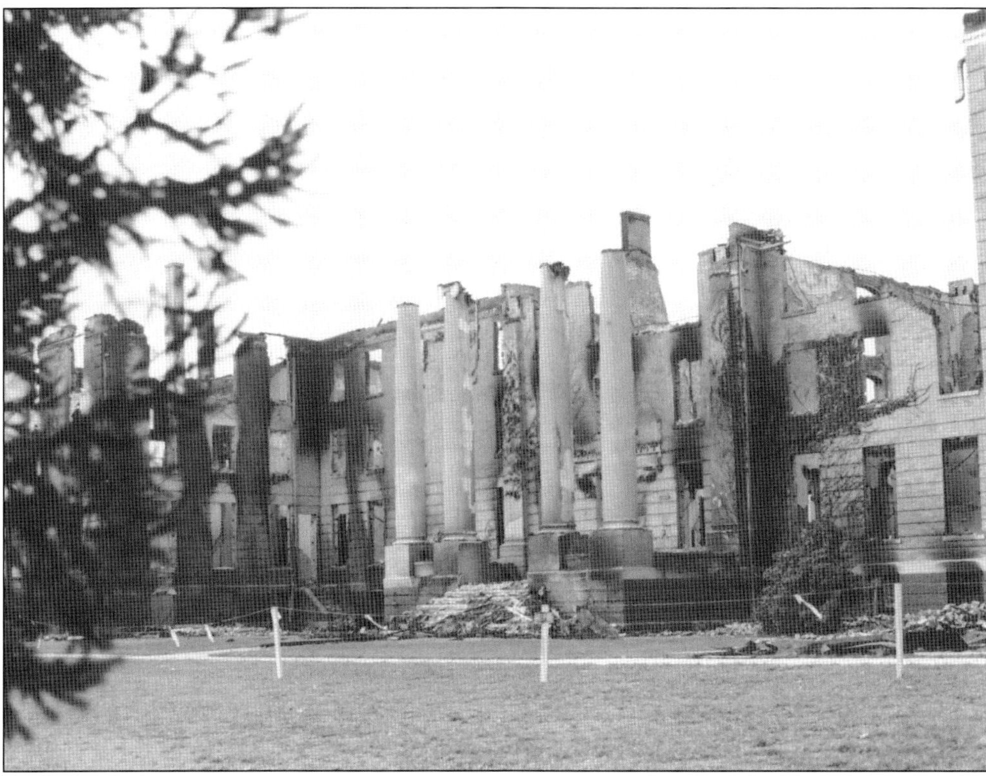

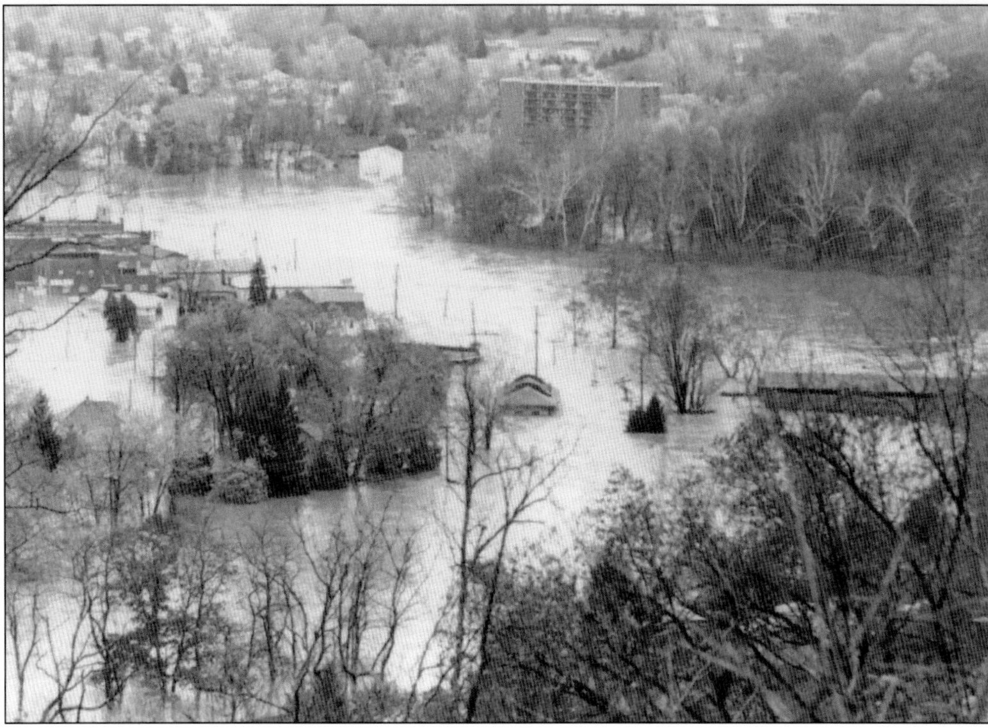

Following several days of hard rain in November of 1985, the Tygart River overflowed its banks. Records indicate that 81 businesses (98%) and 489 homes (50%) in Barbour County were destroyed or severely damaged at a cost of more than $10 million. Five hundred truckloads of debris were removed from various sites. The only working telephone during and after the disaster was located at Broaddus Hospital. (Courtesy Lars Byrne and Joe Mattaliano.)

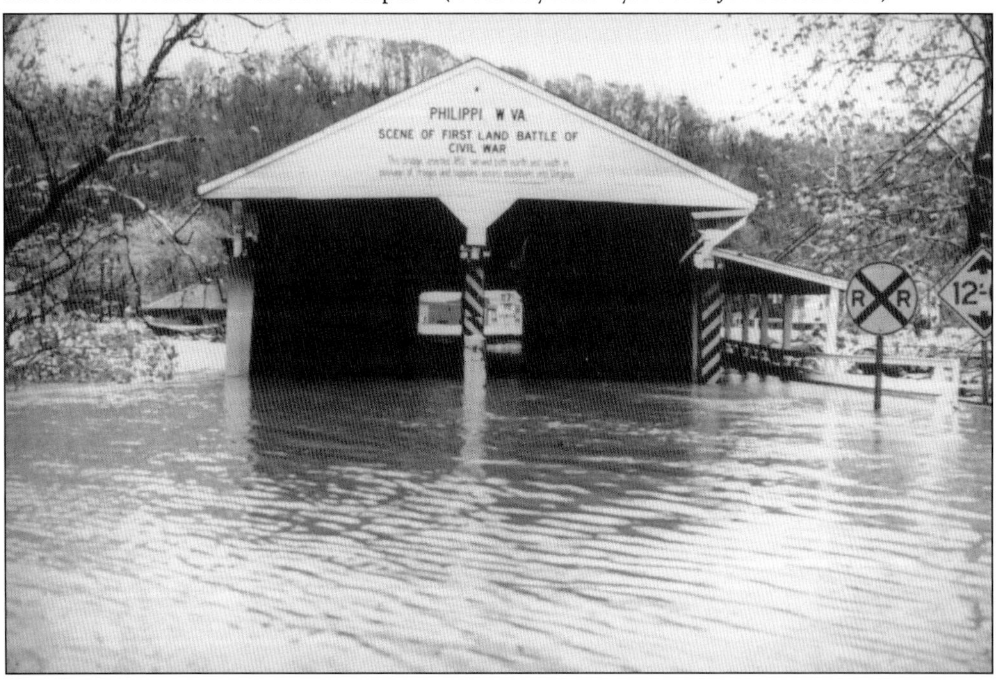

Three

Who Has Made It Happen

Barbour County has produced its share of statesmen, artists, performers, and award-winners. But the real heroes, the most effective leaders, the true shakers-and-movers, are the men and women who till the land, raise the crops, run the stores, raise the children, teach in the schools, preach in the pulpits, and lay the roads. They stand behind and beside those whose public roles and appearances make them famous.

The county would not have flourished without the medical skills of the J.W. Myers family, the legal expertise of Judge Dayton Stemple, the art of songwriters Ida Reed and Henry Everett Engle, the administrative acumen of college presidents E.J. Willis, Elkanah Hulley, and Richard Shearer, and the generosity of philanthropists Michael Late Benedum, Basil Wilcox, and Earl Heiner. Add to them numerous civic and religious and educational leaders, business people, performers—the list is endless.

Here in Barbour County community builders have been and are innumerable. They range from Supreme Court justices to maintenance workers, from social reformers to quilters, from financial wizards to store clerks. Any list will be incomplete, but every list can be representative.

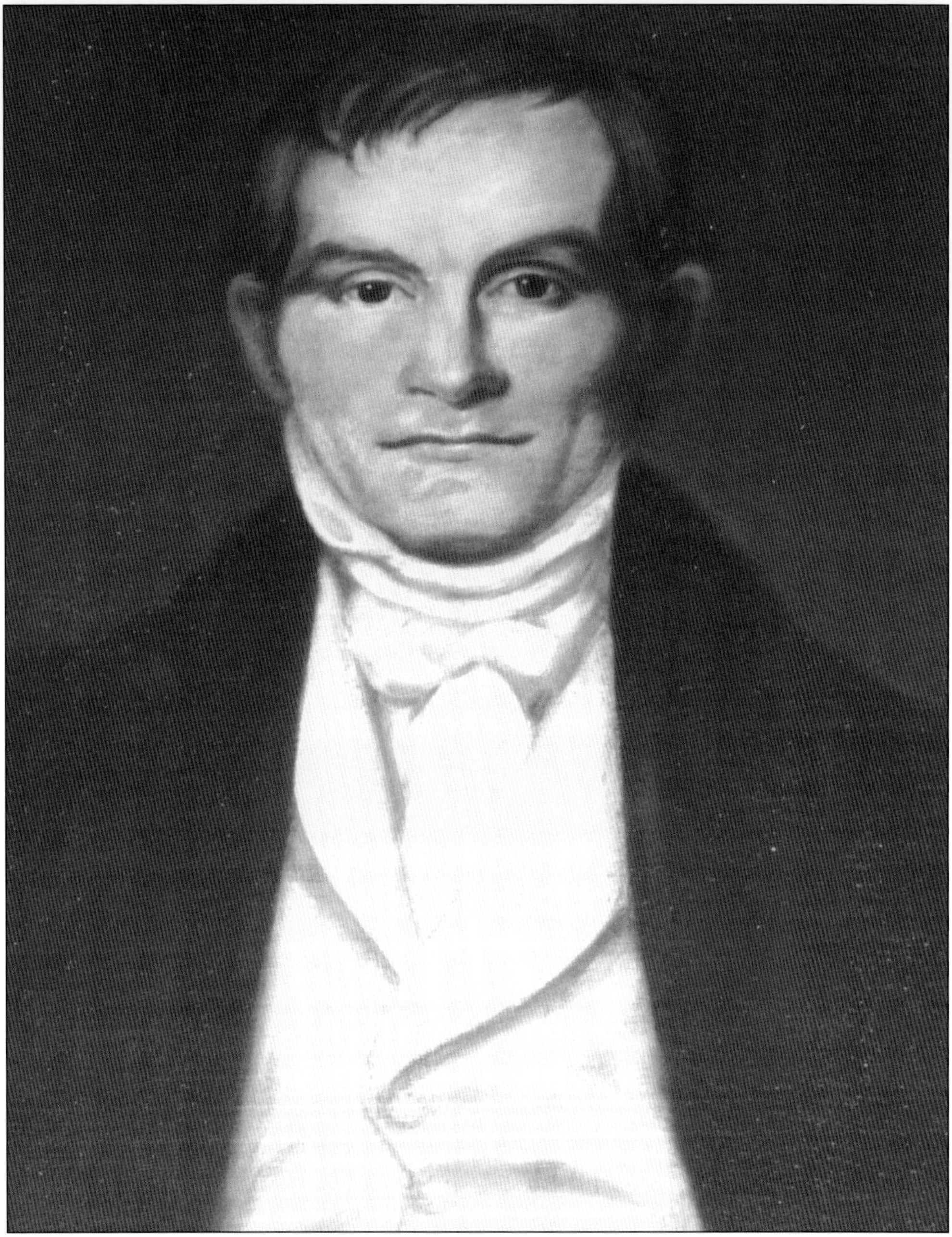

Philip P. Barbour, born in 1783 in Orange County, Virginia, was the son of Colonel Thomas Barbour, patriot of the Revolution. Philip's brother James served as U.S. Senator, Secretary of War under John Quincy Adams, and Governor of Virginia. Philip Barbour, for whom Barbour County and the county seat of Philippi were named, was called "The Pride of the Democracy of Virginia." Serving in the Virginia House of Delegates and the U.S. House of Representatives, he became president of the Virginia Constitutional Convention. He ran for vice president of the United States and later became Associate Justice of the U.S. Supreme Court. He died of a heart attack in 1841. This portrait by an unknown artist hangs in the courthouse in Orange County, Virginia. (Photo Barbara Smith.)

Lemuel Chenoweth (1811–1887), born in Randolph County, became a builder of covered bridges, the best known of which is in Philippi. Chenoweth was also known as a wagon-maker, carpenter, master furniture maker, and home and church builder. This portrait of Chenoweth was done by the late Howard Smith. (Courtesy Eleanor Smith Creed, photo Barbara Smith.)

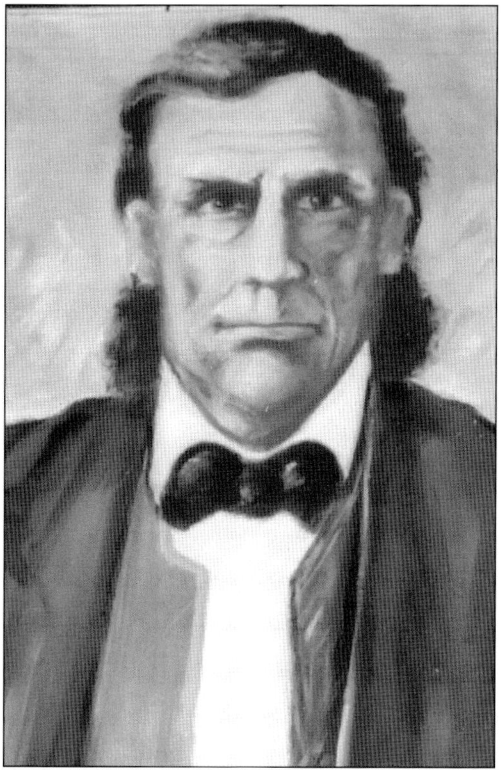

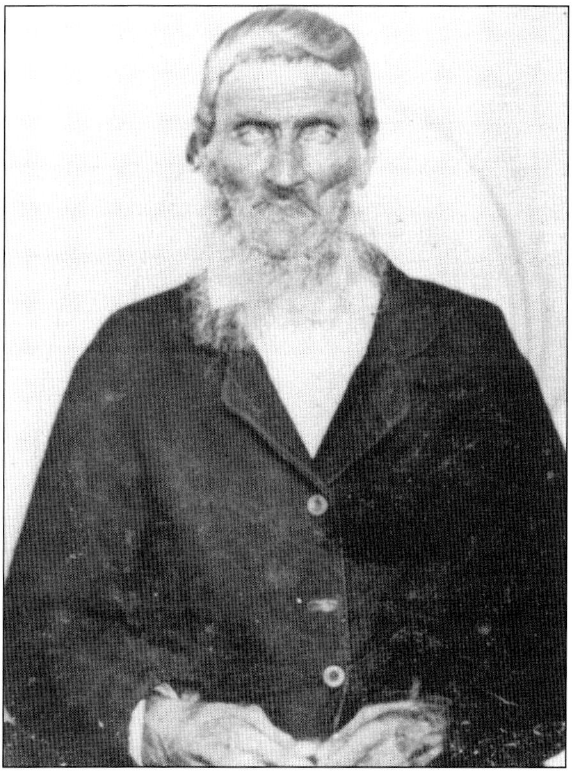

One of the most interesting figures in the history of Barbour County was John Jennings, who was born in England in 1752 or 1753. After being kidnapped into the British army and sent to the American colonies, he migrated to Winchester, Virginia. He deserted the army and made his way to Barbour County and settled in Moatsville, where he died at the age of 96.

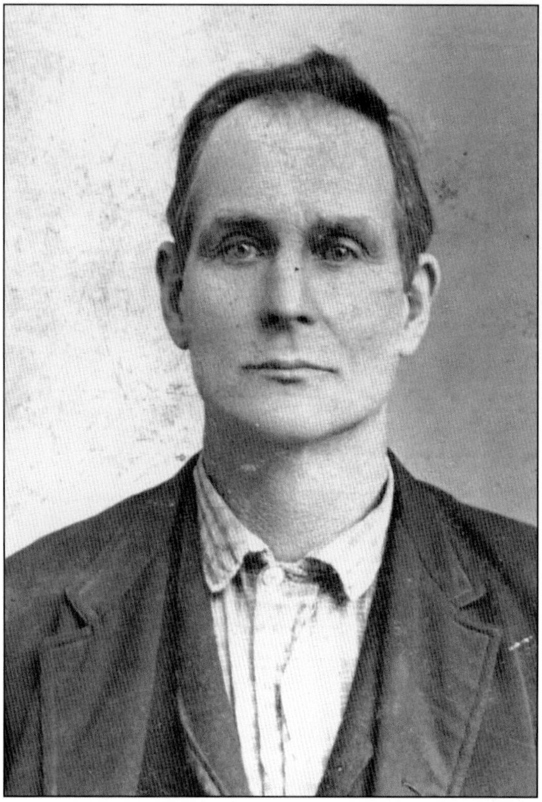

George Johnson was one of the key citizens in the earliest days of Cove Run. His daughter, Eve Johnson Coffman, portrayed in the accompanying photo, posed in front of the Johnson home. She served as postmistress at Cove Run, where the post office, closed in 1927, was called "Johnson." (Courtesy Peggy Robinson.)

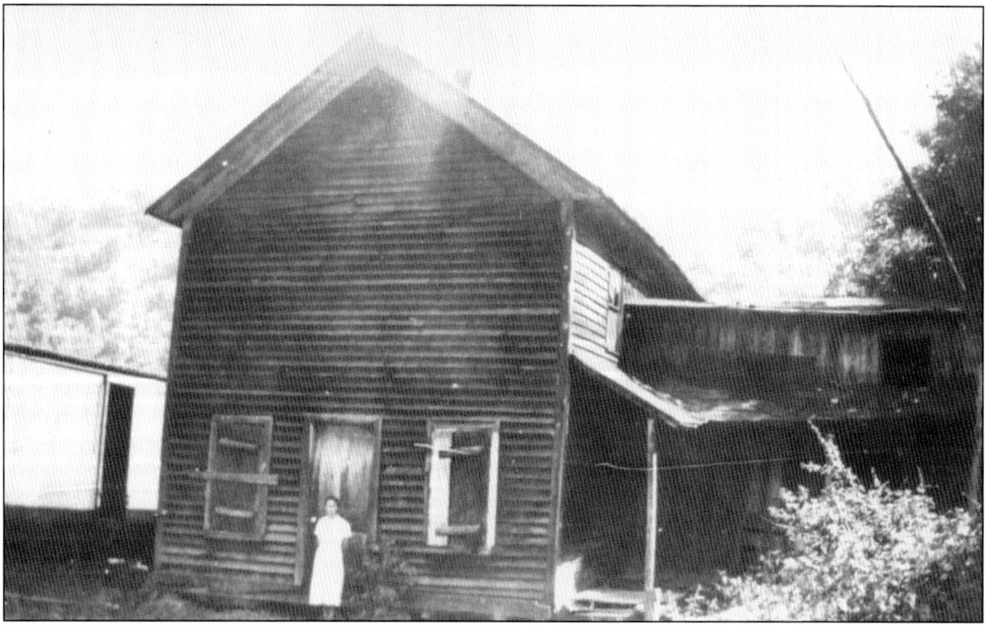

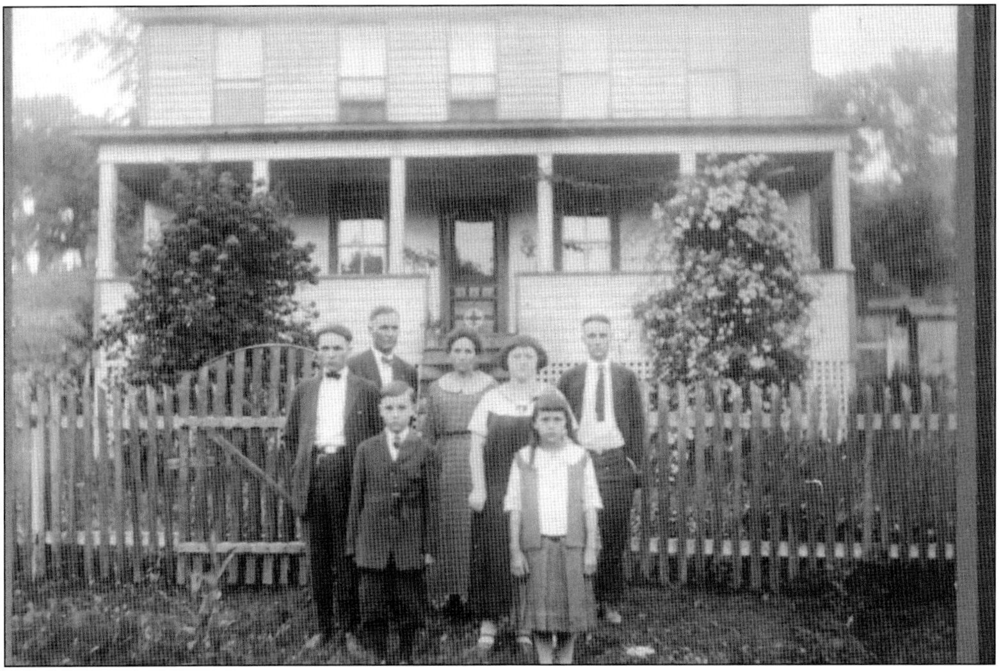

Moatsville was named after the Moats family, several members of which posed for this photo in front of their home. Pictured here are Burke and Eula Moats, their twins, Harry and Hattie, plus their other three children, Delbert, Everett, and Opal. (Courtesy Peggy Robinson.)

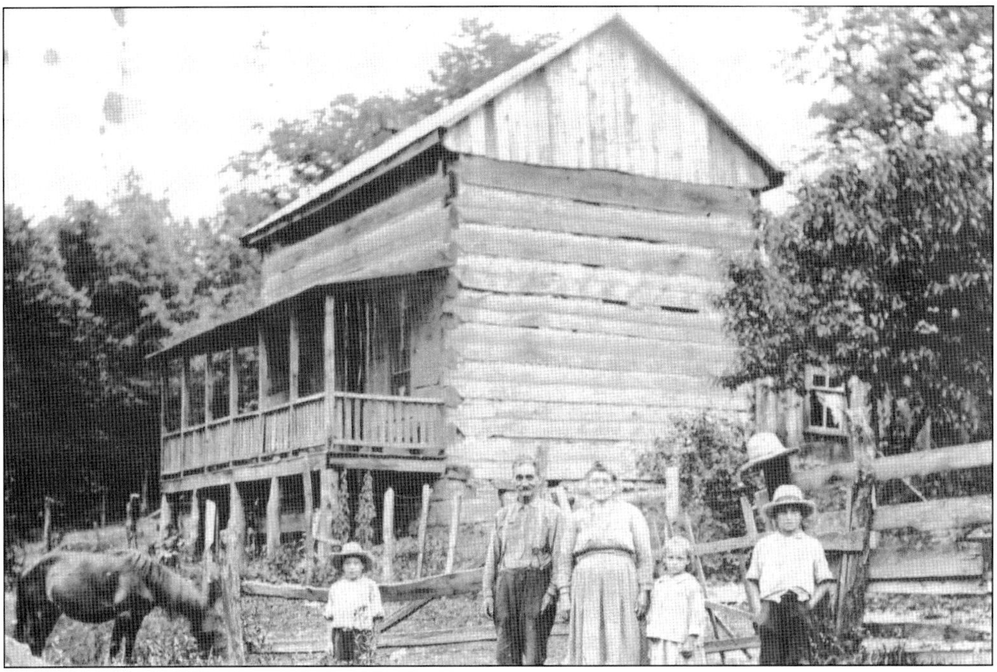

Thomas and Tabitha Zirkle, pictured here in the 1920s, were ancestors of current Barbour County resident Elza Wilson. The small girl pictured is Mildred Wilson Hilton, and the small boy on the left is Lester Saffel. The other boy is Henry Saffel. The Zirkle home was located between Boulder and Audra. (Courtesy Elza Wilson.)

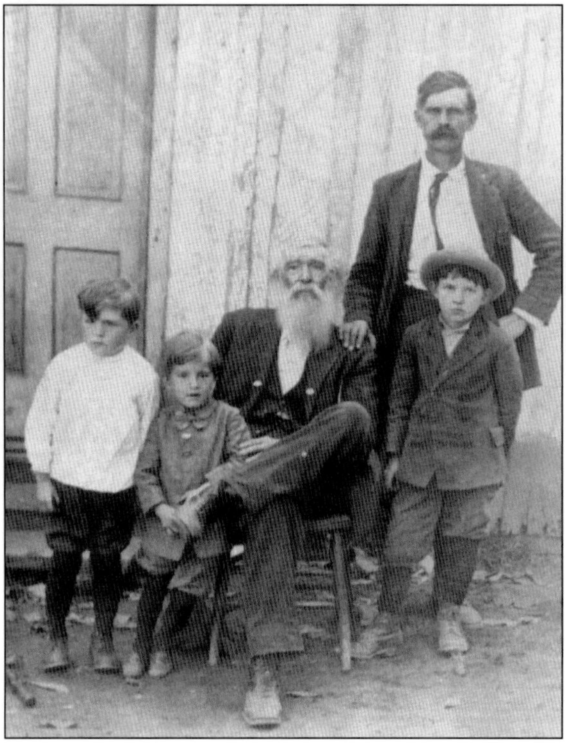

The elderly gentleman in the group picture is Daniel Monroe Williams, who settled in the Mt. Nebo area. Others in the group include Daniel Williams Jr. and his sons (left to right) George, Clayton, and Jacob. The woman in the accompanying portrait is Margaret Rebecca See, who married Daniel Williams Sr., in 1858. They became the grandparents of current Barbour County resident Elza Wilson. (Courtesy Elza Wilson.)

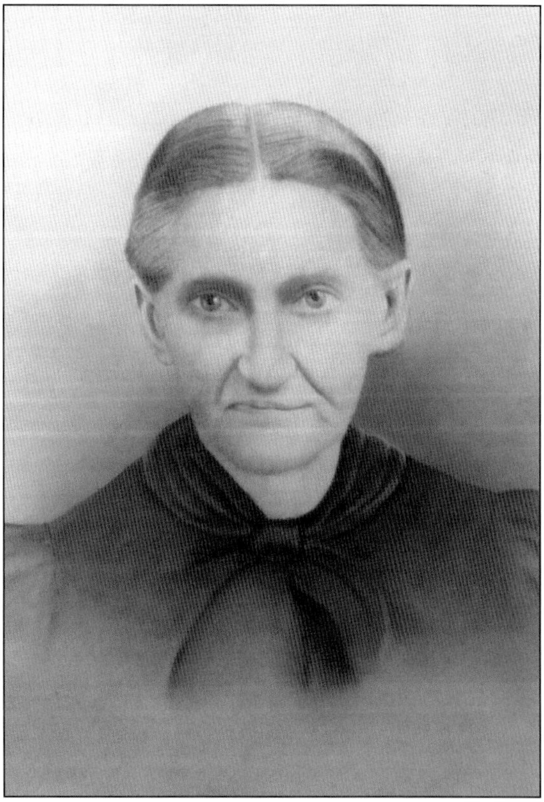

Anastasia and Peter Zubas and their son, Peter, were typical of the families who depended upon coal for their livelihood. In turn, the coal companies were dependent upon workers such as Peter Zubas, who immigrated from Lithuania to work in the mines. (Courtesy Nancy Streets.)

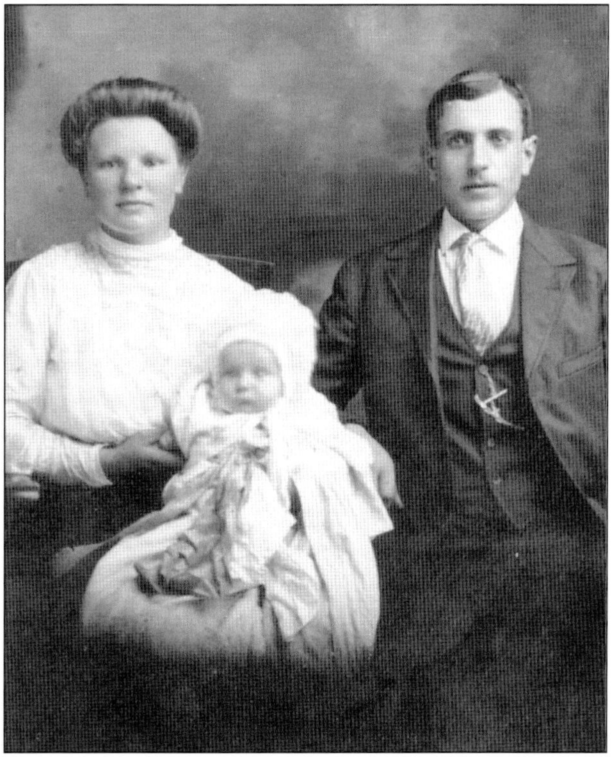

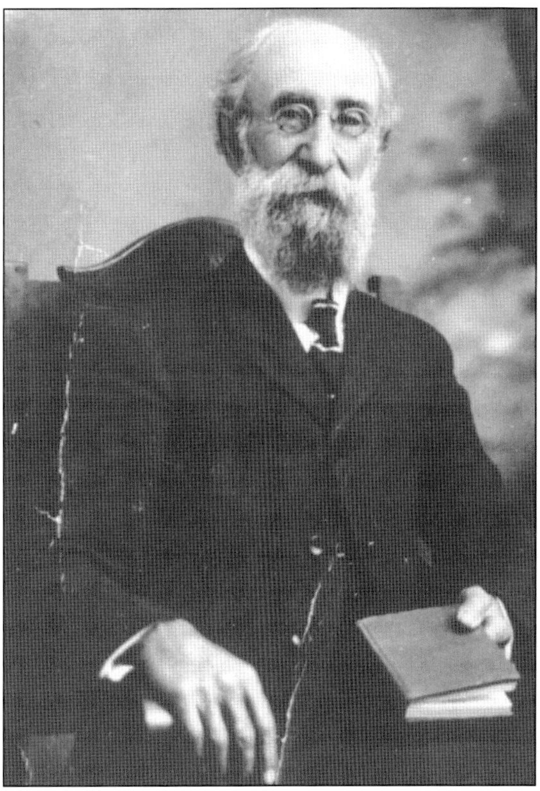

Calvin C. Hart joined the Confederate army in 1861 at the age of 18 and participated in at least 15 skirmishes and battles as a member of McClanahan's Battery. His brother Bunn and nephew John C. Hart served in the same company. Another brother, Hugh, who had migrated to Kansas, fought with Union forces. Calvin C. Hart died in 1924 on the family farm in Barbour County. (Courtesy Neil Irvine.)

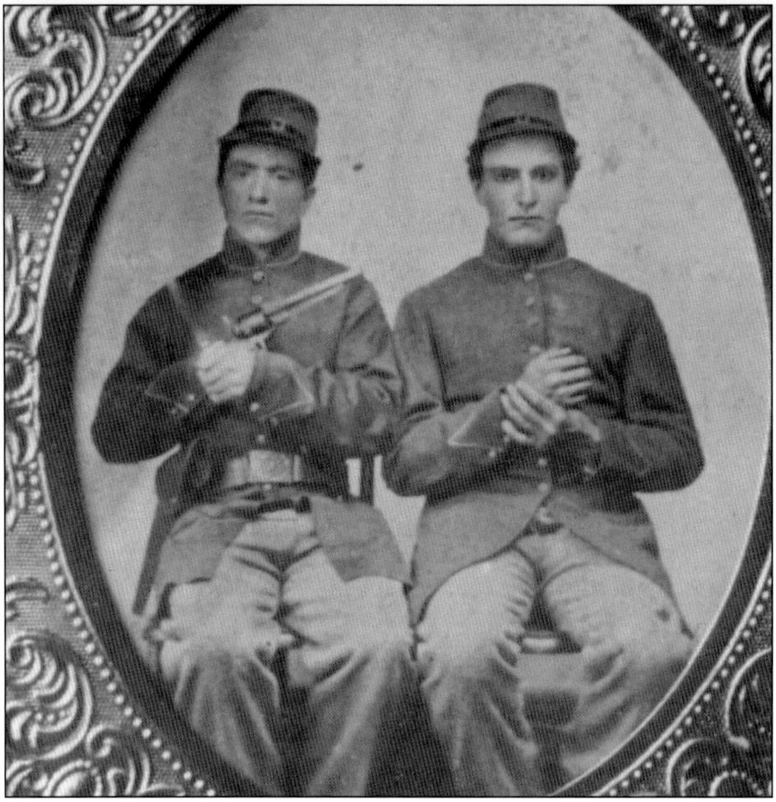

The Civil War brought forth recruits for both the North and the South. Tommy McGinness and Jacob Zirkle volunteered for the Union army in 1862. Zirkle was present at Appomattox when Lee surrendered.

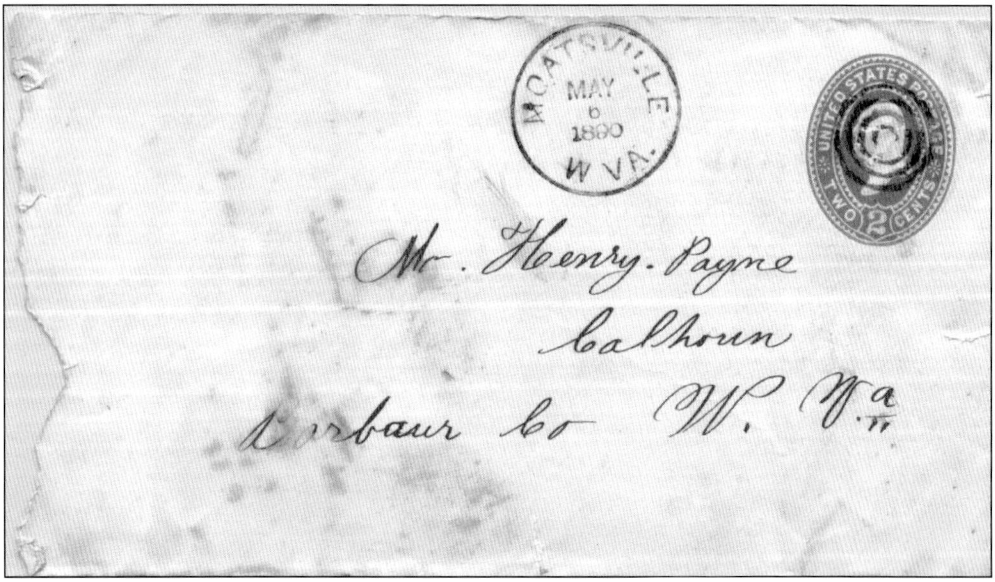

On May 6, 1890, a letter was sent from Moatsville to Mr. Henry Payne in Calhoun, Barbour County, West Virginia. This post office was located directly across from the present Faithway Baptist Church on Route 250. Note the 2¢ stamp. (Courtesy H.A. "Red" Payne.)

Michael Late Benedum, born on Main Street in Bridgeport in 1859, enjoyed a spectacular career as an oil wildcatter and speculator. His highest salary was $150 per month, but he built his earnings and investments into a fortune with which he established in 1944 the Claude Worthington Benedum Foundation. Michael Benedum thereby became the premier philanthropist of north central West Virginia, including Barbour County. (Courtesy Claude Worthington Benedum.)

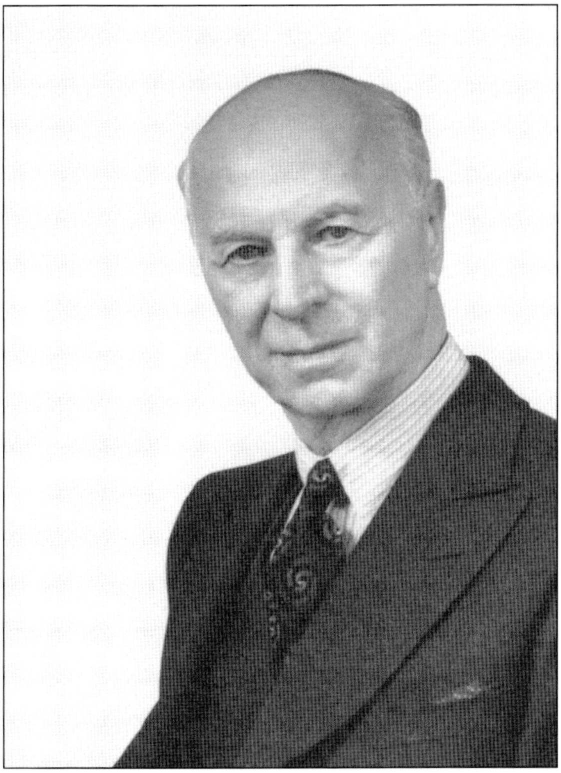

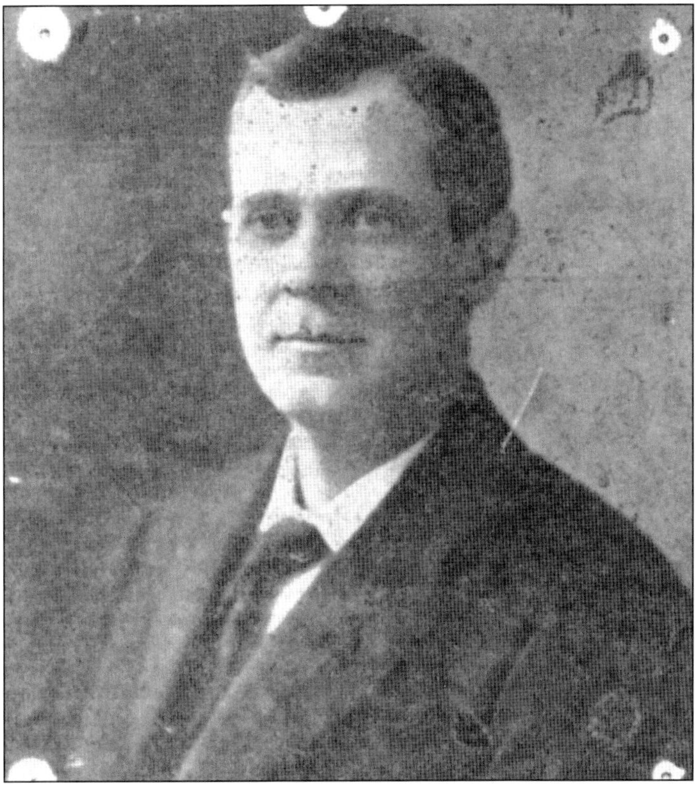

The *West Virginia State Weekly* dated November 23, 1910, notes that in that year, Barbour County had native sons serving as a federal judge, a judge of the State Supreme Court of Appeals, the Secretary of State, the State Tax Commissioner, a state senator, and a judge of the circuit court. Alston G. Dayton was appointed by President Theodore Roosevelt to serve as Judge of the Northern District of West Virginia. (Courtesy Joe Kaiser.)

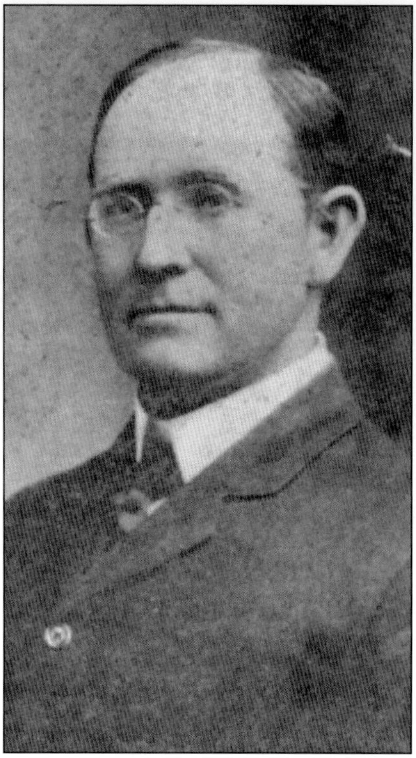

Samuel V. Woods was born in Philippi on August 31, 1856, and was admitted to the bar in 1880. He was a delegate to the National Democratic Convention in 1900 and served as state senator from the Northern District. (Courtesy Joe Kaiser.)

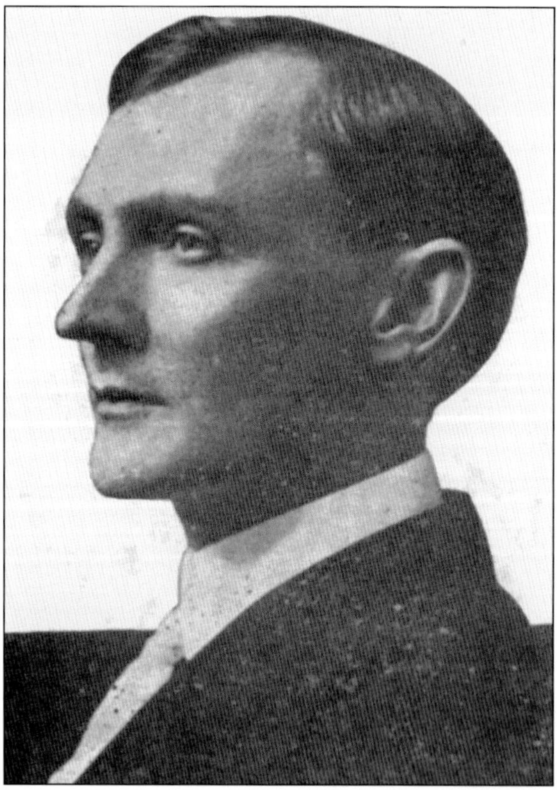

Having grown up in Grafton but living as an adult in Barbour County, Fred O. Blue was appointed State Tax Commissioner by Governor Glasscock. Blue had previously been elected to the state senate. He was married to Maggie J. Ice, daughter of a Philippi judge, and belonged to the Philippi Baptist Church. (Courtesy Joe Kaiser.)

Charles F. Teter was known as "The Big Man from Barbour." A delegate to the National Republican Convention in 1908, he also ran as a Republican candidate for Governor of West Virginia. Born August 4, 1858, near Belington, he was elected prosecuting attorney for the county. He also served as secretary and treasurer of the Philippi Coal Mining Company. (Courtesy Joe Kaiser.)

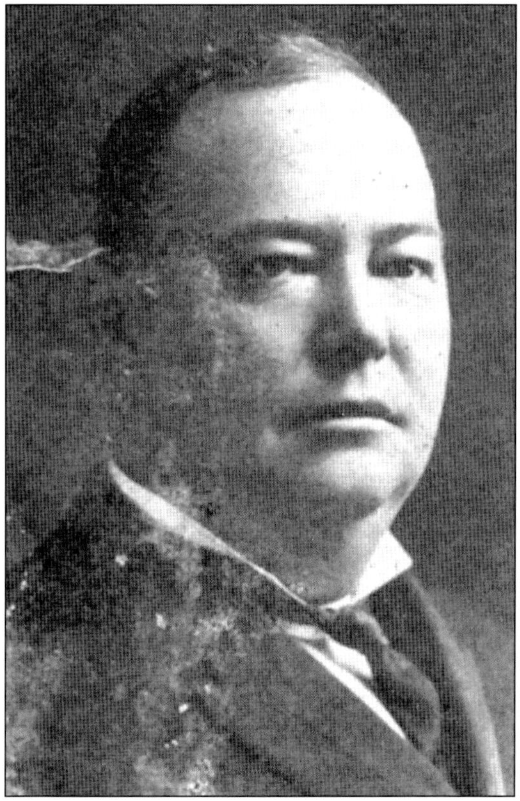

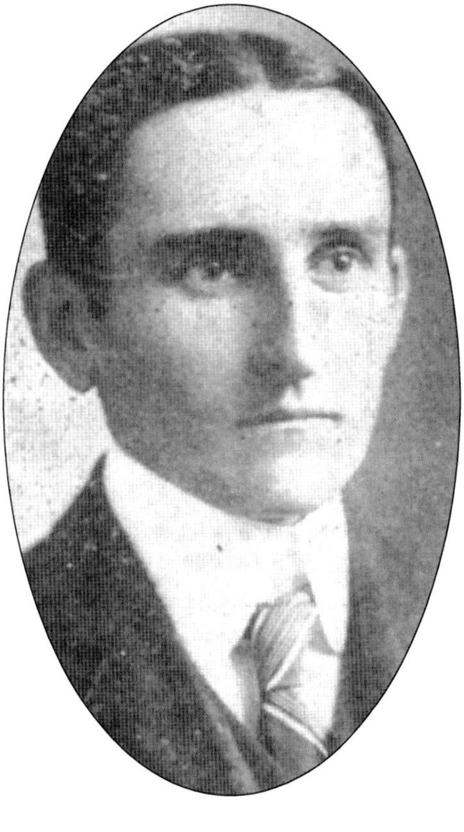

Harry H. Byrer was the secretary and member of the executive committee of the Tygart Valley Marble Works, which was organized in 1905. Other officers were Charles M. Byrer, president, and Edmund Whitehair, treasurer and manager. The plant was one of Barbour County's most successful businesses at the time. The company created statuary, coping, headstones, and tablets. (Courtesy Joe Kaiser.)

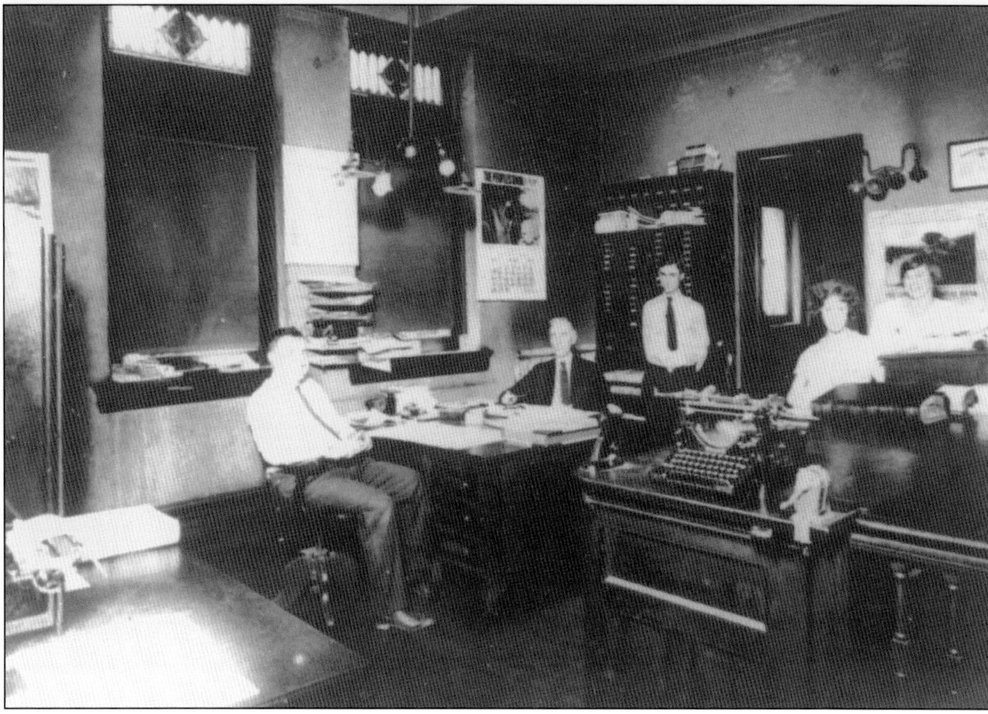

John F. Hewitt, wearing a coat and seated here behind the desk, served as county clerk. This photo was taken at the Barbour County Courthouse in 1925. (Courtesy Jane Mattaliano.)

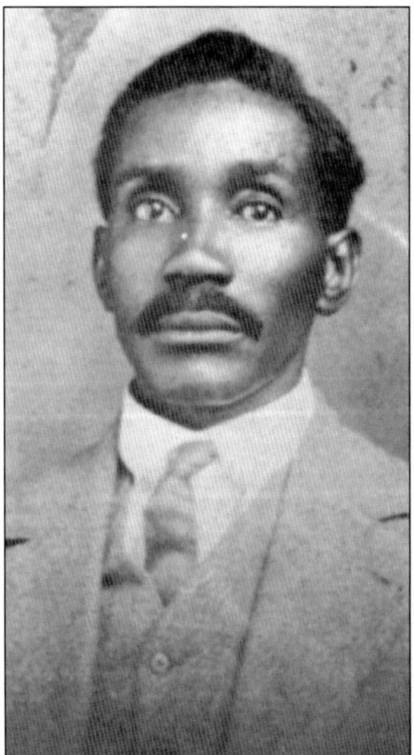

Henry Franklin, a section boss at the Cambria Mine, rode horseback from Brownton to Philippi to request a school for black children. The superintendent required Franklin to find ten pupils and a building. Franklin and his wife converted their Brownton bedroom into a schoolroom and enrolled a dozen students. He later constructed a separate building on his own land. This arrangement served until the mid-20th century.

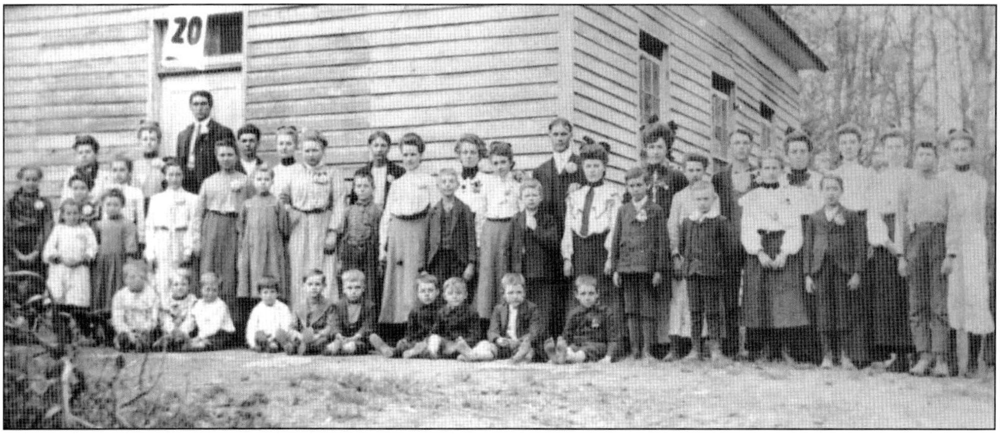

The White Oak School in Glade District was one of the largest at the time this photo was taken. Pictured top left is the teacher, Melville P. Boyles, who at the age of 16 was granted a Number One teaching certificate. He later served as principal of Belington High School, Victory High School in Clarksburg, and several others throughout the state. (Courtesy Joe Mattaliano.)

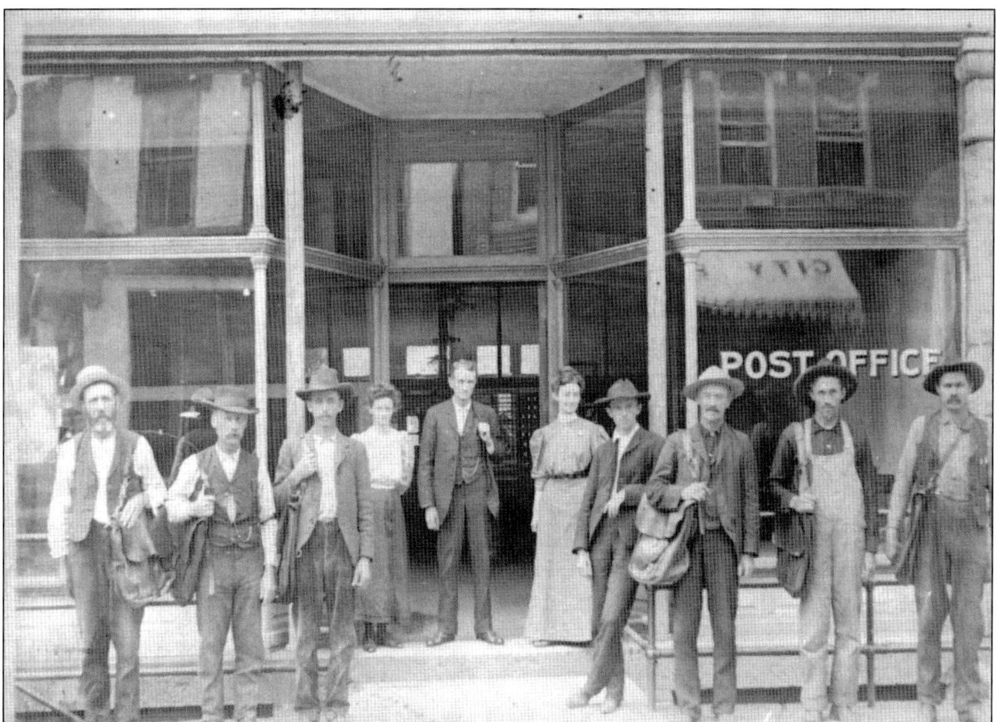

Modern post office employees bear little resemblance to these workers pictured in 1906. On the right and left are the mail carriers, and in the center of the photo are the clerks. (Courtesy Joe Mattaliano.)

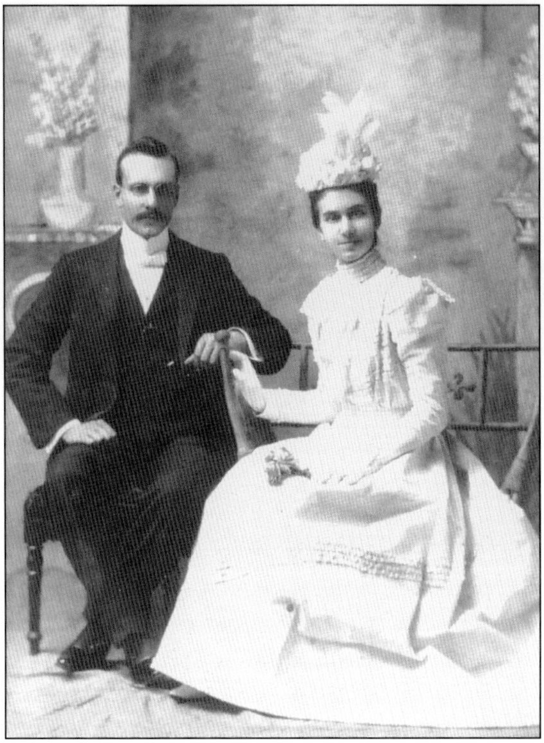

Dr. J.W. Myers, who had been practicing medicine in Nestorville, moved his office to Philippi in 1910, where he founded the Myers Remedy Company, distributing a great variety of medications over a multi-state region. This wedding photo of Dr. Myers and Lennie Crim Myers was taken in 1898. All five of their children, Hu, Elmer, Edna, Karl, and Junior, became physicians and practiced in Barbour County at one time or another. The accompanying photo commemorates Dr. Myers' graduation from medical school. (Courtesy Jane Mattaliano.)

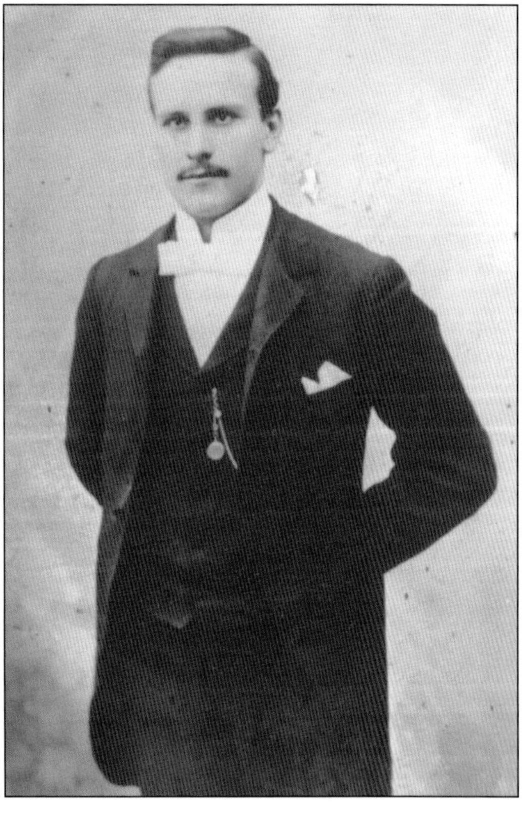

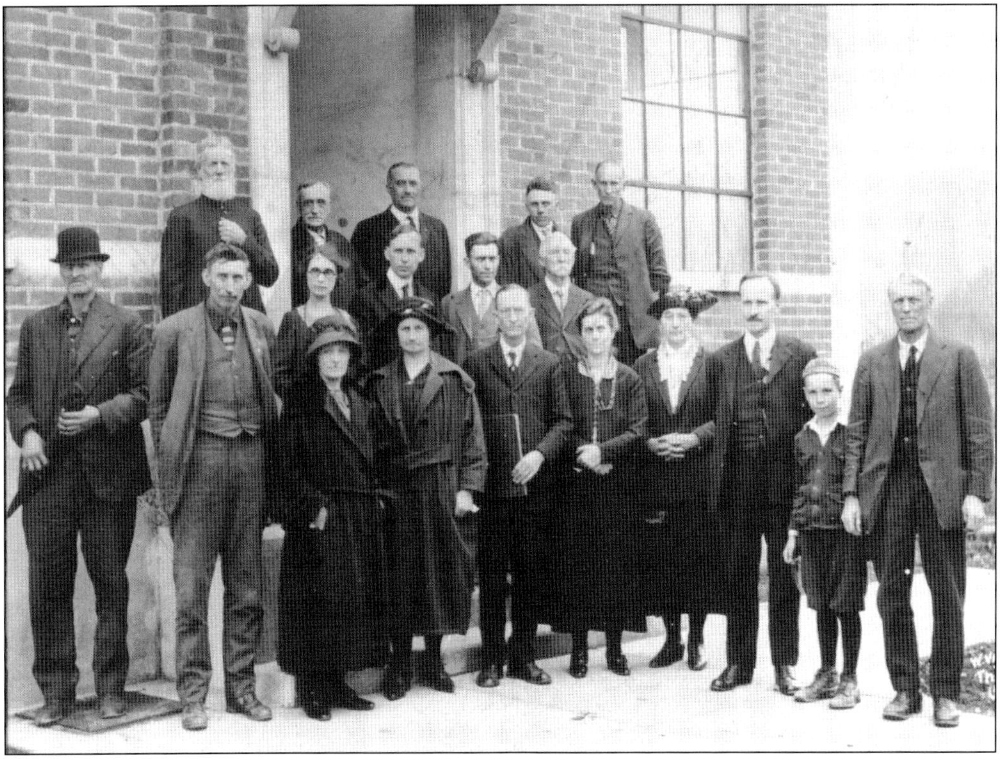

By 1927, the Myers Remedy Company used 3,200 outlets in seven states. Incorporated in 1915, the business was housed in a factory erected in 1923. It served over a million customers. Many of the remedies were based on natural substances such as herbs, and many of the formulas came from folk sources. Pictured here is the Remedy staff. (Courtesy Jane Mattaliano.)

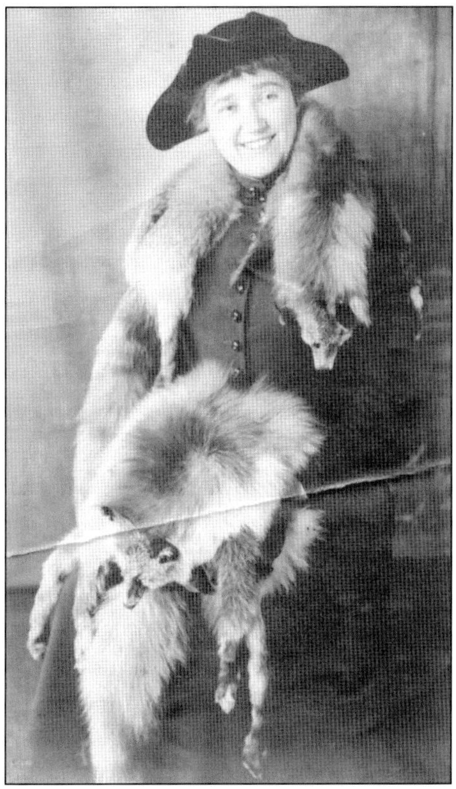

Miss Alma Pitts was one of the best-known citizens of Barbour County in the early 20th century. Pictured here in her 20s, she later became a realtor and insurance broker. Her home, located at the present site of the Hu Myers Center, was a landmark. Present Philippi residents James and Robert Califf are her nephew and great-nephew. (Courtesy James and Robert Califf.)

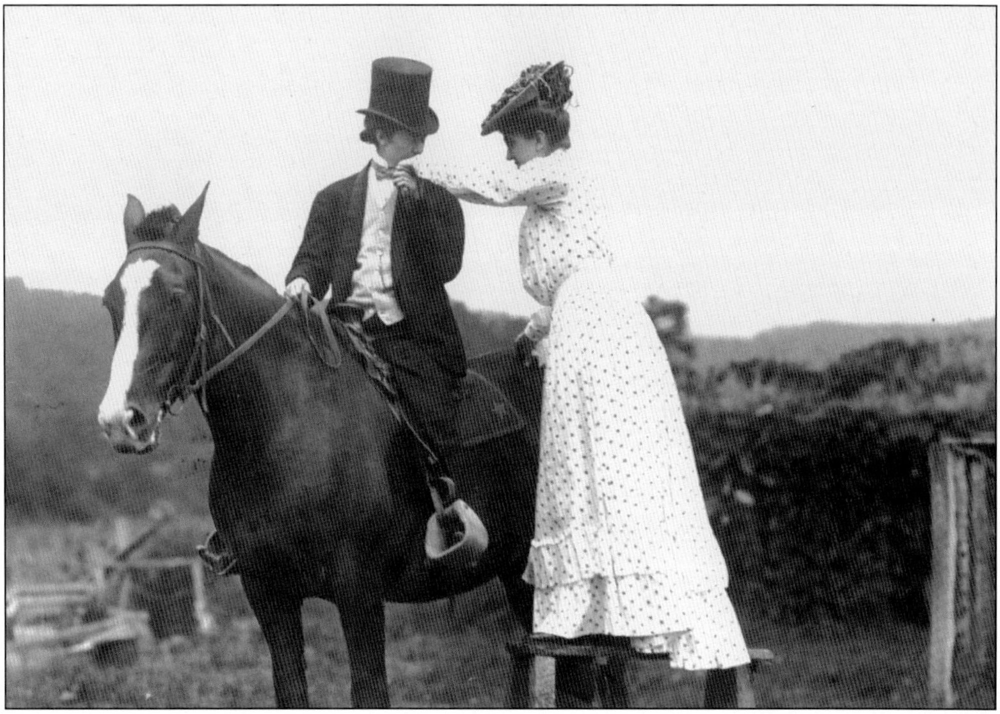

Rita (Reta or Reeta) Pitts later married Jack Califf and became the mother of present Philippi resident James Califf. She taught piano and directed music and drama activities at Broaddus Institute. She is pictured here in 1910 with one of her suitors prior to her marriage. (Courtesy James and Robert Califf.)

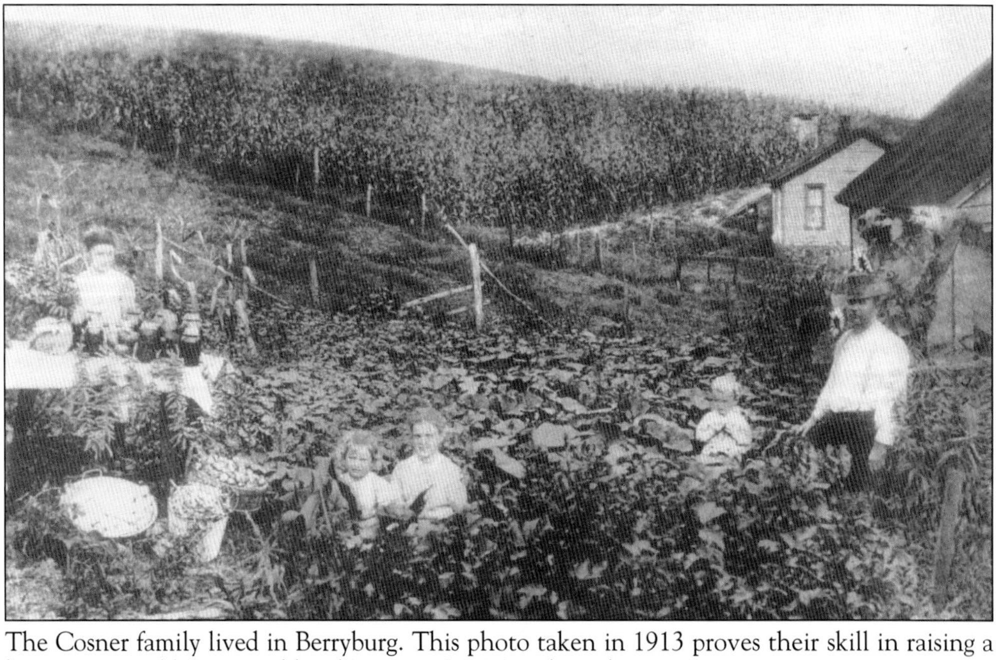

The Cosner family lived in Berryburg. This photo taken in 1913 proves their skill in raising a bumper crop of fine vegetables. (Courtesy Joe Mattaliano.)

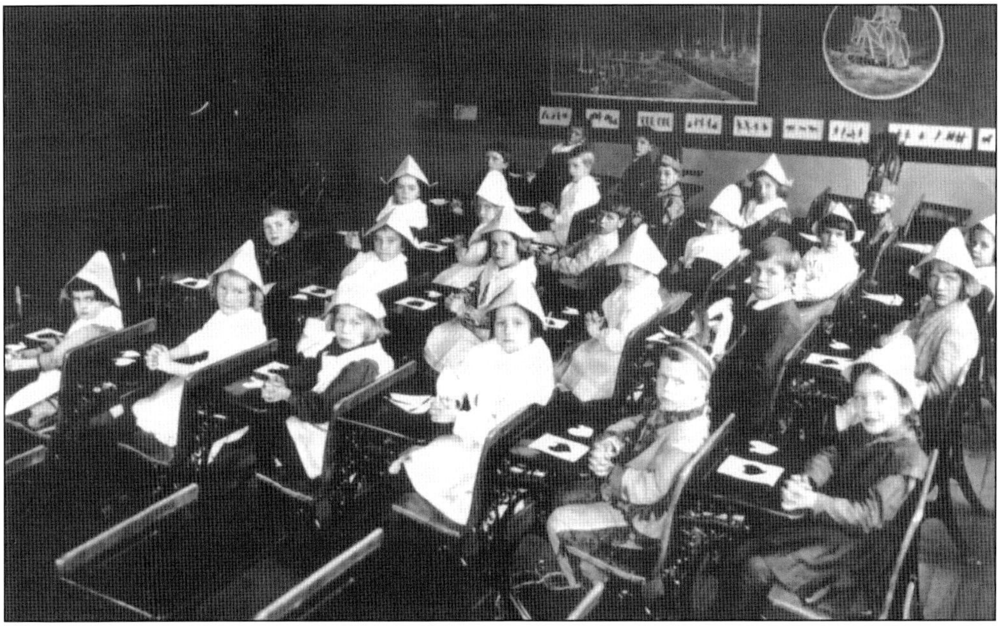

These unidentified school children in an unidentified Barbour County school were all dressed up with no place to go, but they did have their picture taken! (Courtesy Joe Mattaliano.)

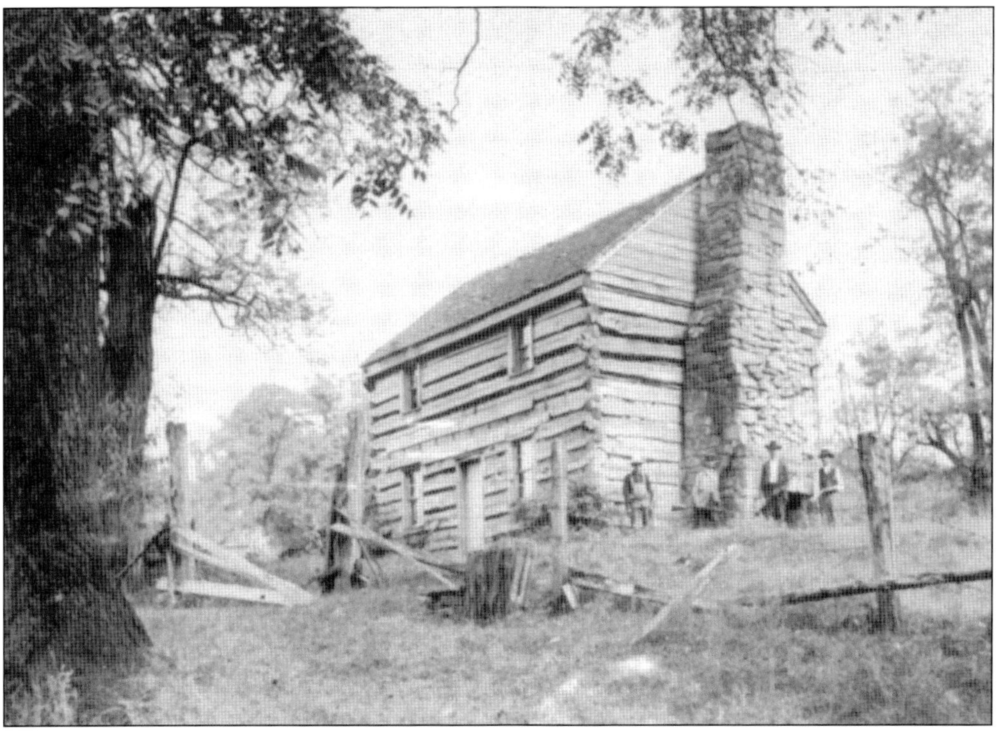

This log house in Elk City was donated in 1976 to Pricketts Fort in Marion County. An Elk City resident, Bud Dickinson helped to hew the corners of the building on property now owned by heirs of H.L. and Laura Gall Roy. Posing for this photo was a family whose name is believed to have been Bear or Baird. (Courtesy Martha Rose Roy.)

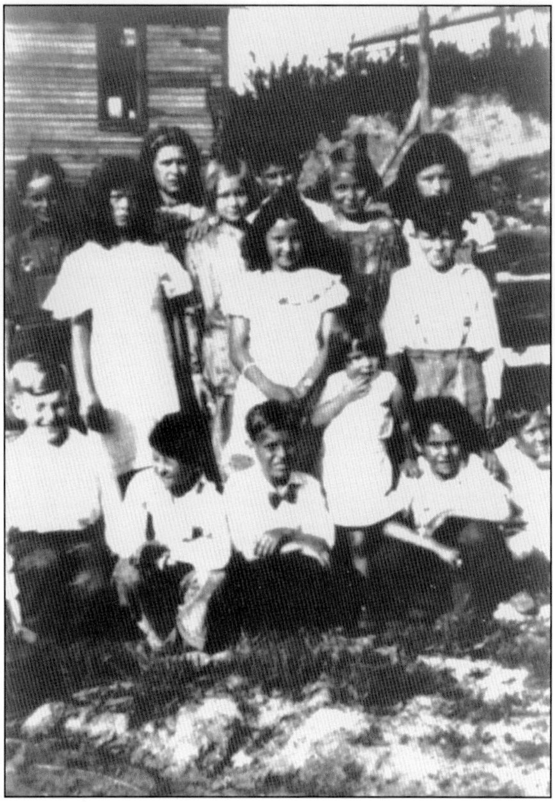

Taken in 1930 at the Galloway crossing and in front of a home occupied by the Meherg family, this photo includes (front to back and left to right) Henry Cavallo, Guido Cavallo, Russell Scott, Stella Dottellis, Bill Dottellis, Louis Girimot, Ilene Meherg, Elizabeth Dottellis, Aldo Cavallo, Frank Markley, Daisy Scott, Geraldine Keener, Louis Barbero, Beulah Markley, and Angie Dottellis. (Courtesy James B. Keener.)

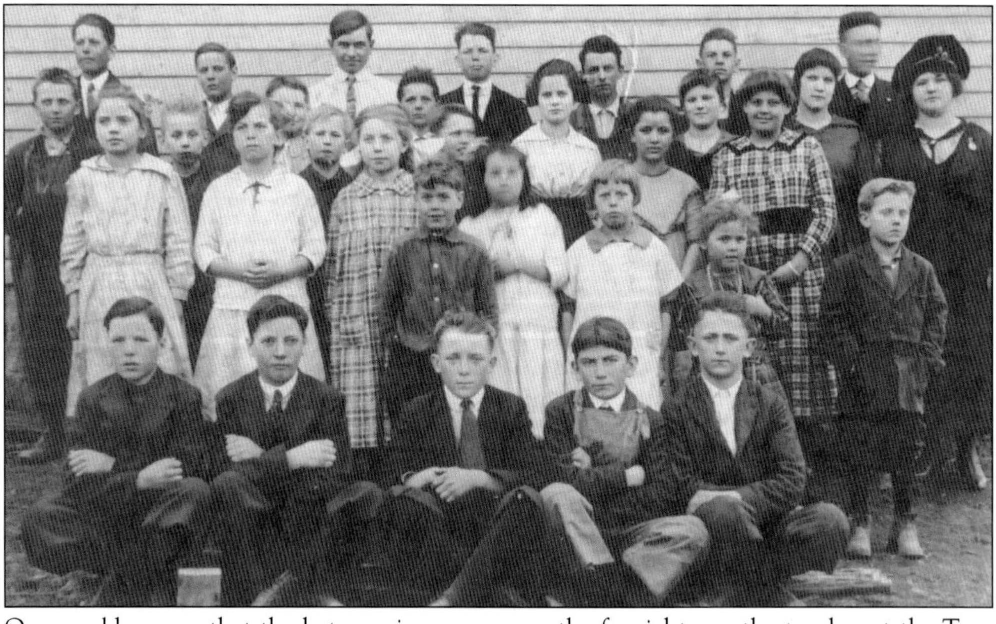

One would assume that the hat-wearing woman on the far right was the teacher at the Tacy School where this photo was taken. Mrs. Gerald Posten was the owner of the picture and was probably one of the students. (Courtesy Joe Mattaliano.)

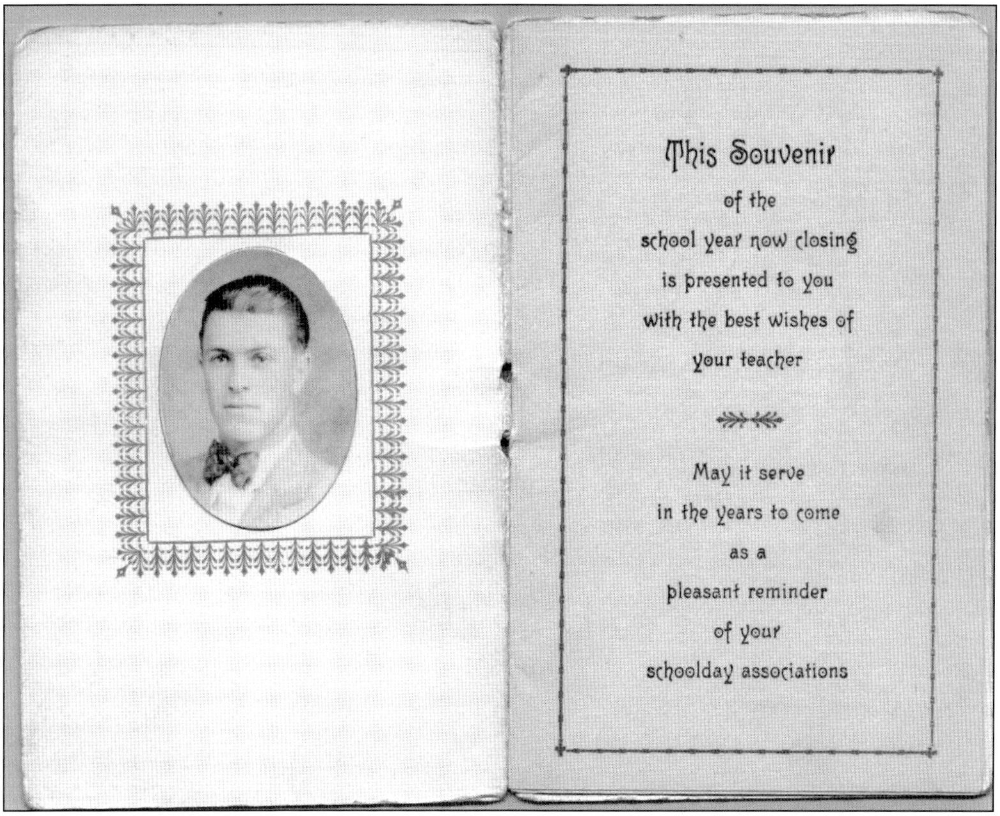

In 1931 the teacher of the Corley School in the Barker District, Obed Poling, gave each student a souvenir booklet containing his picture. The small publication included five poems, a list of the pupils, and the names of the three members of the board of education. Poling later became president of the Board of Trustees of Alderson-Broaddus College and chief administrator of Broaddus Hospital. (Courtesy H.A. "Red" Payne.)

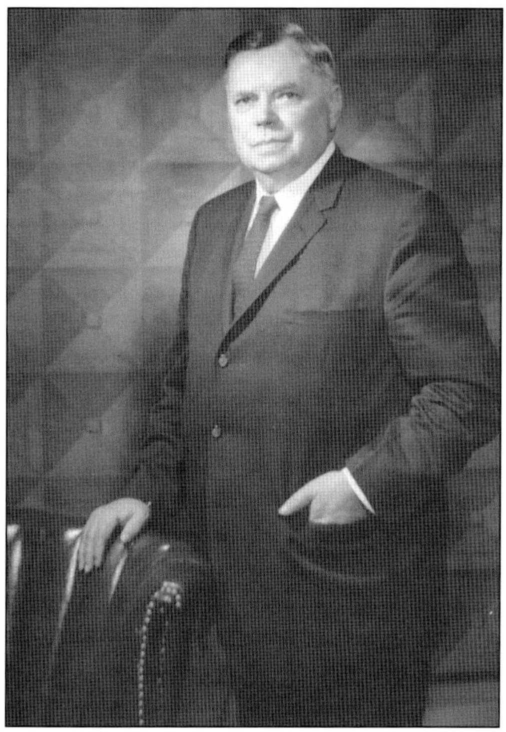

A prominent figure in Barbour County history is Judge Dayton Stemple. Attending Tacy and Philippi public schools and graduating from West Virginia University School of Law, Stemple went immediately into politics, serving 16 years as state senator, as Senate Minority Leader, and later Judge of the Circuit Court for Taylor and Barbour Counties. Judge Stemple died in 1964. (Courtesy Joe Mattaliano.)

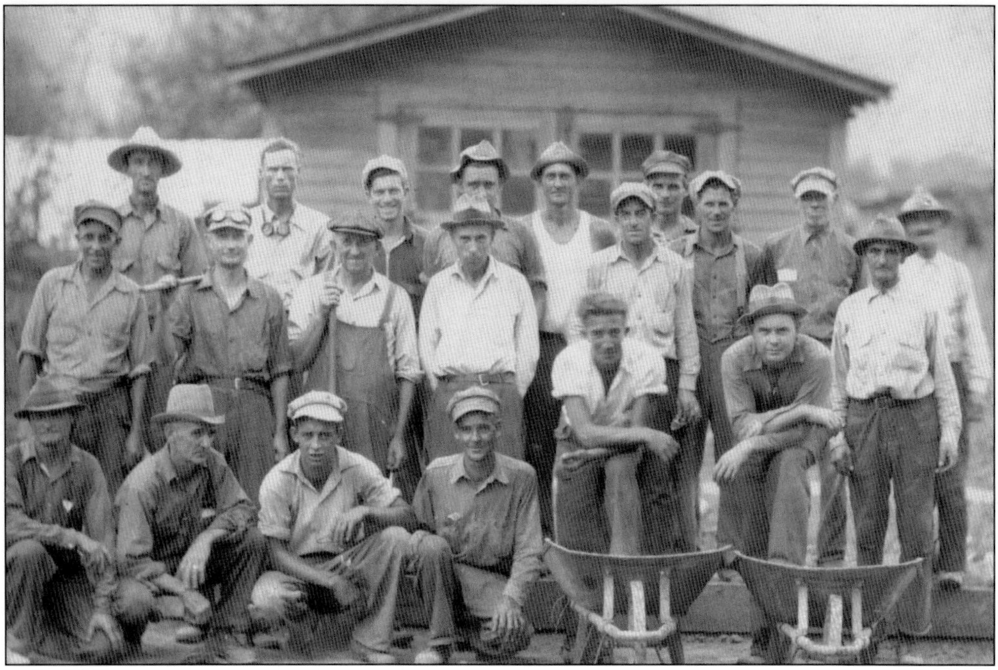

The WPA, a program created by Franklin Delano Roosevelt, was in operation from 1935 to 1942. This particular crew worked on the streets of Belington. Included among these men are Charley Ervin, Harry Jones, Theodore Teter, and Ode Ervin. (Courtesy H.A. "Red" Payne.)

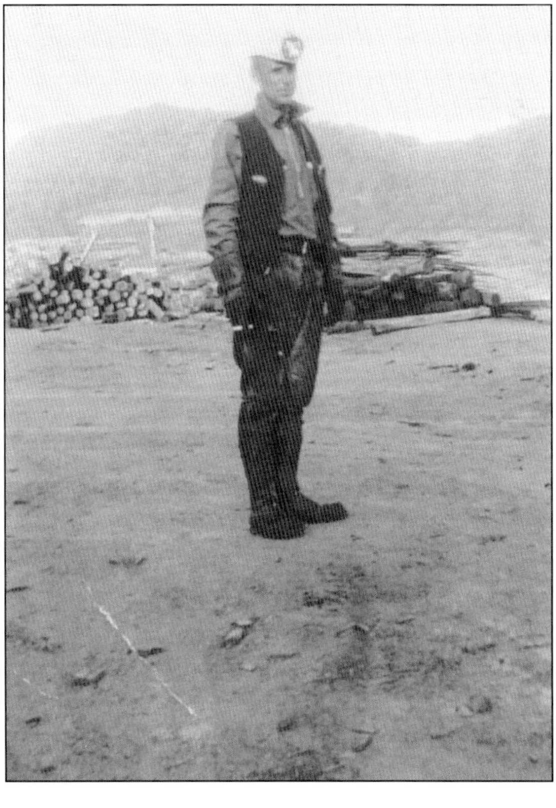

Stark Humphries was employed by Simpson Creek Colliers. This picture, taken in the early 1940s, suggests that Humphries at the time worked above ground rather than in the mine. (Courtesy Alice "Bonnie" Rowan.)

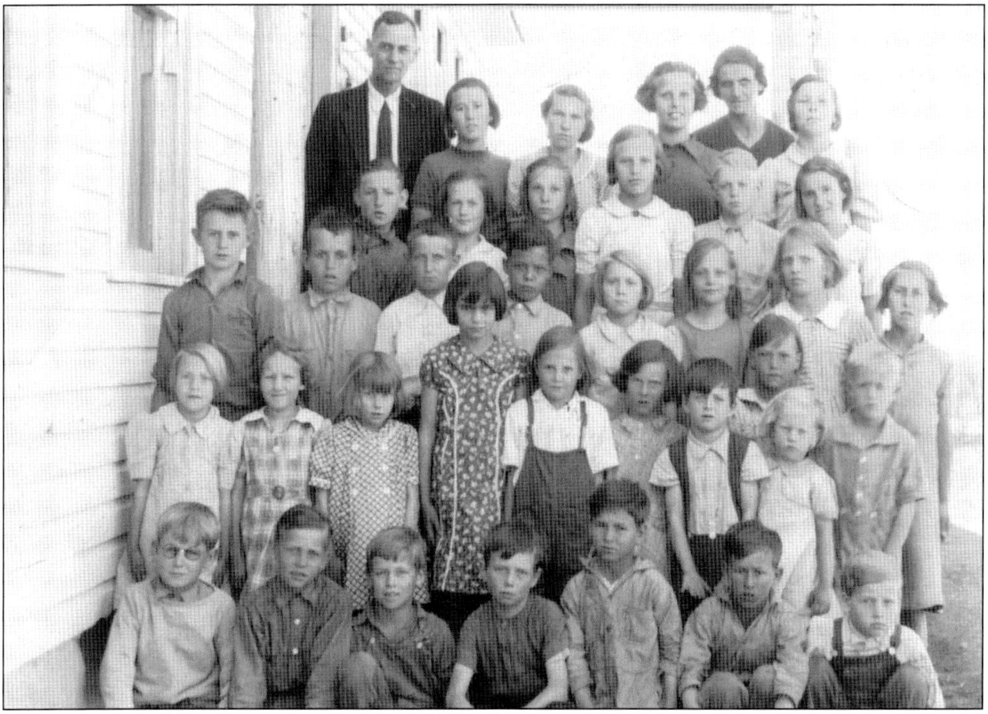

Pictured in 1937, this fine group of Barbour County students attended the Union School. Teachers were W.T. Cross and Mrs. Lantz (back row, left and right). (Courtesy Joe Mattaliano.)

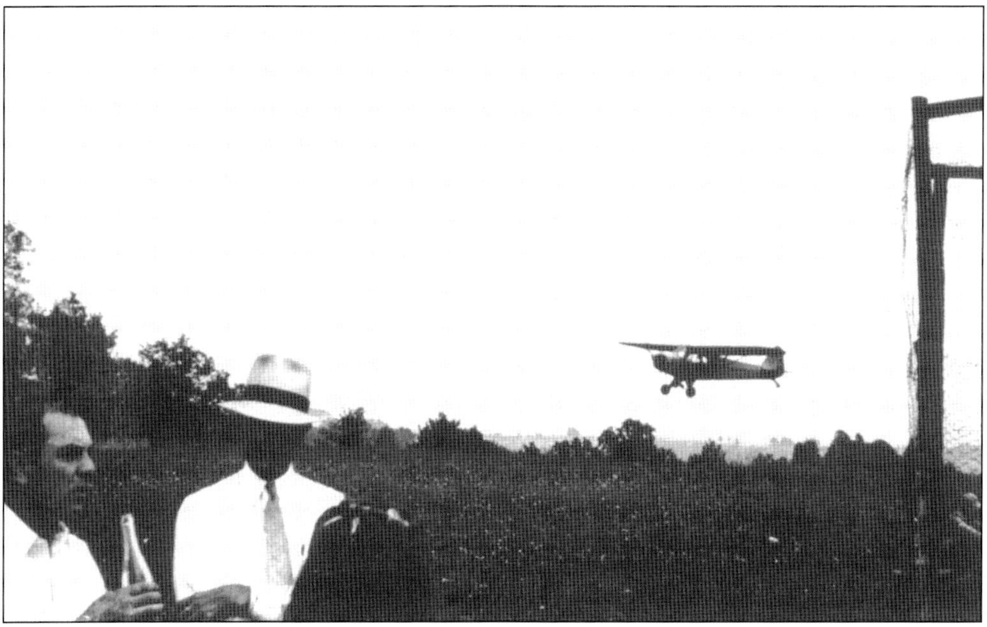

Wilbur Simpson owned and operated small planes and a private airport in Barbour County. He gave flying lessons to a number of county residents, including Dr. Richard Shearer, president of Alderson-Broaddus College. Air mail was bagged and dropped to the ground from biplanes such as the one seen here. (Courtesy H.A. "Red" Payne.)

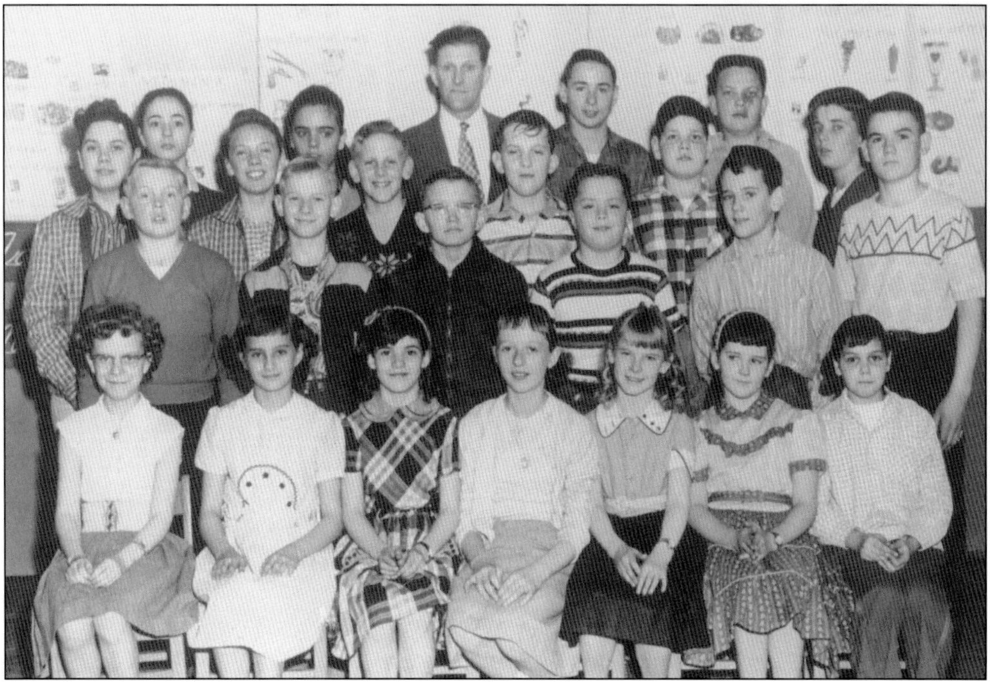

This Century School class picture of 1956–57 includes a number of individuals who later became Barbour County leaders, including Jim True, John Cvechko, and Gary Cunningham. (Courtesy Nancy Streets.)

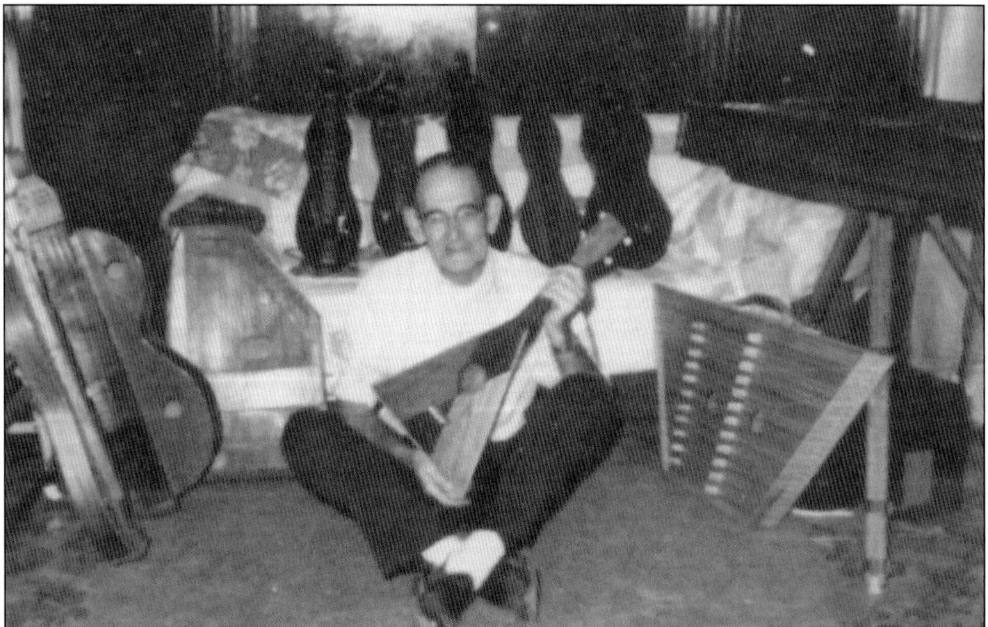

Born in Volga in 1913, Charles Maxson became famous throughout the state and region as a master dulcimer builder. He described himself also as inventor, musician, teacher, storyteller, fiddler, guitarist, pianist, organist, and player of mandolin, autoharp, banjo, humle, balalika, saw, and chimes.

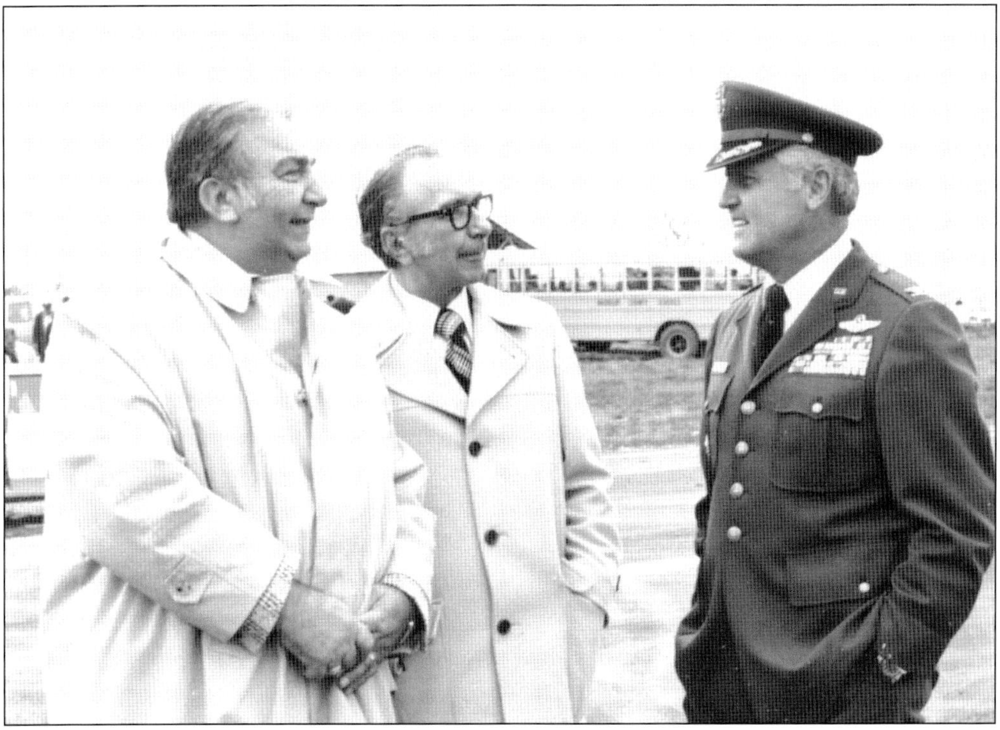

The most famous person to grow up in Brownton is Colonel Ralph Albertazzie, pilot of Air Force One under four presidents. He has received many honors from Barbour County organizations, including an honorary doctorate from Alderson-Broaddus College in 1973. Pictured with Colonel Albertazzie are Al and Frank Mellie. (Courtesy Lars Byrne.)

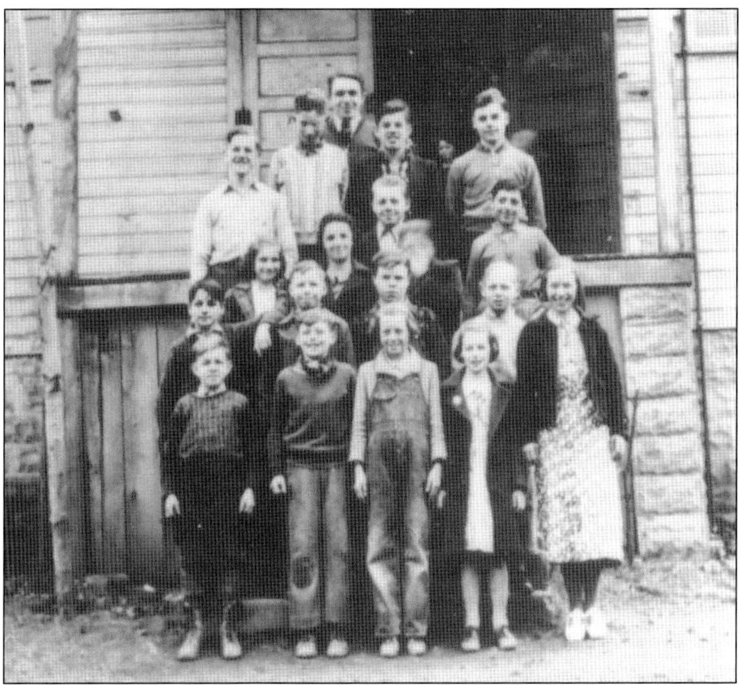

Loyd Hall taught at the Bear Mountain school when this picture was taken. Included in the group is Ralph Albertazzie, far right, second row from the back. Albertazzie went on to play football for Philippi High School and West Virginia University before joining the Air Force and becoming pilot of Air Force One. (Courtesy Helen and Albert Gleza.)

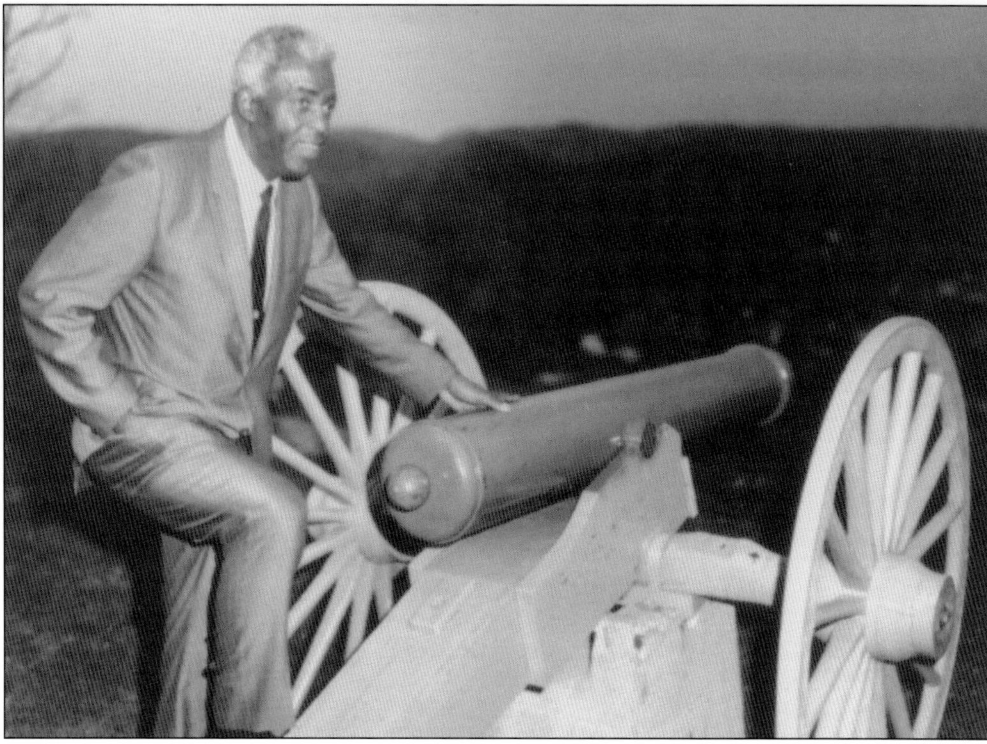

Baseball Hall-of-Famer Jackie Robinson was present for the opening baseball game of the Alderson-Broaddus 1969 season. He posed for pictures on the crest of Battle Hill, the site of the college. For many years, cannons which were replicas of the originals designated the location of the first land battle of the Civil War.

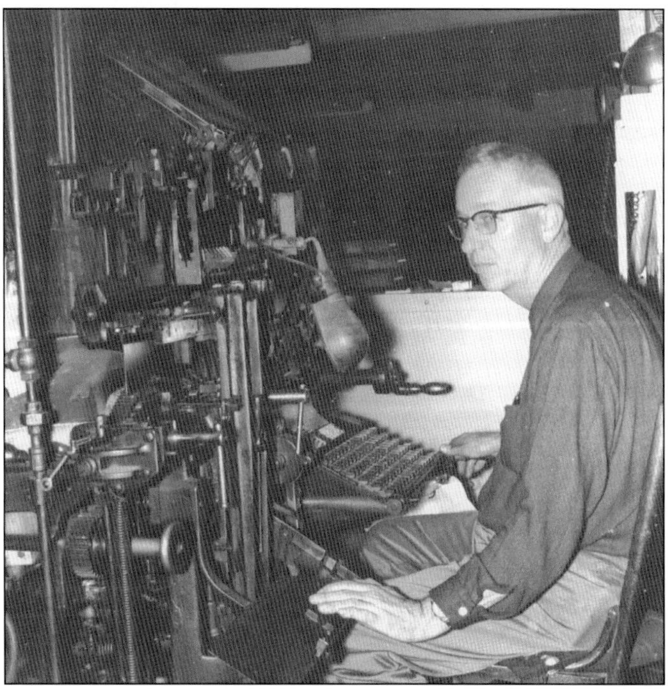

Allen Byrne owned and edited *The Barbour Democrat* for 55 years. Byrne was known as one of the fastest and most accurate Linotype operators in the country. Although he surrendered leadership of the paper to his sons in 1975, Byrne continued to work at the paper and to serve the community in a great variety of ways. (Courtesy Lars Byrne.)

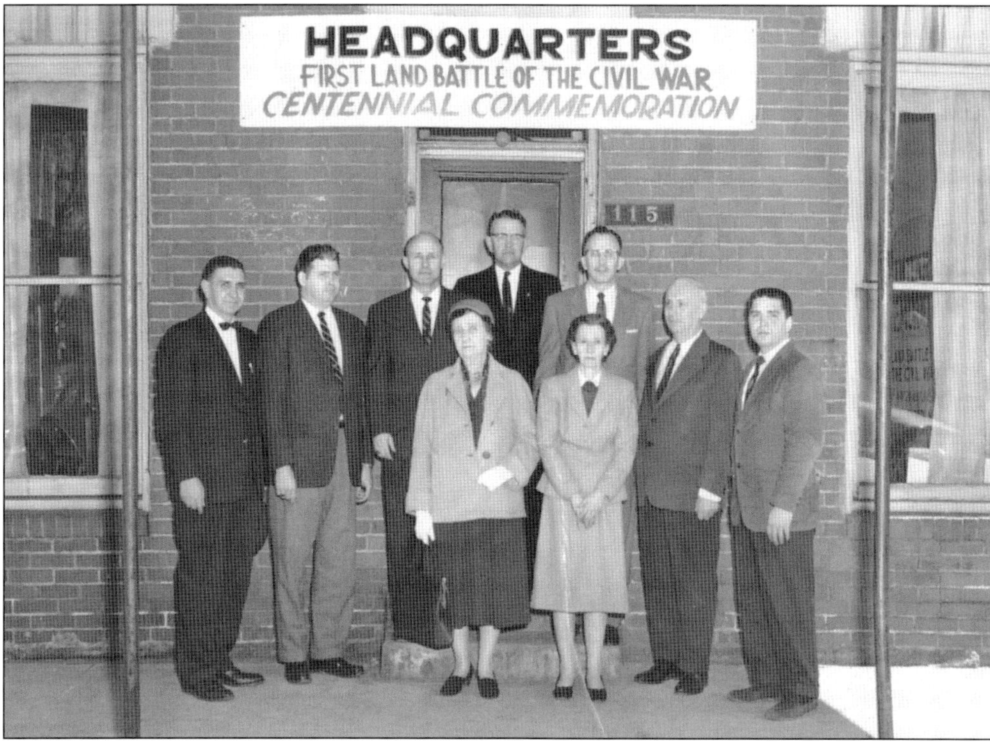

The centennial commemoration of the first land battle of the Civil War was held in 1961. Included in the arrangements committee were (left to right) Bill Woodford, John Phillips, Dr. Richard Shearer, Alma Pitts, Frank Sigley, Dr. Elmer Myers, Mary Chaffee, Dr. Karl Myers Sr., and Dr. Elliot Bryant. (Courtesy Joe Mattaliano.)

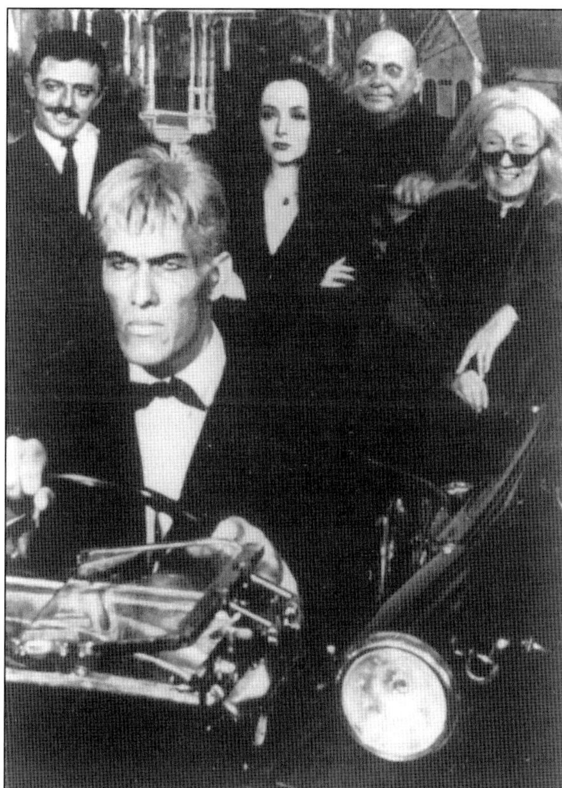

One of Barbour County's best-known citizens was Ted Cassidy, a native of Philippi, who played the role of Lurch on the very popular television series *The Adams Family*. Cassidy is pictured in the lower left of the photo. (Courtesy Joe Mattaliano.)

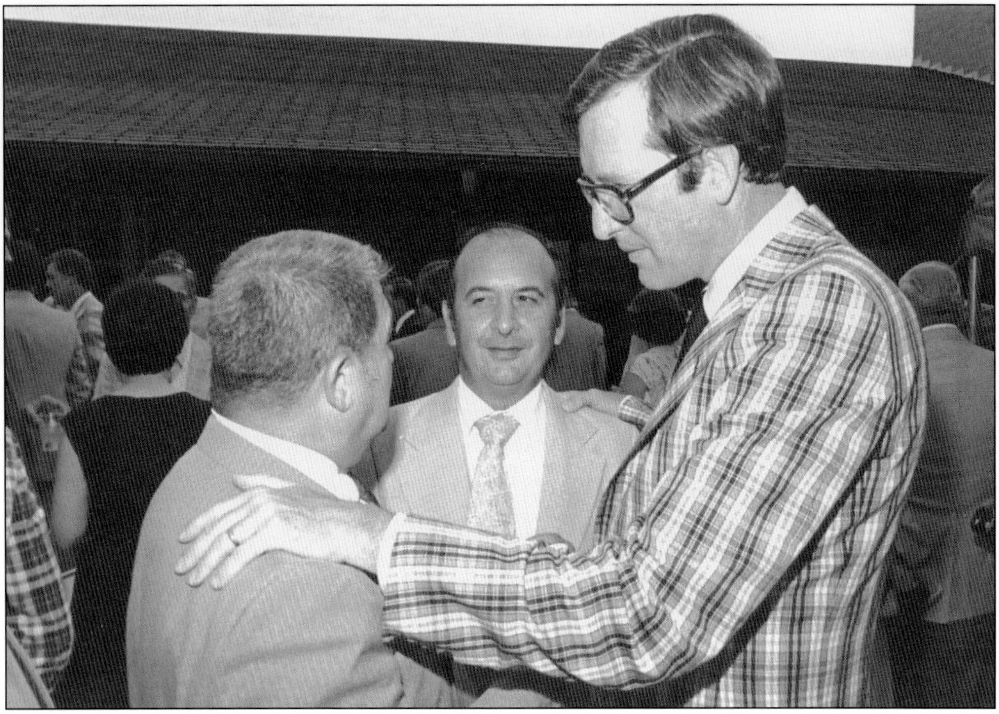

Wearing a fashionably bold sport coat in this particular photo, then-governor Jay Rockefeller greeted and befriended many Barbour County residents, including Joe Mattaliano, who served as city manager in Philippi for 38 years before becoming a representative to the state legislature. (Courtesy Joe Mattaliano.)

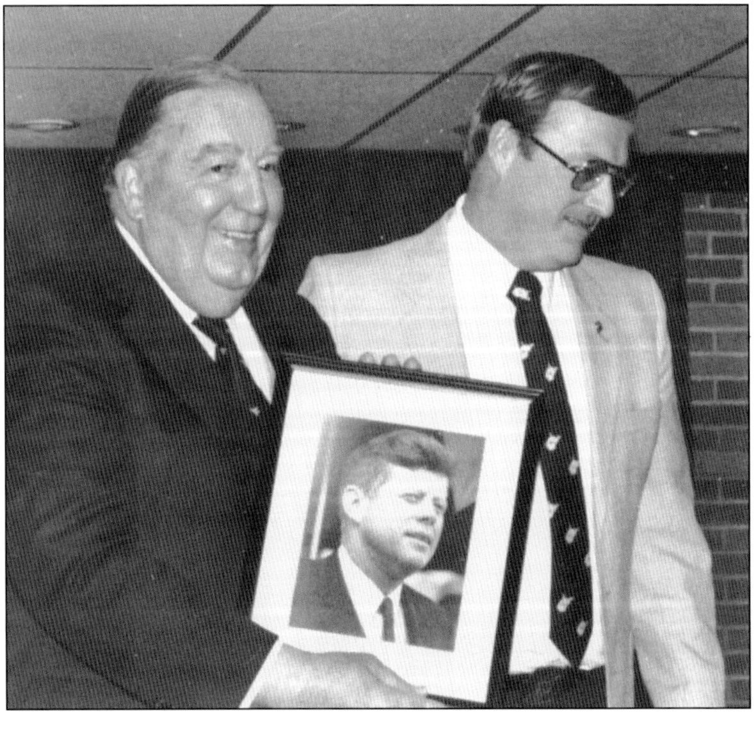

U.S. Senators Robert Byrd, Jay Rockefeller, and Jennings Randolph have been great friends of Barbour County. Senator Randolph was presented with a portrait of John F. Kennedy at a Kiwanis meeting in the early 1980s. Lars Byrne made the presentation. (Courtesy Lars Byrne.)

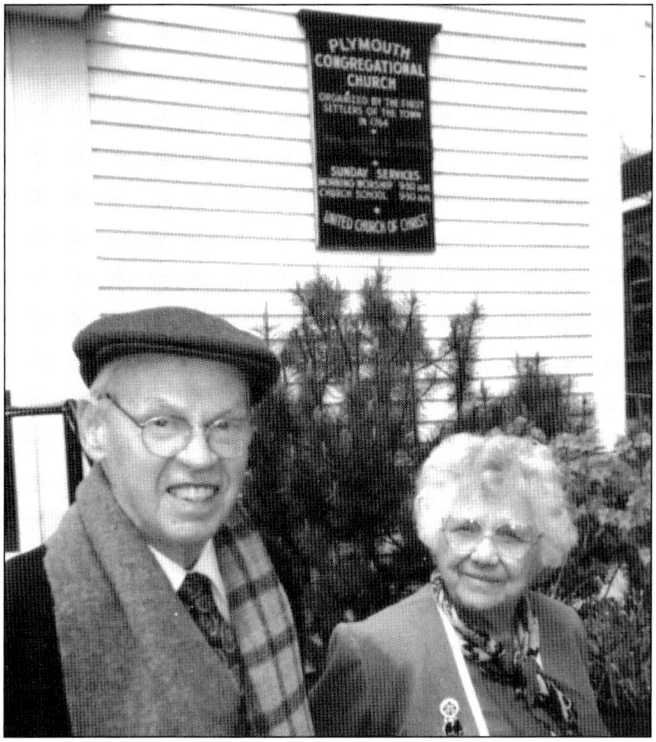

Born of missionary parents in China, Herbert and Bertha Waters met and married after their families returned to the United States. They taught at Alderson-Broaddus College for many years, Herbert specializing in printmaking and watercolor, Bertha in pottery and weaving. Herbert's work has been recognized internationally. It is his print that serves as the frontispiece for this book. (Courtesy Leonard LoBello.)

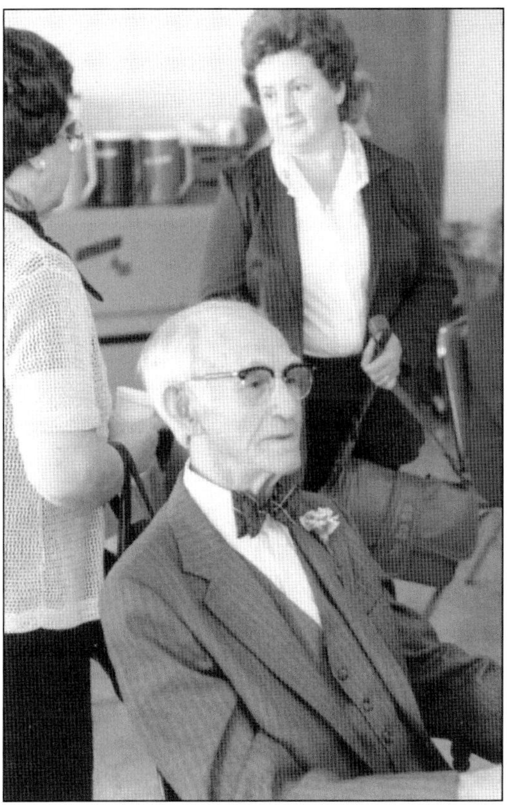

One of the longest-lived residents of Belington and Barbour County was Fred Thompson, shown here at his 100th birthday celebration in 1983. State legislator, government printer, and editor of the *Belington Republican* newspaper, he lived to be 103 years old. (Courtesy H.A. "Red" Payne.)

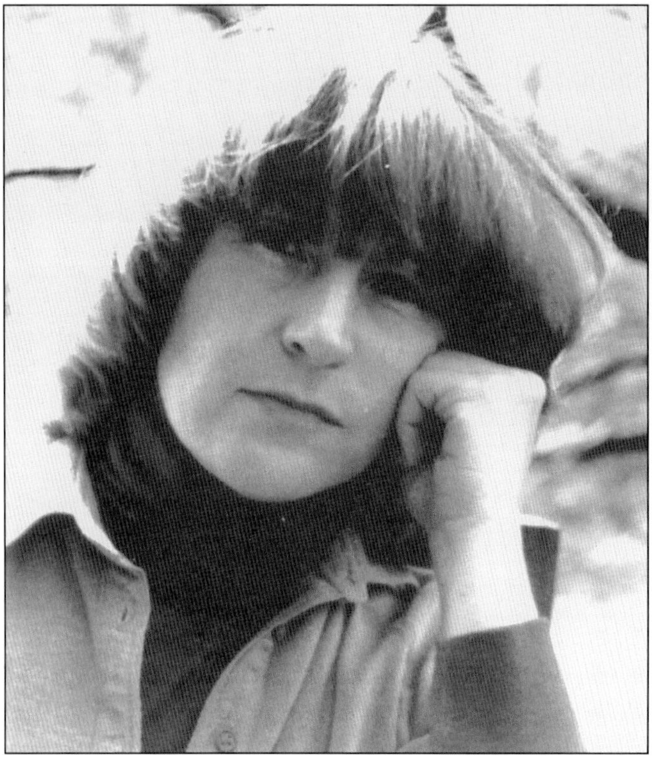

Poets Laureate of West Virginia have included Karl Dewey Myers (1927–1937), Roy Lee Harmon (1937–1943), James Lowell McPherson (1943–1946), Roy Lee Harmon (1946–1960), Vera Andrew Harvey (1960–1961), Louise McNeill Pease (1979–1993), and (pictured) Irene McKinney (1993–), native and current resident of Talbott Community in Barbour County.

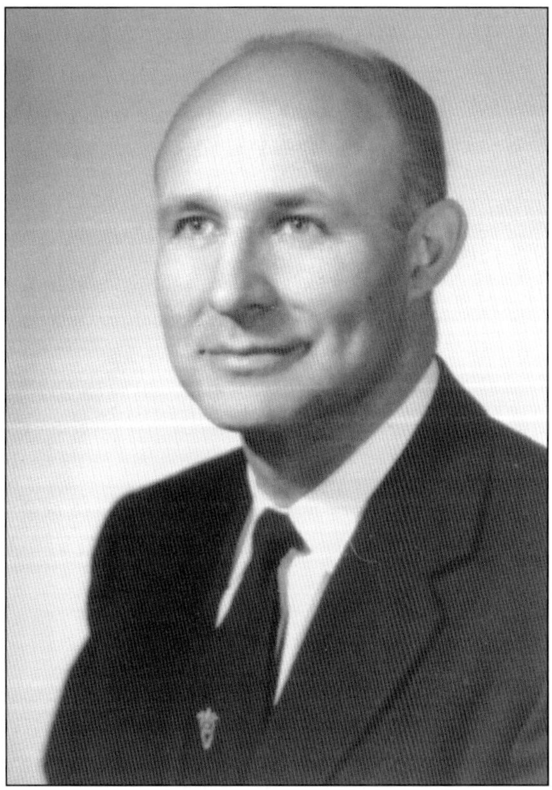

Richard E. Shearer served as president of Alderson-Broaddus College from 1951 to 1983. During his tenure the college gained its first North Central Association accreditation. A dozen buildings were constructed during Shearer's presidency, and enrollment more than doubled. Since his retirement, Shearer has continued to be a leader in community affairs.

Four

WHERE IT HAS HAPPENED

Who does not remember the first school attended, the church where one was baptized or confirmed, the houses where playmates gathered, grandparents died, pets were fed and pampered, carried or ridden? Who, if asked, could not name the three most significant locations of his or her life? Each person's list will be distinctive, personal, and highly memorable, for those buildings and hillsides, those paths and mountain peaks, become a part of our identities.

No matter where Barbour Countians go, there are certain landmarks with which they describe "home"—the Tygart River, Laurel Mountain, No Business Hill, Grab-a-Nickel Hill, Battle Hill, the college, the bridges, the model fairgrounds, Audra State Park, the riverfront at Arden—the list goes on and on. For most natives, moving away from the hills means moving away from a sense of shelter, security, beauty, and "home."

Schools and churches, banks and grocery stores, roads and railroads are built and eventually collapse or are torn down. The constants are the land, the river, and the mountains, the "places" where we belong. For many, the place of belonging is Barbour County.

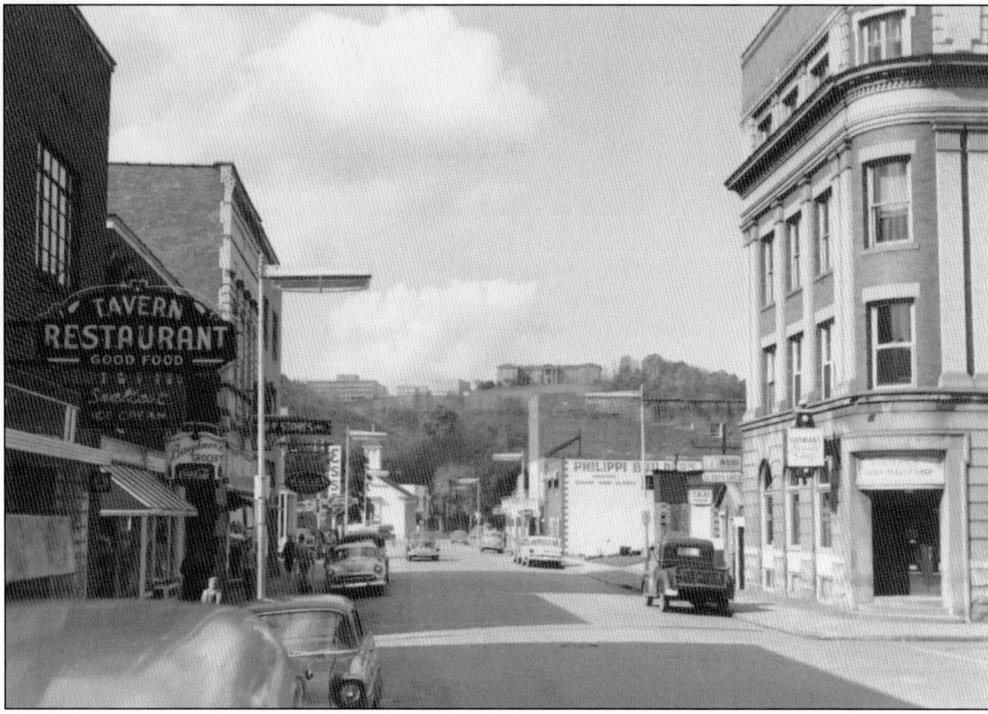

Although car models and storefronts have changed over the years, the general character and appearance of Barbour County have remained constant. This is a rural community of hard-working individuals whose values are symbolized by its schools, its churches, its college, its businesses, and its many civic organizations. (Courtesy Joe Mattaliano.)

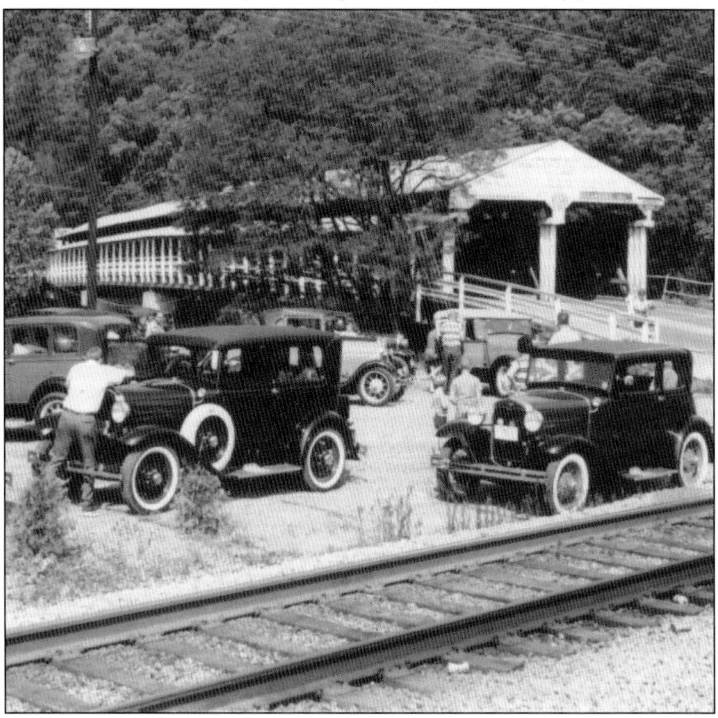

The covered bridge in Philippi has been a focal point of Barbour County. It served both the Union and the Confederate forces during the Civil War, but its long-term value has been the service it has rendered as part of the northcentral West Virginia highway system. The site occupied by the fancy vehicles in this photo has been established as a veterans' memorial park. (Courtesy Joe Mattaliano.)

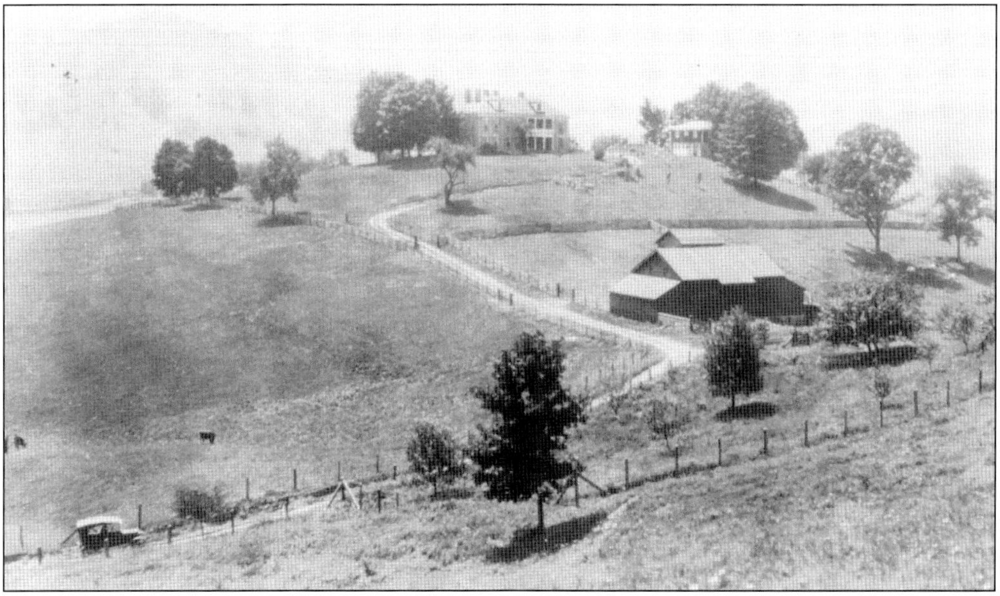

The land on which Adaland is located was land granted to James Thompson after the Revolutionary War. Built in 1870, the present mansion was eventually owned and named for his wife by Judge Ira E. Robinson. After being held by several other owners, the property was donated by Anker Energy Corporation to the City of Philippi. Now restored, it was placed on the National Registry of Historic Places in 1995. (Courtesy Ann Serafin.)

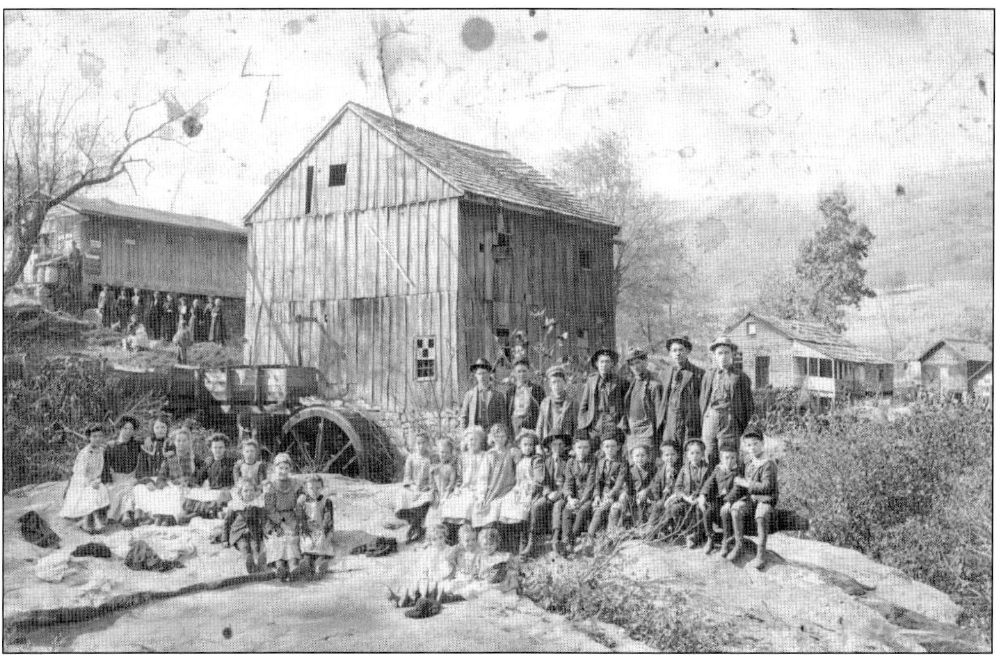

Pictured in 1903, this school group, whose teacher was L.L. Hershman, posed near the Moatsville Mill, which was located on the banks of Teter Creek. Benjamin Myers built the mill by hand, including a mill race and an overshot water wheel. Rebuilt after a fire, the mill ground grain until the early 1930s, when modern technology caused it to be abandoned. (Courtesy Rose Frey via Joe Mattaliano.)

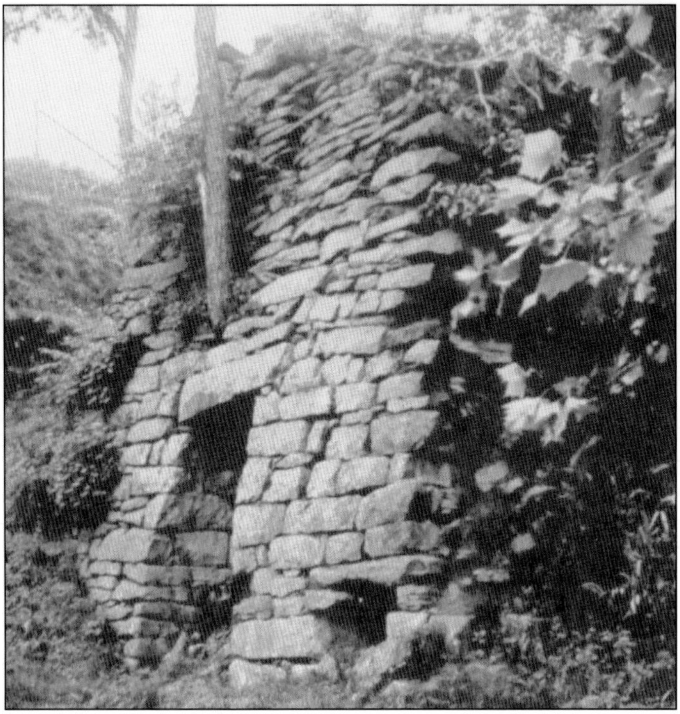

The unincorporated community of Valley Furnace was named for its chief feature, a 39-foot sandstone furnace which was built in 1848 to process iron ore found nearby. Charcoal was used for fuel, and the furnace produced about 5 tons of purified iron each day. Ox sleds hauled the product to nearby waterways, whereby the iron was delivered, primarily to Pittsburgh.

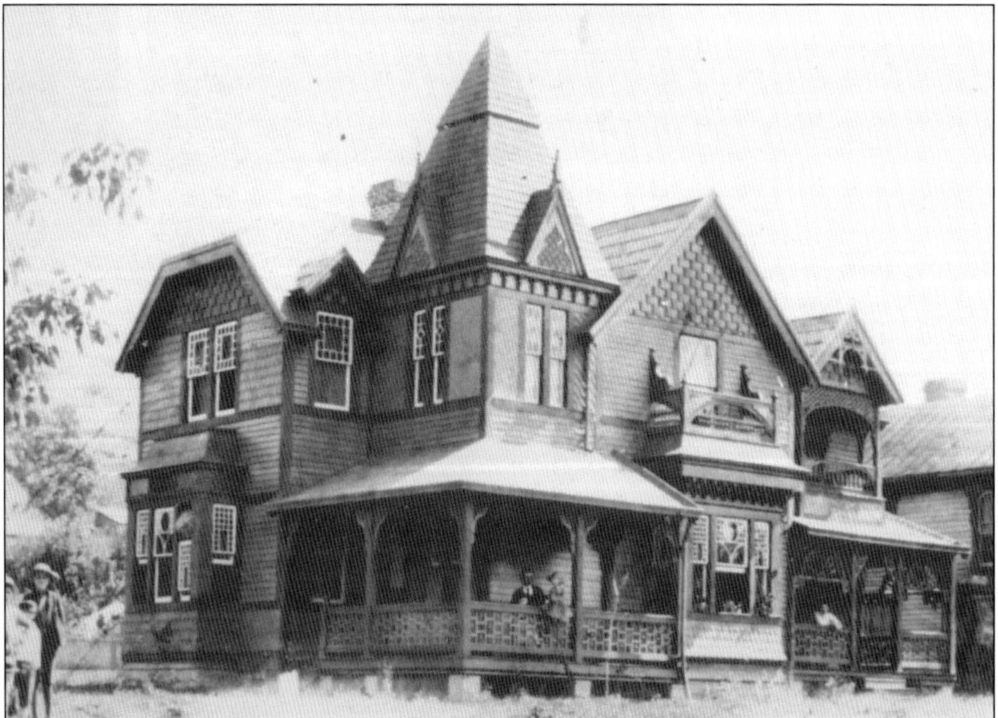

One of the most interesting structures still standing in Barbour County is the old Gall House, built by Dr. E.D. Gall in 1885. It has served as an inn as well as a private home. Most recently it has housed a jewelry business.

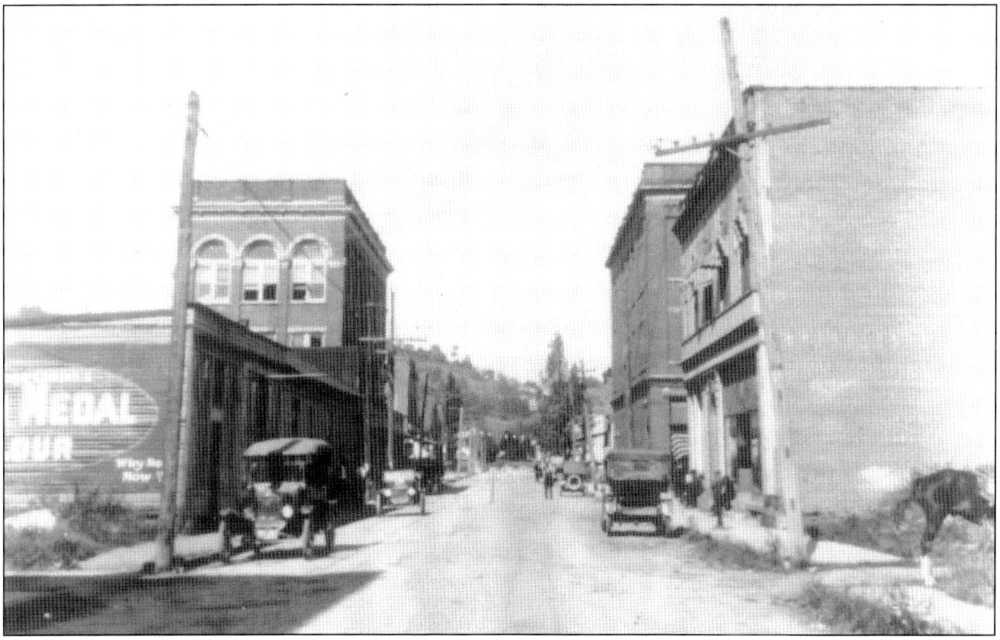

Settling in the Belington area by 1772 were Daniel Booth and Elias Barker, who developed adjoining acreage. Both men built and operated mills. From being a crossroads for Native American trails, Belington became a major junction on the B&O railroad. This is an early picture of what was later named Crim Avenue. (Courtesy Stephen Rautner.)

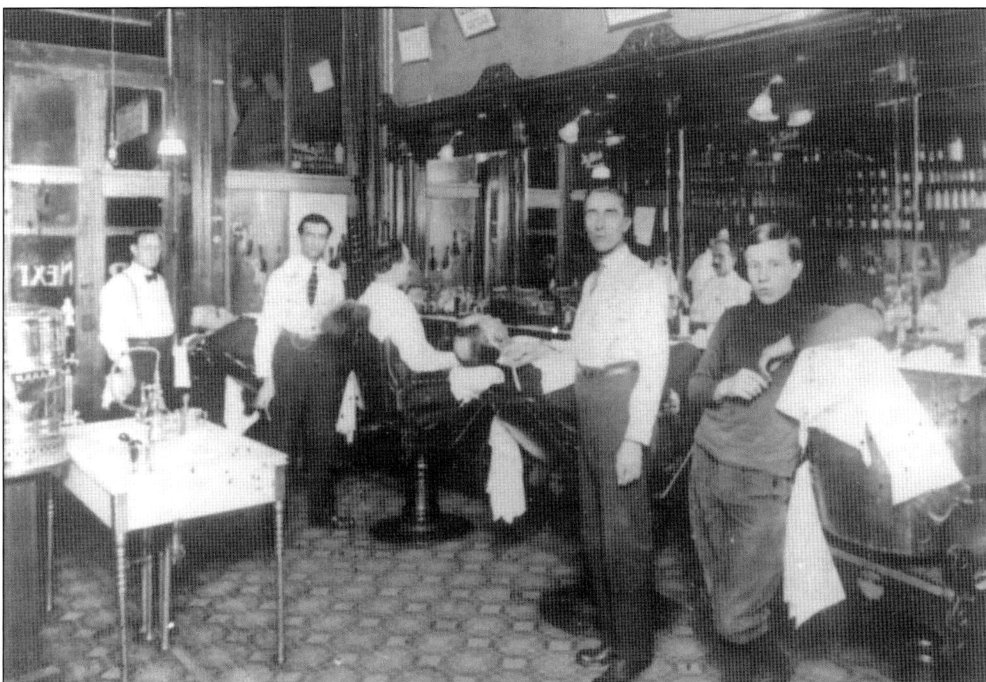

This barbershop, like most at the turn of the 20th century, was clean and neat. Most of the customers were local businessmen and their sons. Note the certificates high on the wall. (Courtesy Jane Mattaliano.)

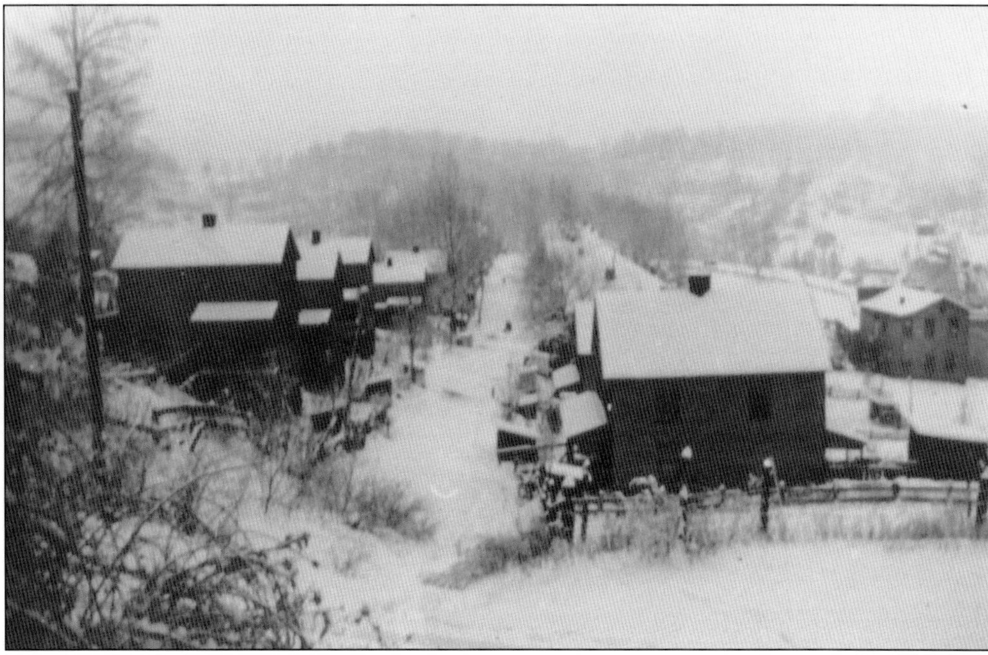

At the time this photo was taken, almost all houses in Century were company-owned, as were most of the other buildings. Many of the houses were two-family dwellings, some of them later being converted to accommodate single families. (Courtesy Nancy Streets.)

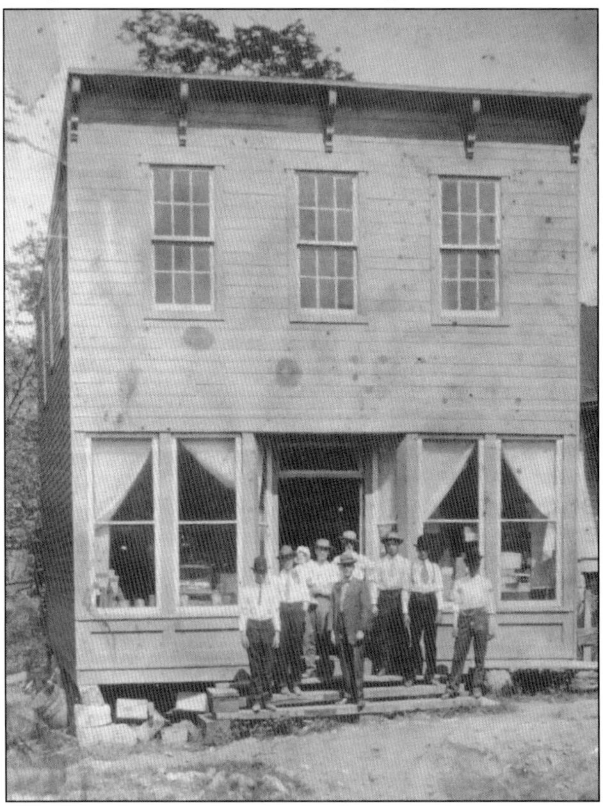

This store at Moatsville was considered a major enterprise at the time, and its owners and clerks held enviable positions in business and in the community. (Courtesy Peggy Robinson.)

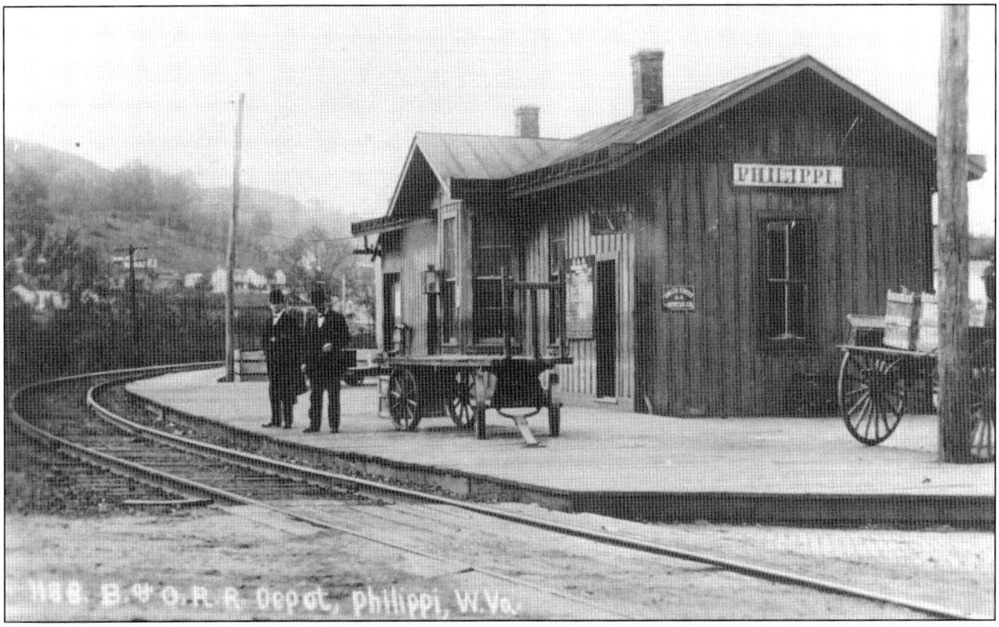

The importance of railroads to the development of Barbour County and the entire United States cannot be overstated. This photo taken early in the 20th century indicates that the depot also housed the United States Express Company. Train schedules were posted on the front of the building. (Courtesy Don Funk.)

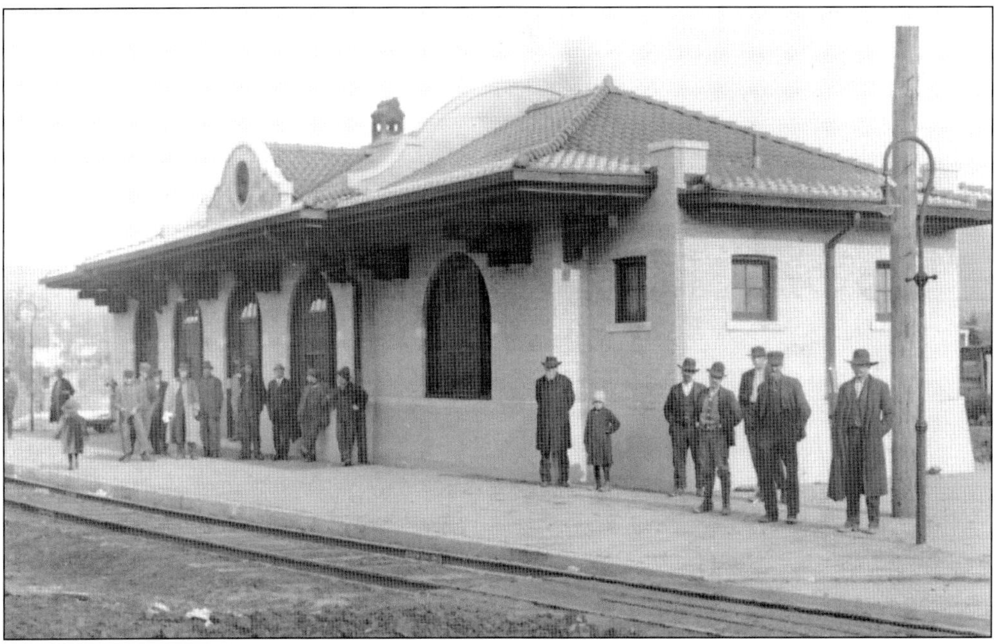

Many of the residents of and visitors to Barbour County arrived by way of the B&O station in Philippi, the new depot having been constructed in 1911 using brick and hand-carved wood. Passenger service ceased in 1957, and the building now serves as a museum. (Courtesy Joe Mattaliano.)

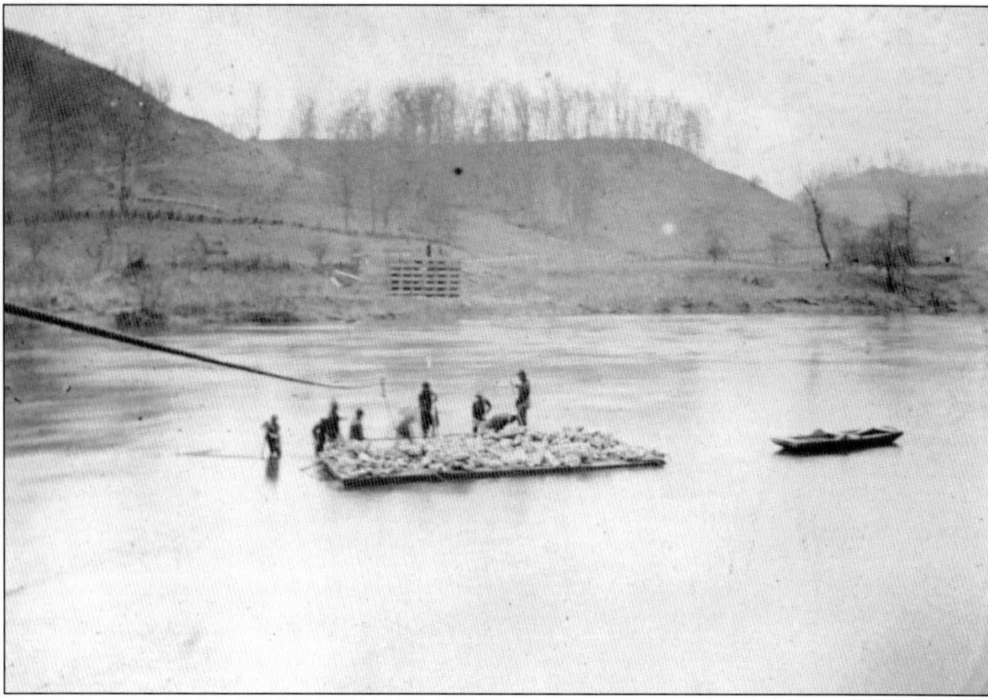

A truly major undertaking at the time was the building of "the iron bridge" in Philippi. The barge in the photo was laden with stones to be used in the building of the pillars. (Courtesy Joe Mattaliano.)

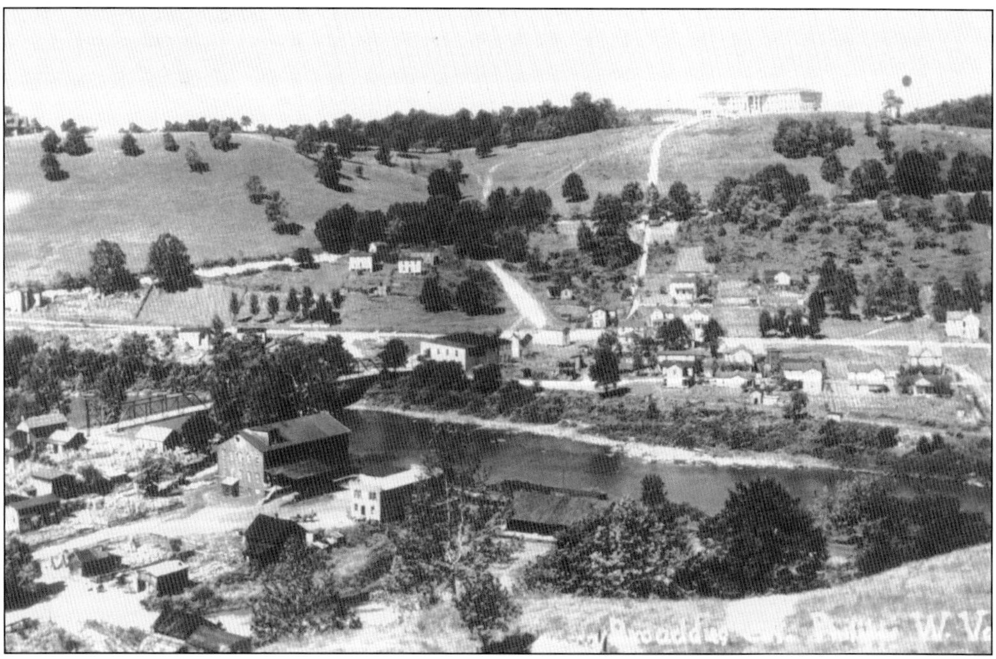

When this photo was taken in 1911, the only college buildings visible on the almost-bare Battle Hill were Old Main and the president's home (far left). Spanning the river was "the iron bridge." (Courtesy Joe Mattaliano.)

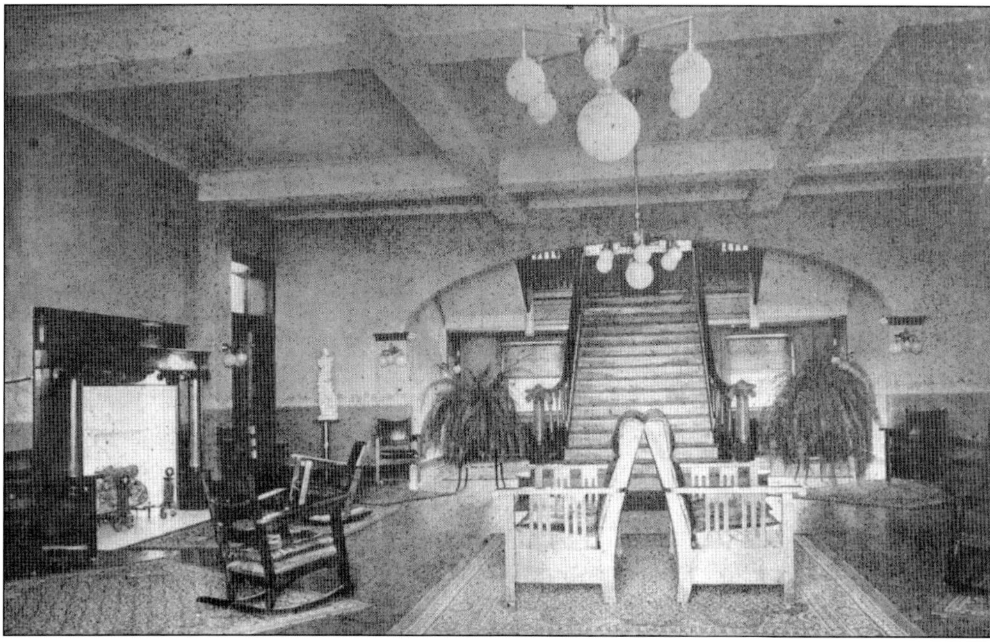

Soon after the dedication of the building, this photo was taken and made into a postcard to demonstrate the attractive appearance of the lobby of Old Main Hall. The photographer, far ahead of his time in style, had set a light inside the fireplace in order to show off that amenity. (Courtesy James and Robert Califf.)

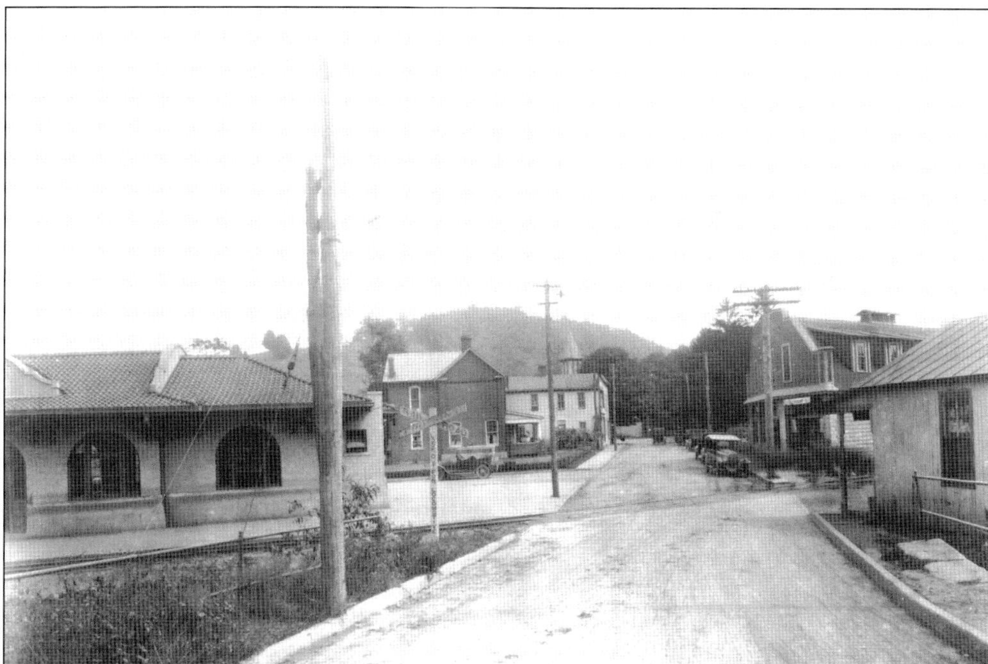

Current residents of Barbour County will recognize only one of the buildings in this early picture of Main Street, Philippi. On the left is the railroad depot. Other buildings include the Kines Hotel (far left) and the City Restaurant (far right). (Courtesy Lars Byrne.)

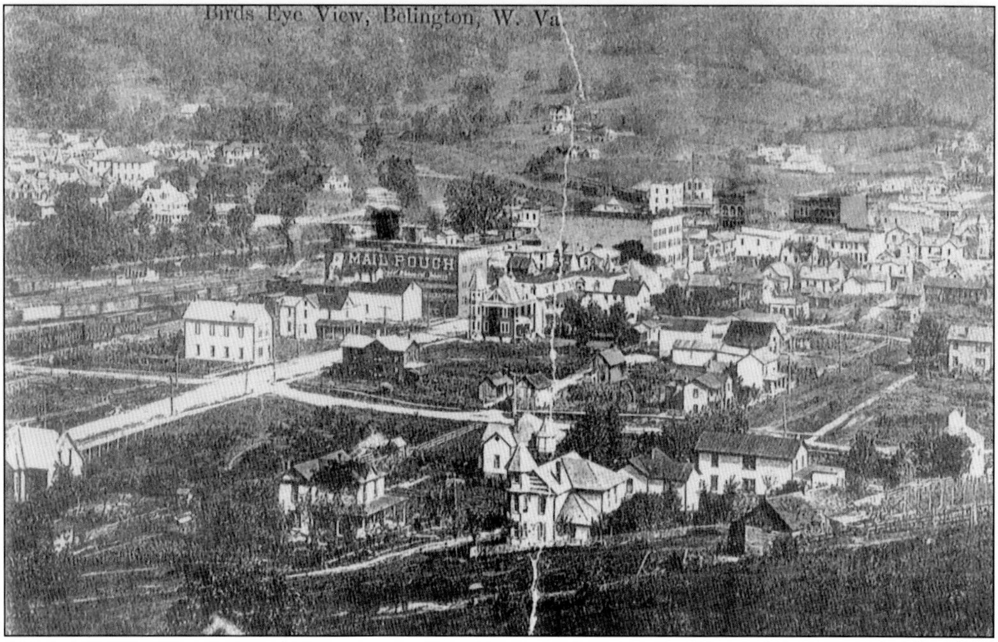

The town of Belington was a thriving railroad center until the World War II period. Both coal and timber were transported by the Grafton and Belington Railroad, later absorbed by the B&O system. (Courtesy Don Funk.)

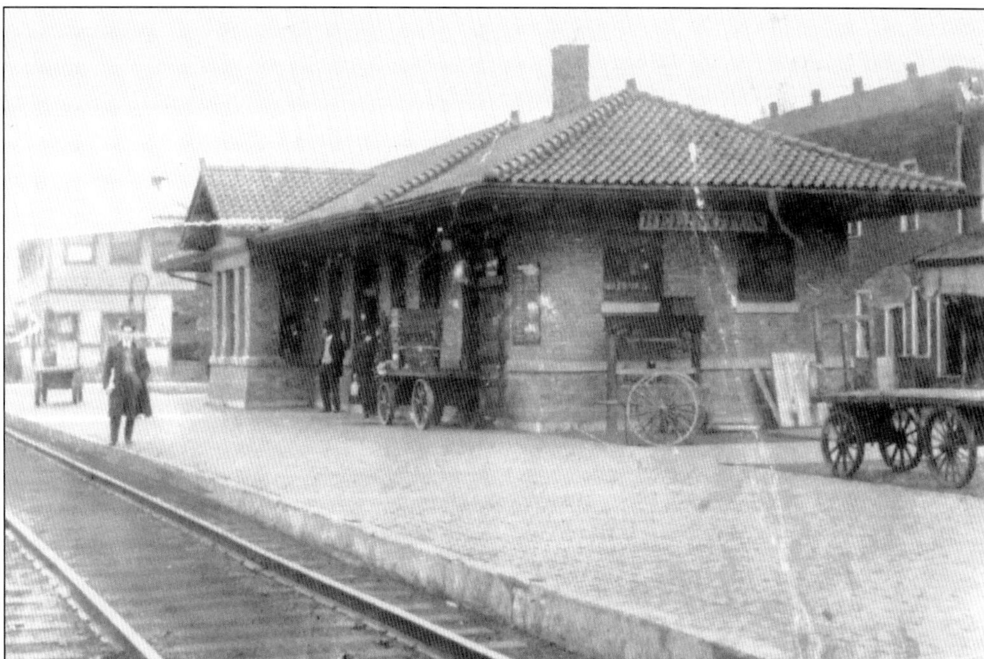

For many years the focus of the Belington community was the railroad depot. After regular passenger service was discontinued in the 1940s, a rail bus ran on the line for several years. (Courtesy Stephen Rautner.)

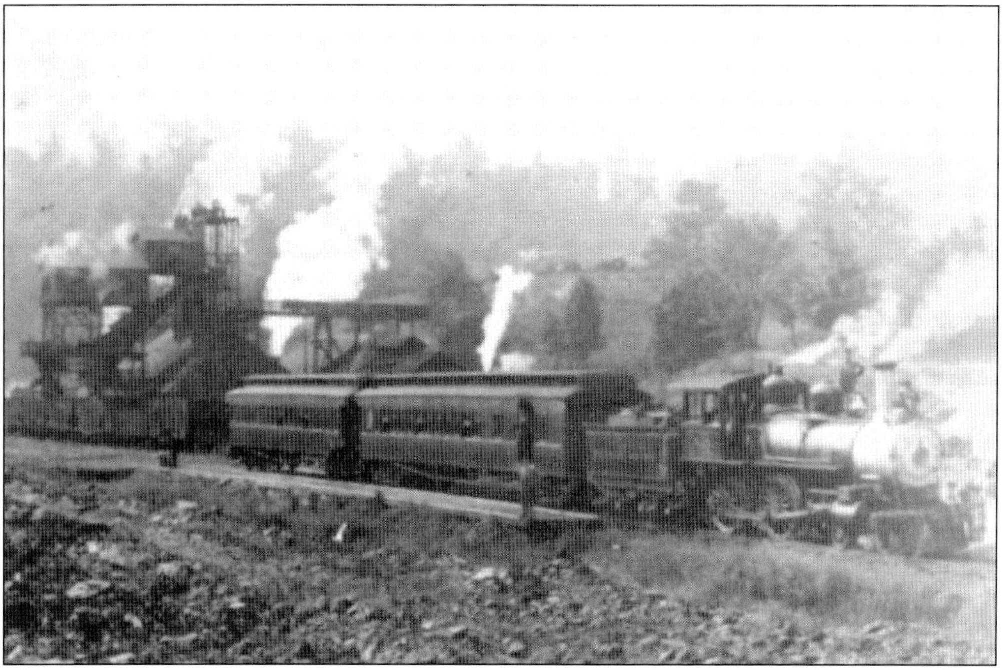

The community of Century was, in its most prosperous period, a bustling coal town located on a spur of the B&O railroad. Records of 1925 indicate that four trains serving both passengers and the coal mines ran daily except on Sundays.

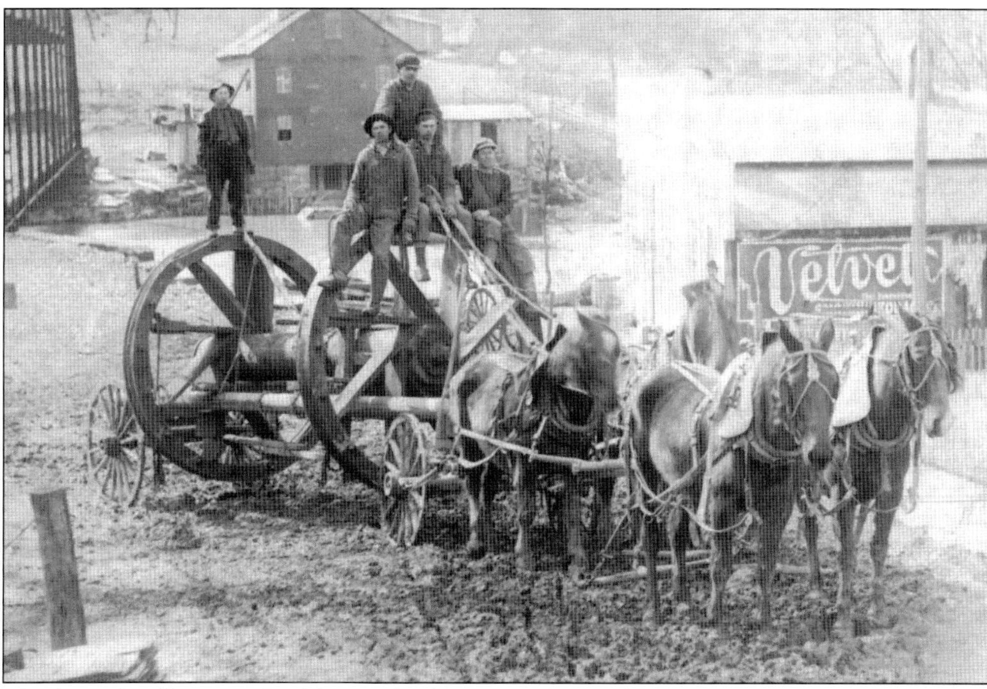

The first schoolhouse in Boulder was built in 1881. Pictured here are Russell, Carl, and Dalton Sandridge and Guy Ritter, who were hauling materials for the building of the Methodist church in 1911. Services are still held there every Sunday. (Courtesy Amanza Nitz.)

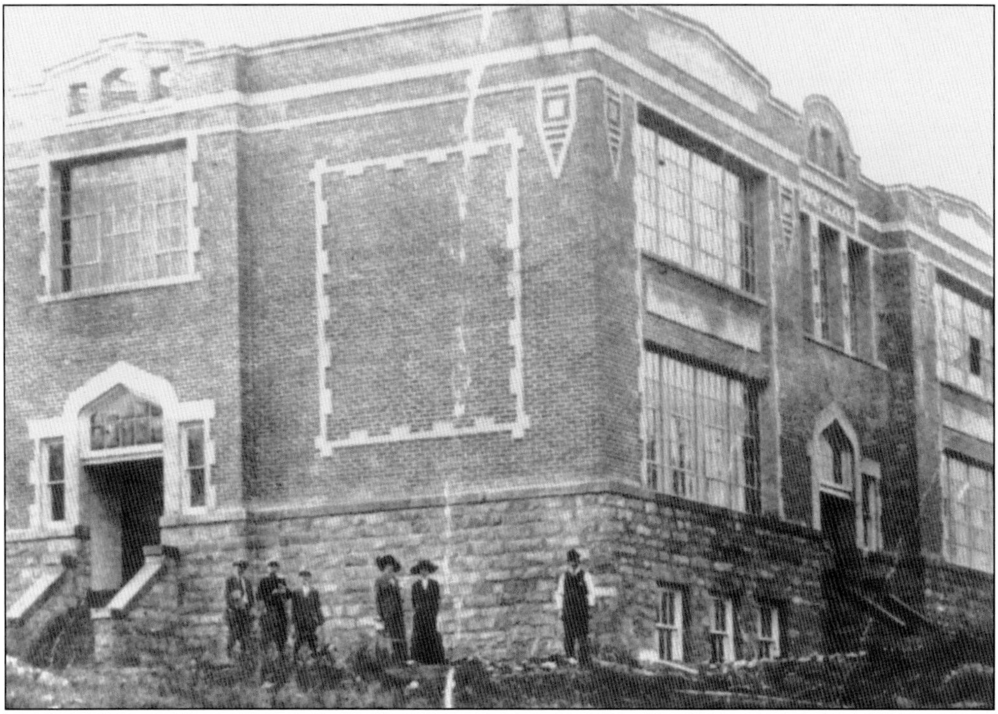

Belington High School, built in 1913, served the community well until it was closed in 1963 when the consolidated school, Philip Barbour, opened. (Courtesy Stephen Rautner.)

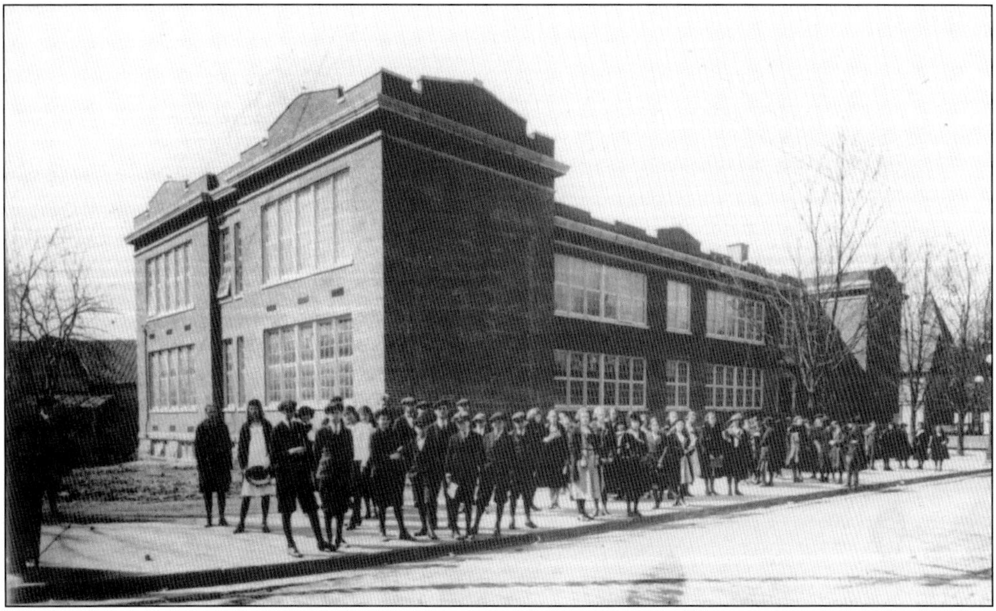

Built in 1921, the Philippi School was demolished in 1963 and students transferred to Philip Barbour High School. The site of the old building is now occupied by a pharmacy.

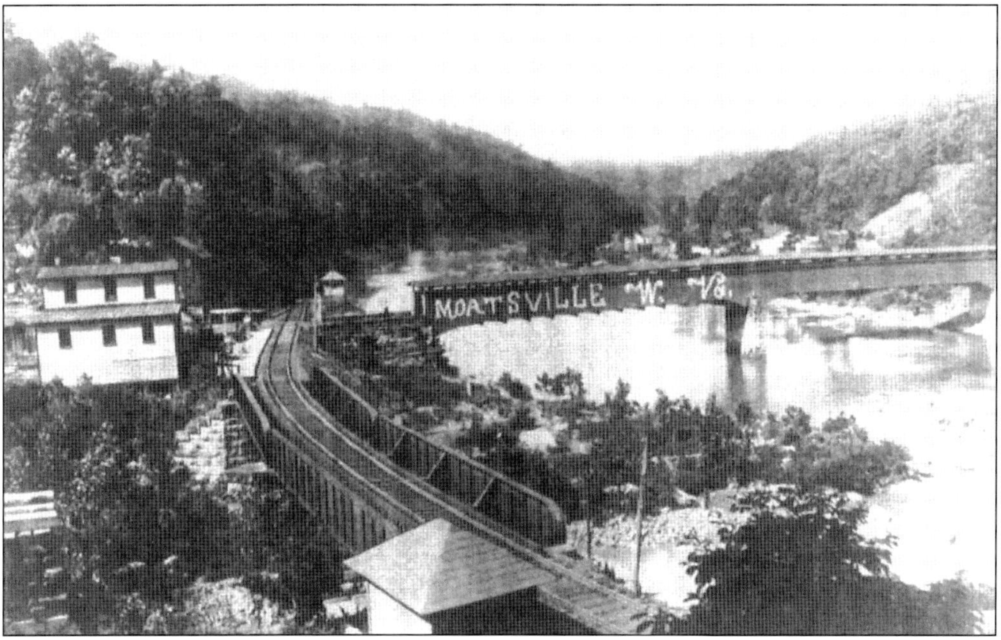

Moatsville, one of the very first communities in Barbour County, was located near a Native American village, reportedly called "Painted Camp" in recognition of the painted wigwams. Moatsville boasted a long covered bridge which spanned the Tygart River. A trestle also was constructed to accommodate the railroad line. (Courtesy Patty Marsh.)

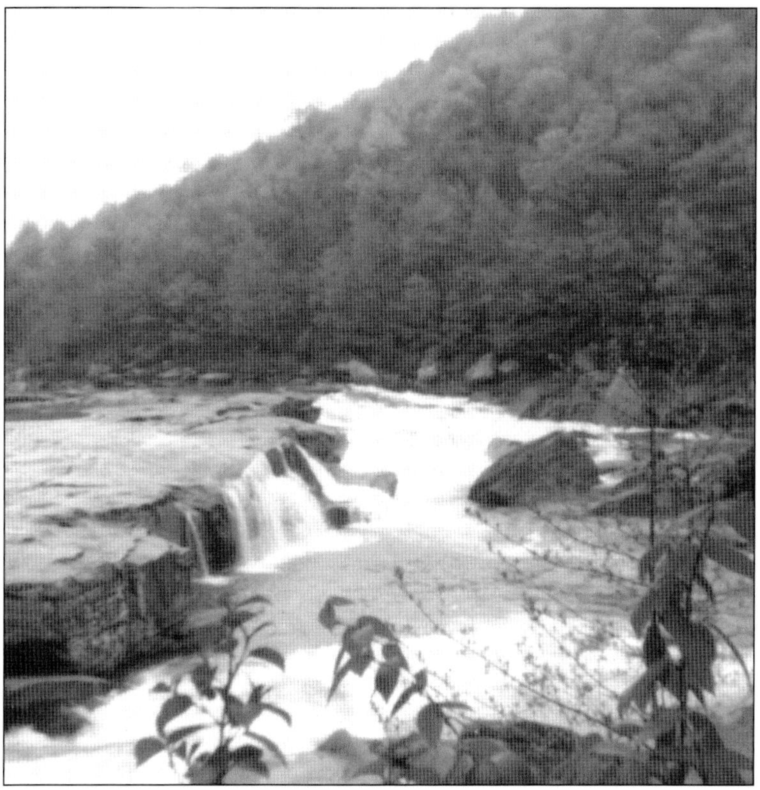

Moats Falls is claimed by many local residents to be the most beautiful area in Barbour County. For years it could be accessed only by paths through the woods. The road leading to it today, still unpaved, is the old railroad grade between Arden and Moatsville. (Courtesy Peggy Robinson.)

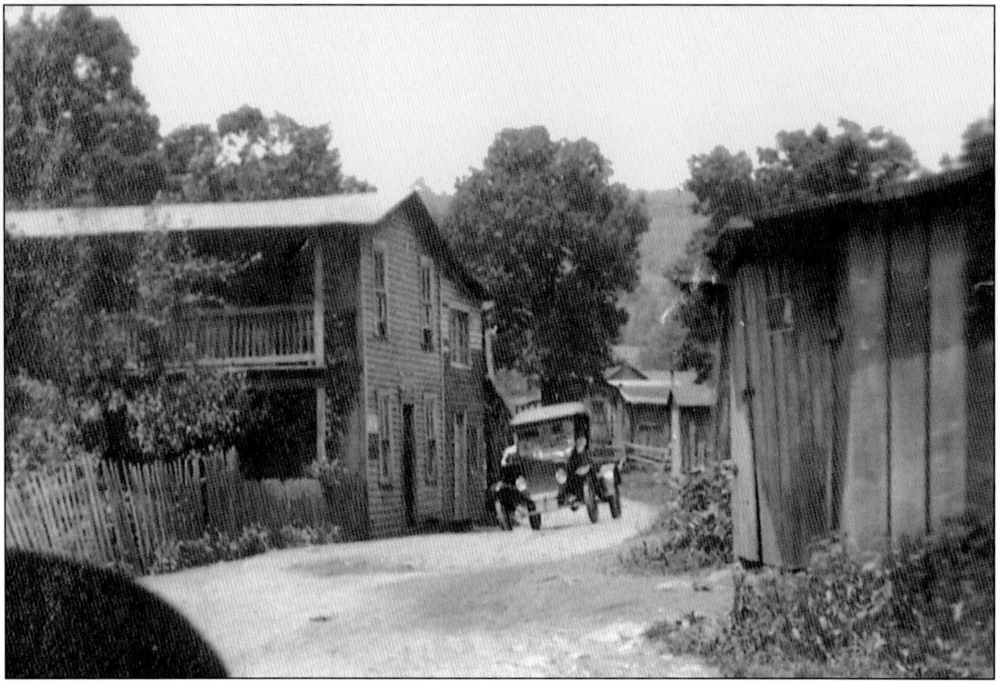

The building on the left was the home of the Weaver family, including Patty Weaver Marsh, who now resides near Arden. Her grandmother ran a store on the lower floor of the building and sold gasoline in addition to food and supplies. (Courtesy Patty Marsh.)

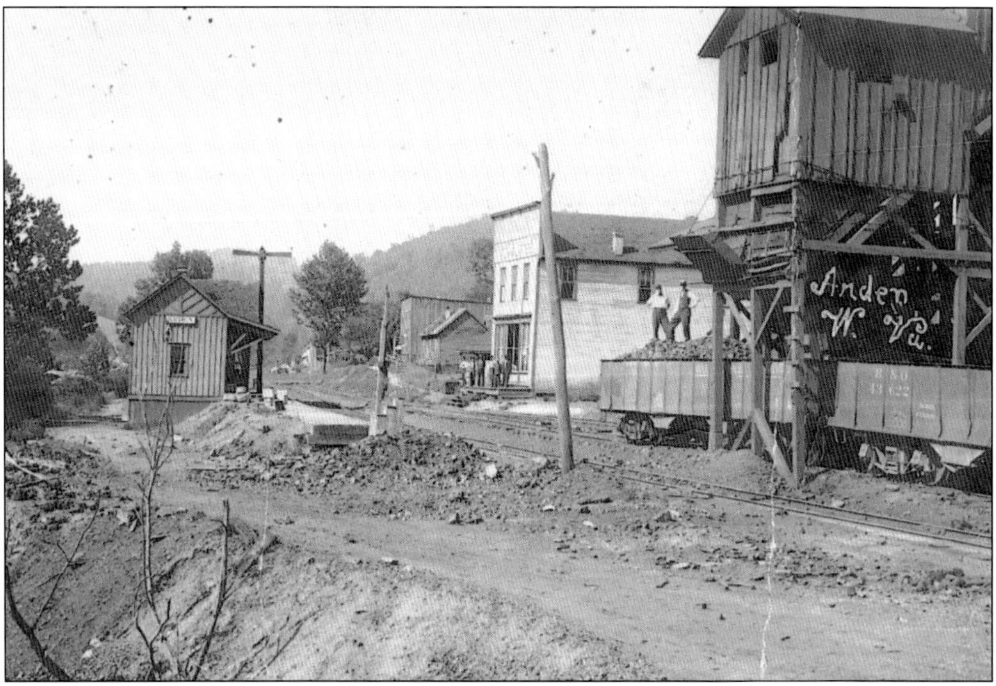

On the left in this photo, taken in 1925, is the Weaver home/store. The building on the close right is the coal mine tipple. Behind it are the post office and the company store. Paving of the street was a long way off. (Courtesy Patty Marsh.)

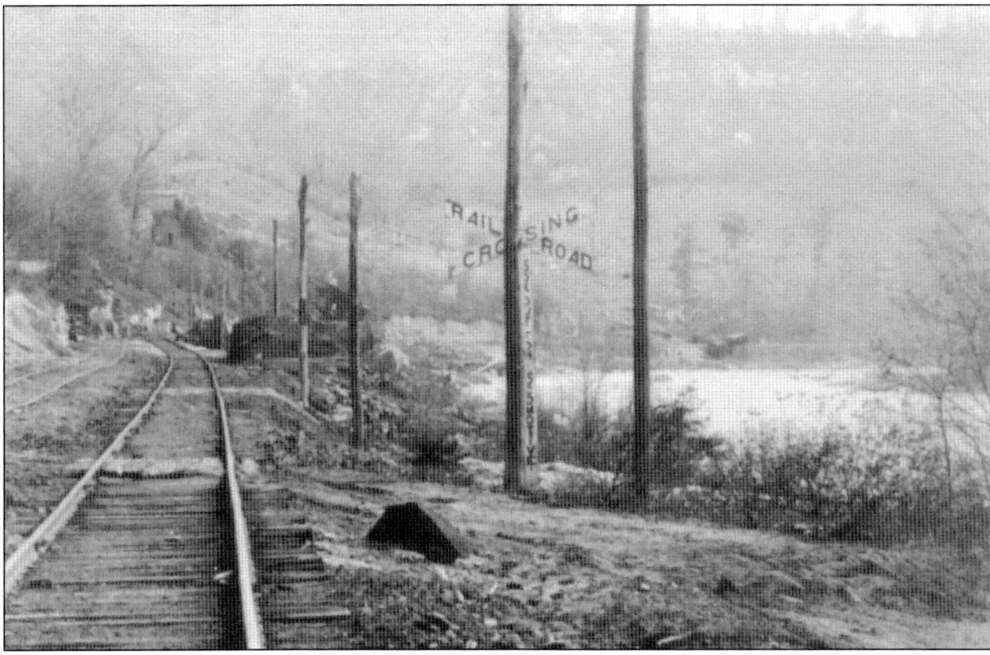

The first wagon road on the east side of the Tygart River was built in 1800 and ran approximately 7 miles from Anglin's Ferry to Bill's Creek and Billsburg. Over 100 years later, a still-unpaved road in Moatsville crossed the railroad tracks and led up to Felton Hill. (Courtesy Patty Marsh.)

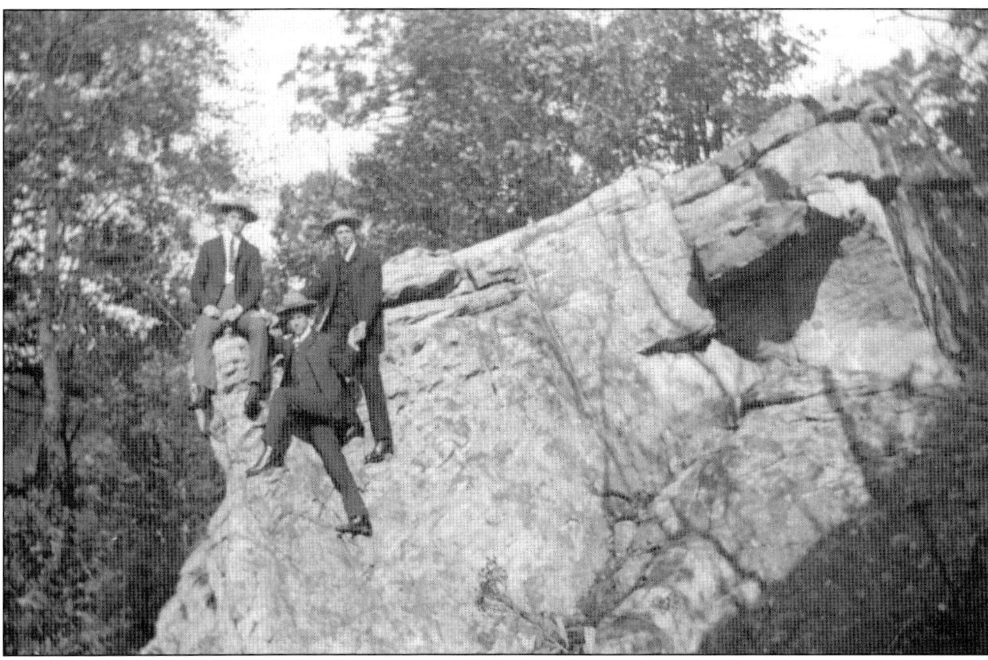

"Suicide Rock" has long been a favorite get-away spot for local residents and students from Alderson-Broaddus College. Located in the cliffs above Route 119, it has been the scene of many daring adventures and a few broken bones. The dandies here are unidentified. (Courtesy Joe Mattaliano.)

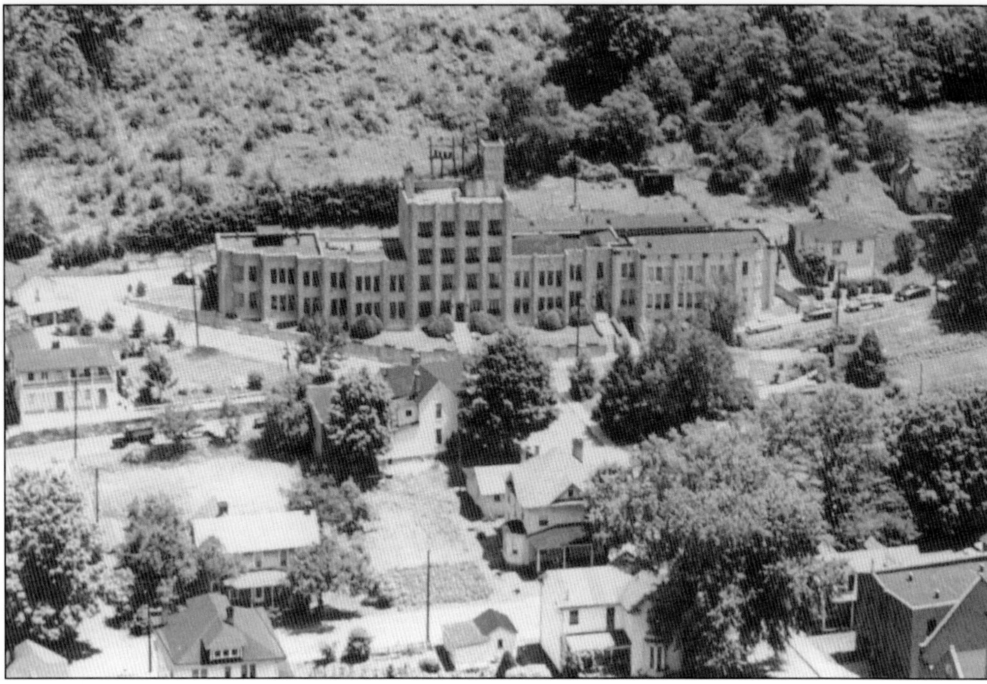

Dr. J.W. Myers donated the land for Barbour County's first hospital. Built in 1933, Myers Clinic served both in- and out-patients for the 20 years before Broaddus Hospital was constructed, after which it became an out-patient clinic. Many pieces of medical equipment and a great variety of universally accepted treatments originated at Myers Clinic.

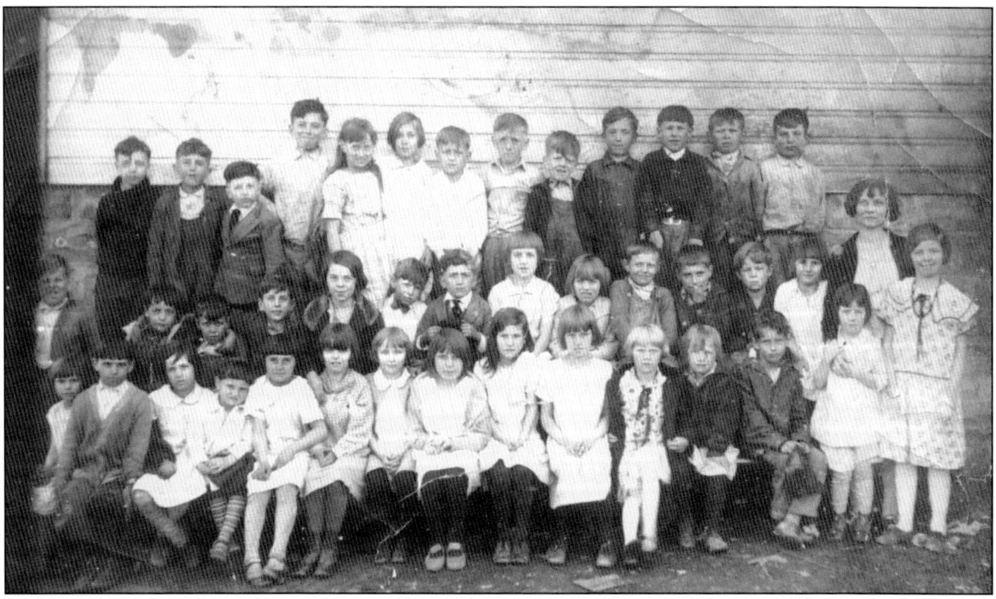

The Bear Mountain School in Browntown produced many fine students and student athletes. Mines operating on this and nearby hills opened in 1916 and used inclined tracks. Several incidents of "runaway" coal cars have been reported. In 1925, when production amounted to 200 tons per day, top daily pay amounted to $4.08. (Courtesy Helen and Albert Gleza.)

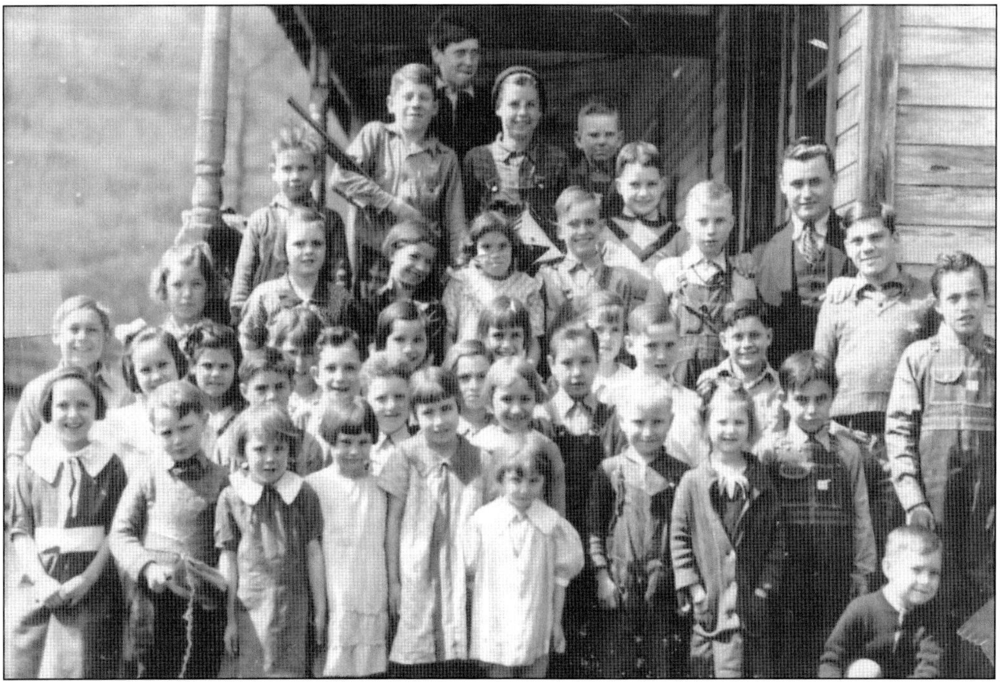

There were two theaters in Brownton during its heyday. The Star Theater was the location not only for movie showings but for school classes such as this one. The Galloway-Brownton community at the time also boasted 11 stores, 3 barbershops, and 3 pool rooms. (Courtesy Helen and Albert Gleza.)

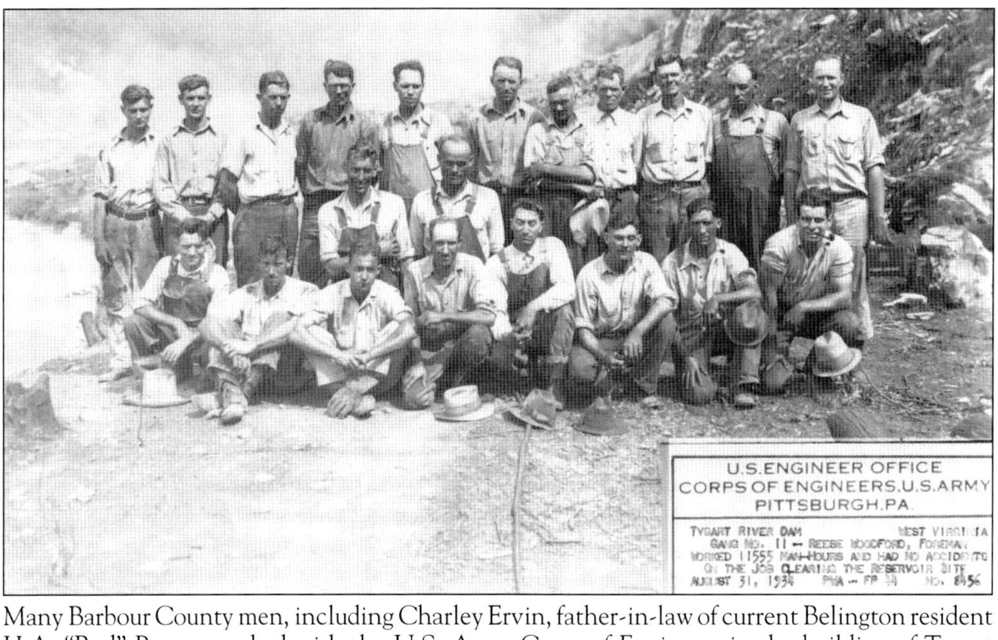

Many Barbour County men, including Charley Ervin, father-in-law of current Belington resident H.A. "Red" Payne, worked with the U.S. Army Corps of Engineers in the building of Tygart Dam in Taylor County, the backwaters of which extend into Barbour County. This photo, taken in 1934, records the fact that these men had worked 11,555 hours without accident. They were in charge of clearing the reservoir site. (Courtesy H.A. "Red" Payne.)

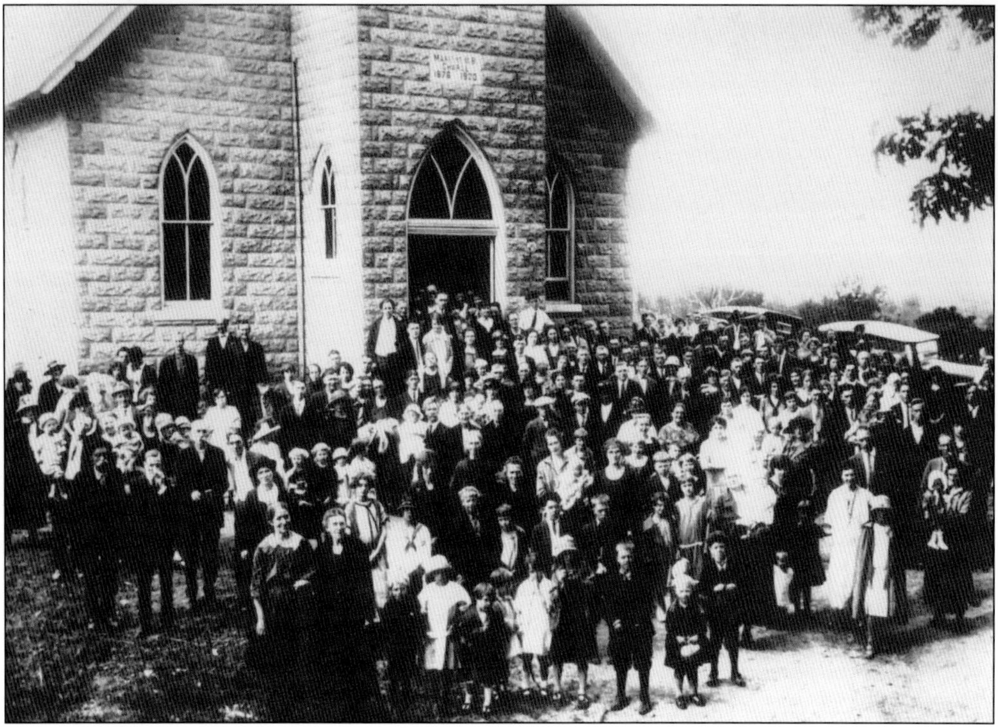

Pictured here is a reunion of the Murphy family in Clemtown. The sign on the church indicates that the congregation was established in 1876, the building constructed in 1920. It was called "Mariah's U.B. [United Brethren] Chapel." (Courtesy Peggy Robinson.)

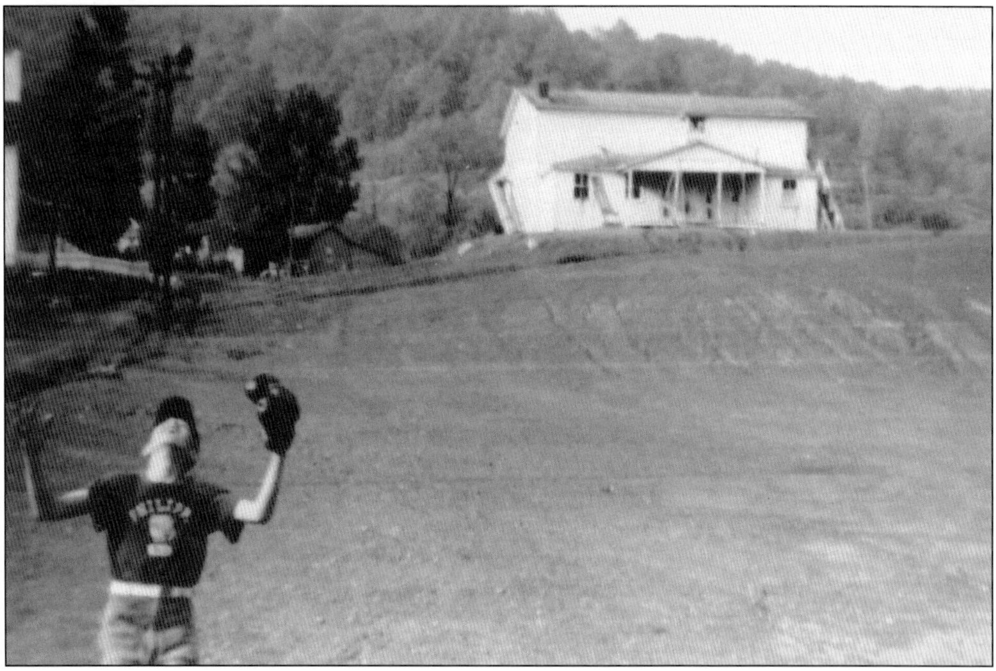

Albert Toth was photographed in 1950 playing on the grounds of the Galloway school, which was located up the road behind the present post office. (Courtesy Helen and Albert Gleza.)

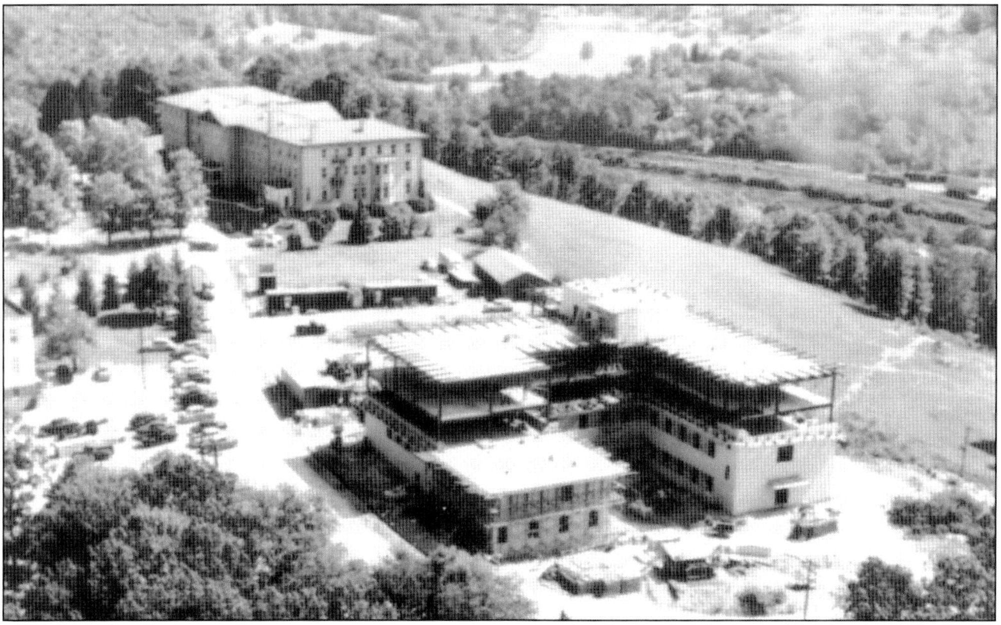

For many years, Broaddus Hospital, built in 1953, was widely known as a cancer treatment center. At the same time that it housed patients, it served as a clinic setting for student nurses and physician assistants from Alderson-Broaddus College. Students in other academic fields met work-study requirements by working in the hospital.

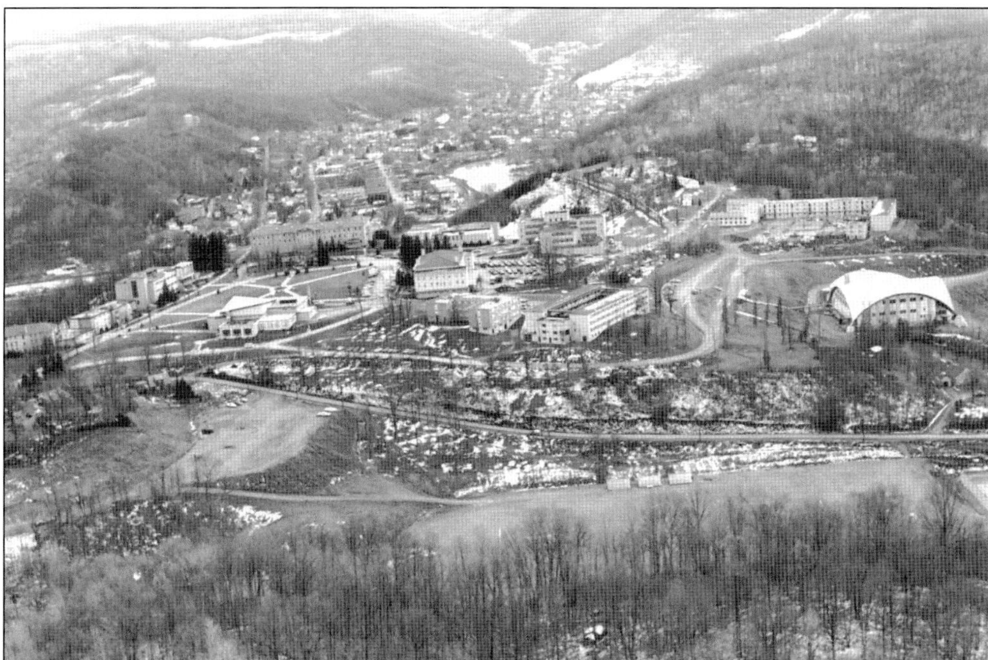

This photo was taken in the drab months of winter before the building of the Hu Myers Health Sciences building and Wilcox Chapel on the Alderson-Broaddus campus. Land was being cleared for Shroath and Kincaid Halls. Still in place were the World War II barracks which housed male and married students. (Courtesy Joe Mattaliano.)

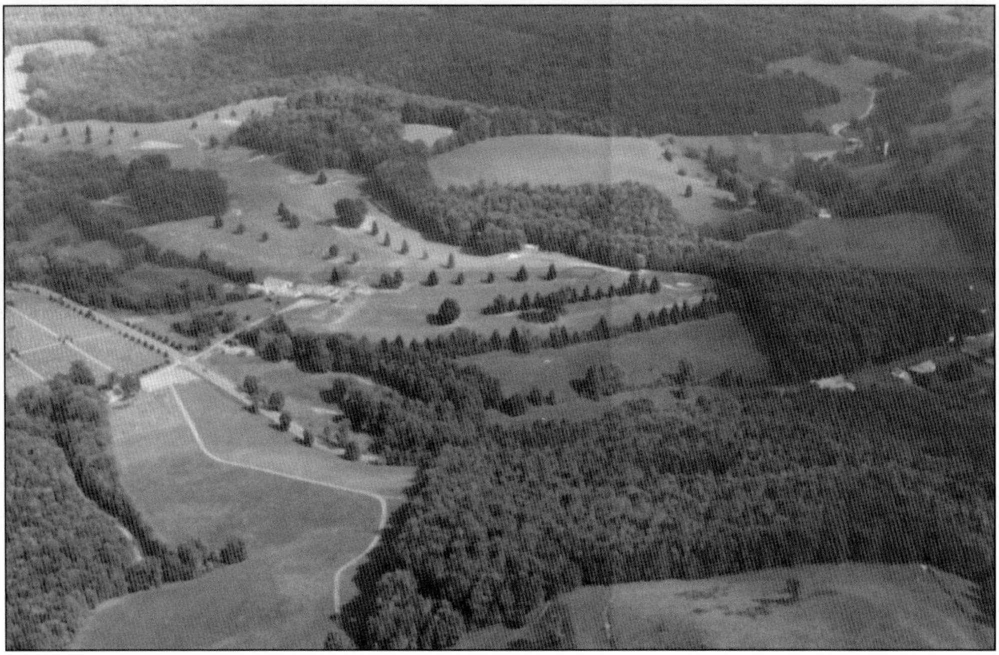

One of the most popular recreational facilities in Barbour County is the Barbour Country Club, formerly farm land. Golfers enjoy this nine-hole "mountain goat" course which lies next to Route 119 south of Philippi. (Courtesy Joe Mattaliano.)

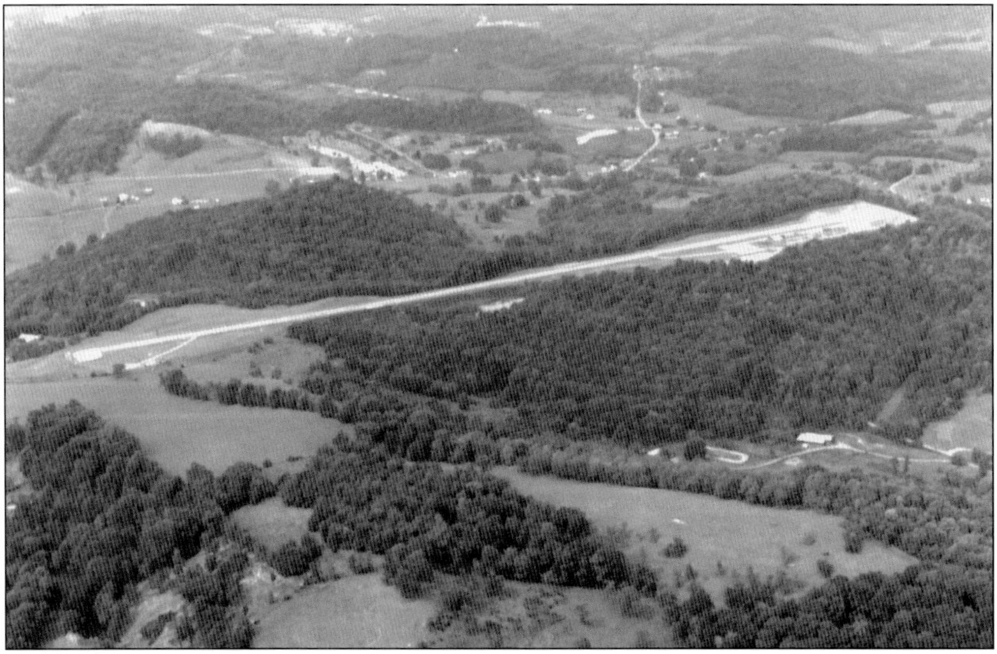

The Barbour County airport serves small, private planes. Its development was promoted by city and county officials and by one of the county's best-known pilots, Dr. Richard Shearer. Nestled in the hollow below the airport are the Carl Tideman home and Carleigh Farms. (Courtesy Joe Mattaliano.)

Five

And in the Meantime

Customs and rituals identify a culture and distinguish a community. In Barbour County those activities have ranged from berry picking to Commencement exercises, from quilting to quarry swimming, from baton-twirling to musket shooting, from church worship to mountain biking. The annual county fair, the Blue and Gray Reunion, the college Homecoming weekend, the Christmas decorations on the courthouse lawn, all contribute to an atmosphere of stability and common values.

Although efforts are made to preserve the symbols and artifacts of local culture, and although immeasurable energy goes into restorations and reconstructions, many important and basic habits and customs have been lost forever. Some chores disappear gladly, some customs regretfully. There are few pictures or written records of the ancient habits of butter churning, clothes-washing in the creek, and bullet molding. Nor is there likely to be, 100 years from now, much attention given to the wearing of analogue watches, hand-writing of personal letters, and dependence upon gasoline engines. What records we have and what photographs have been preserved are crucial to an understanding of who we are and who we have been. Let us hope that someone, somewhere, even today, is taking pictures—and labeling them!

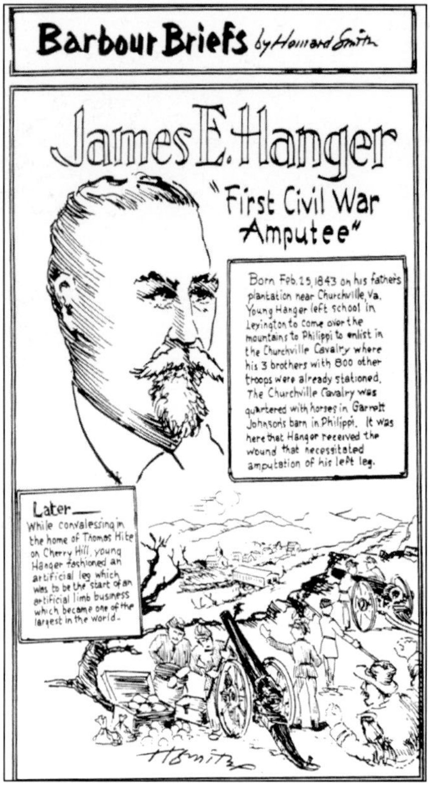

One of the most interesting events to occur during the first land battle of the Civil War was the wounding of James E. Hanger. His leg had to be amputated, after which Hanger designed the first prosthesis, an artificial leg, and founded a company which developed business worldwide. This cartoon was created by Howard Smith, Barbour County pharmacist, humorist, painter, and cartoonist par excellence.

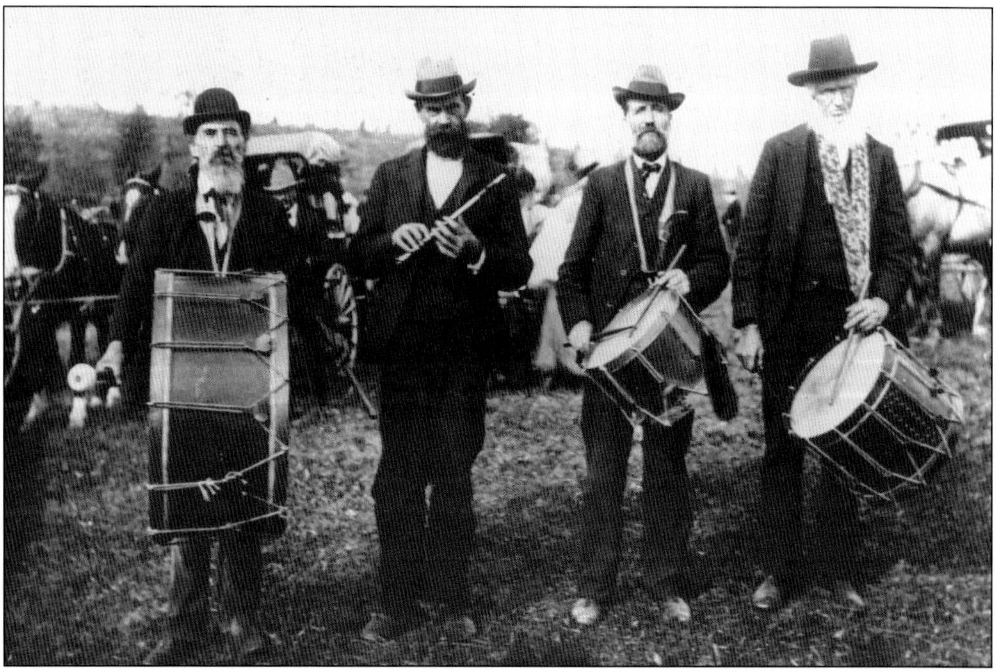

Among the most popular activities in Barbour County over the years have been the street fairs. The first such was held in 1899, when entertainment included this small band. Members were Jacob S. Harsh, Aldernon Crim, Joseph L. Johnson, and Anthony Vannoy.

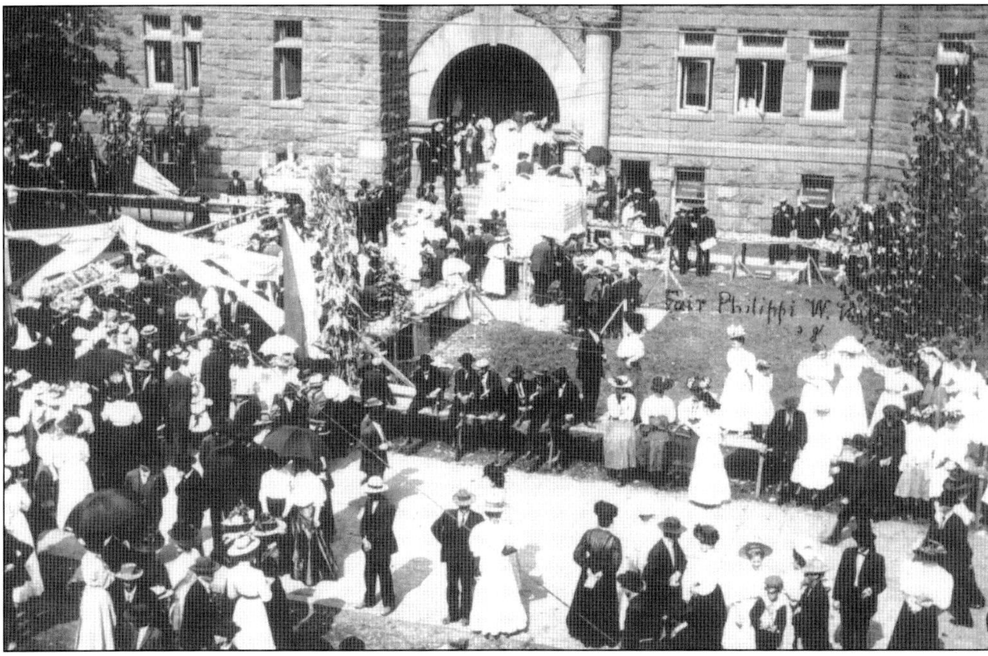

The county courthouse served as the central location for the annual street fair. Activities lasted for several days and included exhibits, organized games, contests of skill, and foot and horse races. This photo was taken in 1908.

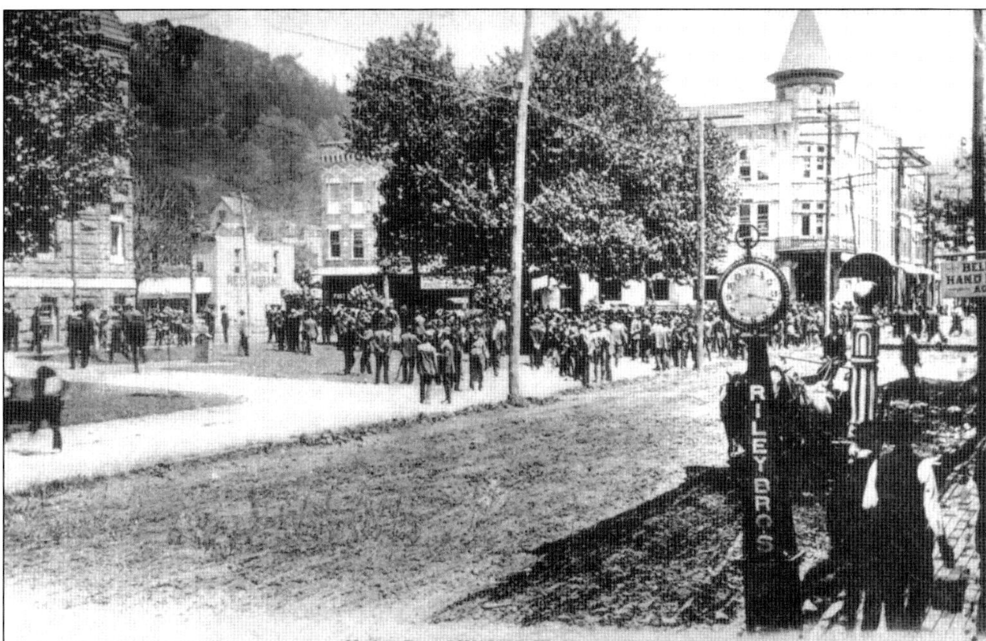

Another important occasion was market day. This photo, taken in 1905, indicates that shops along Main Street in Philippi included a jewelry store, a barbershop, and a laundry, all of which burned down in 1908. Across from the courthouse was a popular gathering place, the Acme Restaurant. (Courtesy Joe Mattaliano.)

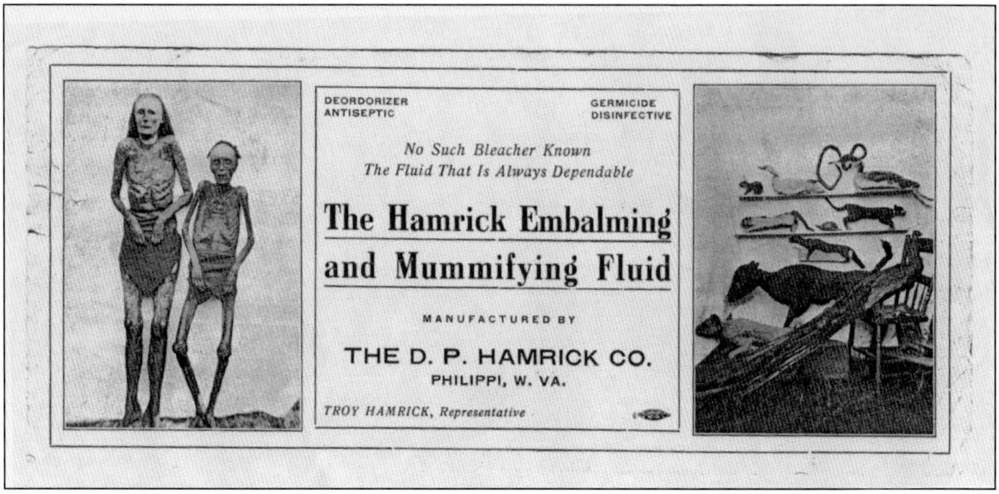

The most unusual business ever to locate in Barbour County was that of an undertaker, Graham Hamrick, who developed an embalming fluid. Several mummies on which this fluid was used in 1888 are on display at the Barbour County Historical Museum.

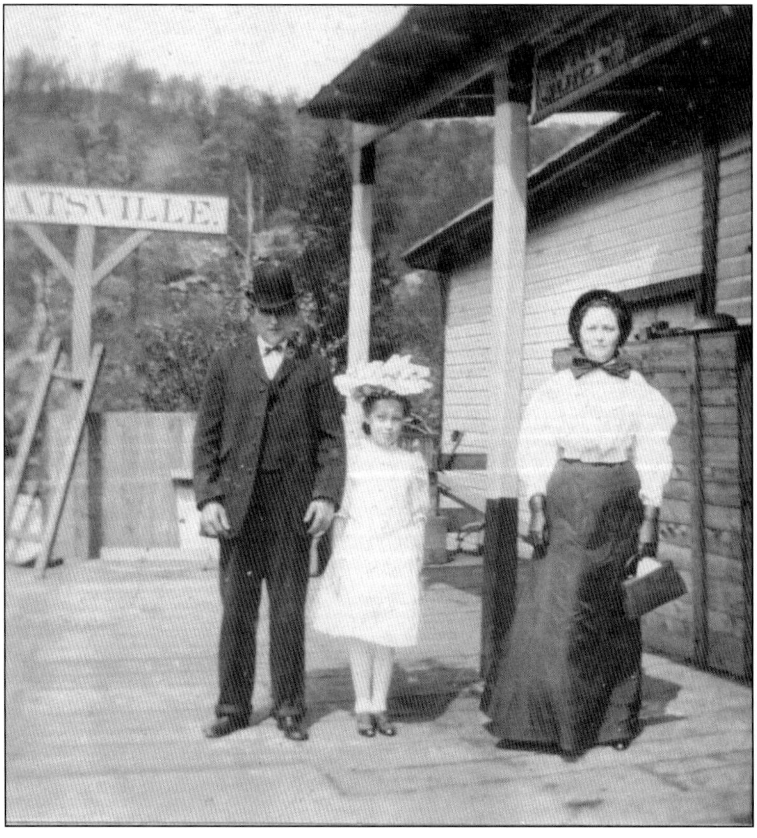

Ready to set off from the Moatsville depot for an unknown destination were Martin Nicola, Edna Nicola Miller (Martin's daughter), and her daughter, Helen Miller (Harr). (Courtesy Peggy Robinson.)

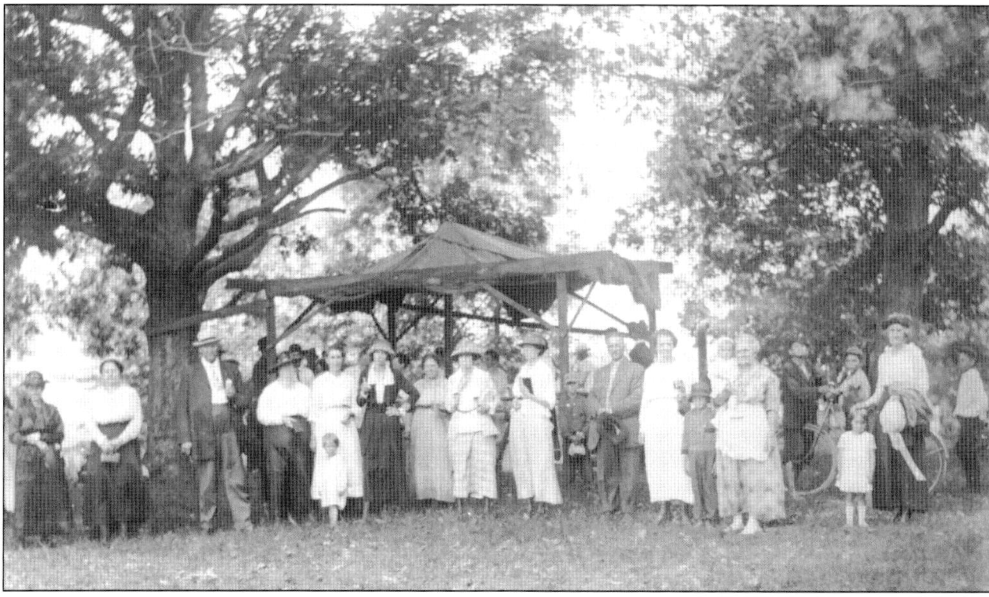

Social occasions of this type at the United Brethren church in Belington (now the Westside United Methodist Church) provided summer entertainment. Included in this photo are ? Price, ? Bush, Becky Thomas, Vernon Tompson, Ettie Cross, Stella Hall, Mrs. ? Richardson, Valley Fitzwater, and Faust Fitzwater. (Courtesy H.A. "Red" Payne.)

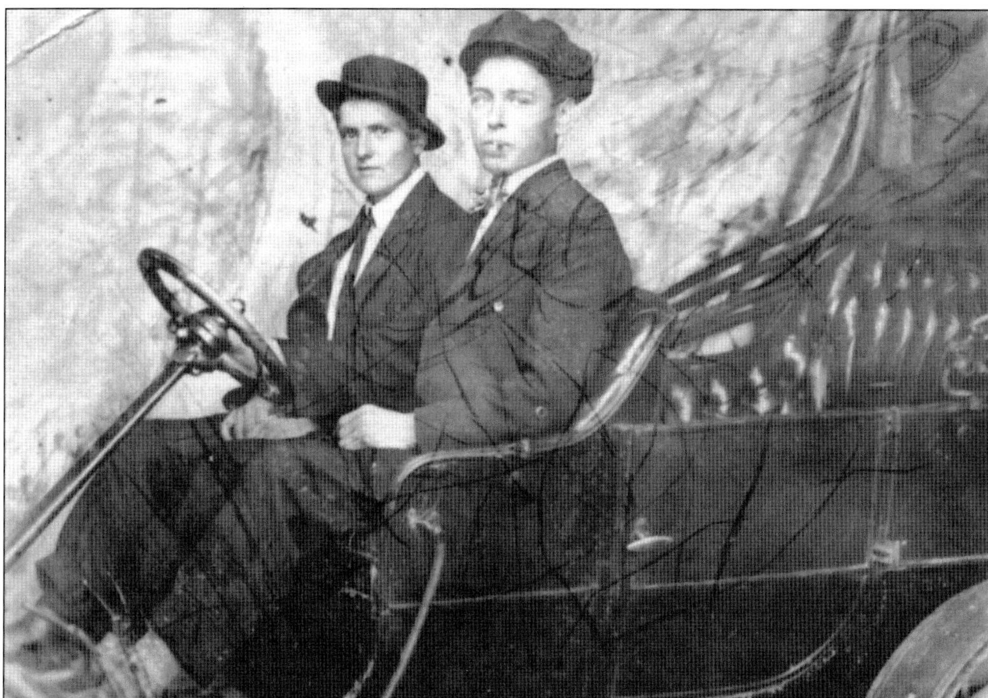

Typical of the studio photos in the early 20th century is this one of two young dandies in what was then a state-of-the-art vehicle. Although the photo was apparently taken in Elkins, Willie Jones and Darl Phillips were natives of Jonestown in Barbour County. (Courtesy H.A. "Red" Payne.)

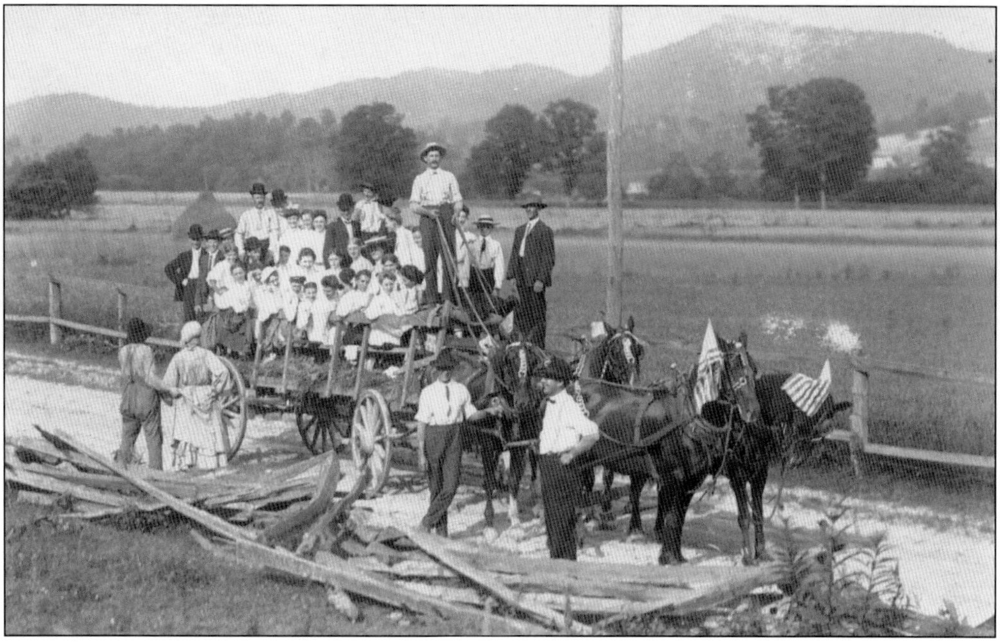

Hayrides were once a popular feature of social life. Carefully chaperoned, they provided a wholesome opportunity for meeting and dating members of the opposite "persuasion." This photo dates back to around 1910. (Courtesy James and Robert Califf.)

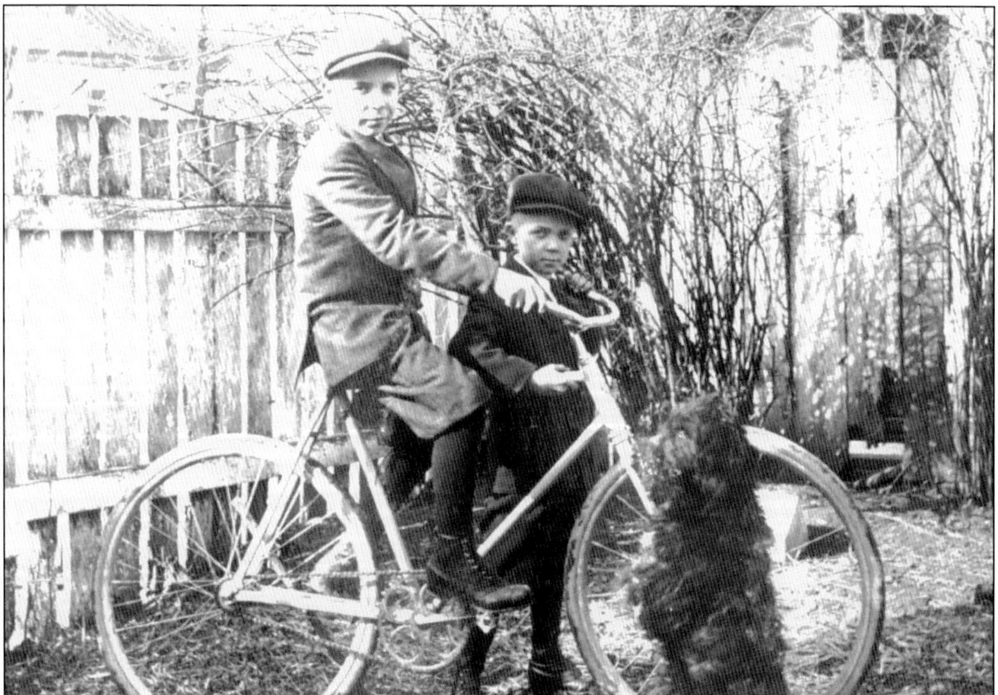

Bicycles and dogs never go out of style. This photo, taken around 1910, is labeled simply "George and Jack." One would assume that George is the boy. (Courtesy James and Robert Califf.)

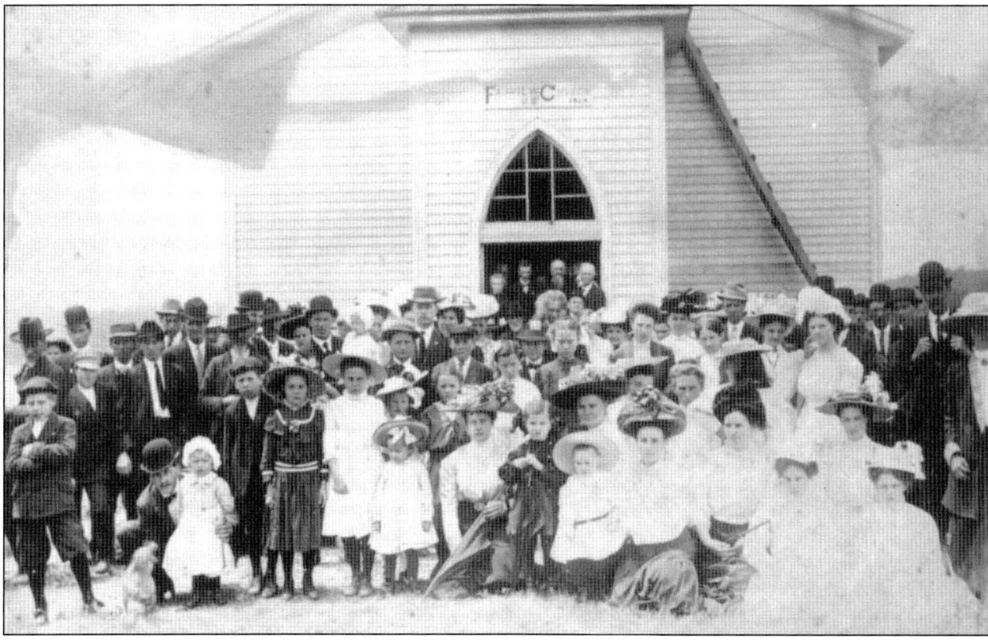

A popular gathering place for both worship and social events, the Fairview Church carried the date of 1909 over its entrance. Individuals pictured here were obviously dressed in Sunday best. Included in the photo are the mother and grandmother of Peggy Robinson, a current resident of Grafton. (Courtesy Peggy Robinson.)

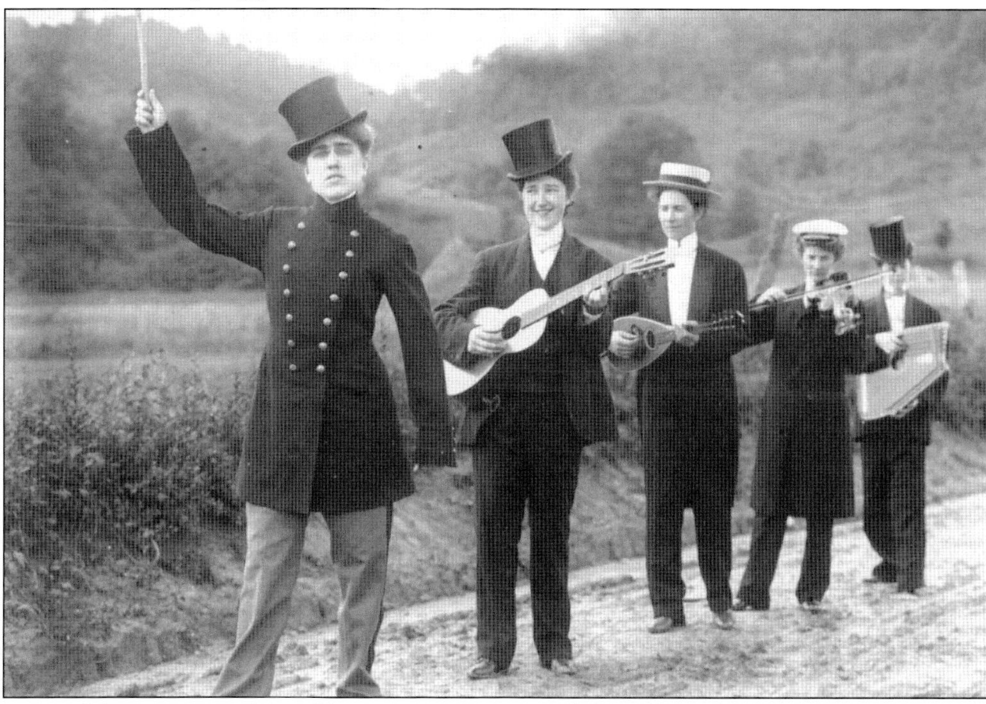

Many of the activities of Broaddus Institute were touted throughout the community and county. This quintet of drama and music students was drumming up attendance for an upcoming performance. The photo was taken around 1910. (Courtesy James and Robert Califf.)

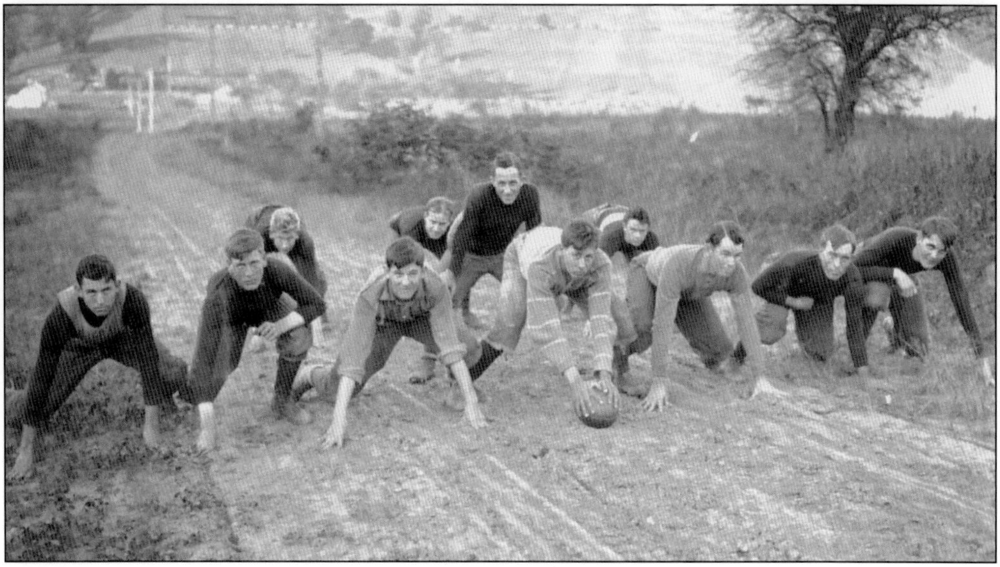

Looking quite unlike the St. Louis Rams of Super Bowl XXXIV, the Broaddus Institute football team of 1910 was probably just as determined and, in their own circle of competition, nearly as successful. (Courtesy James and Robert Califf.)

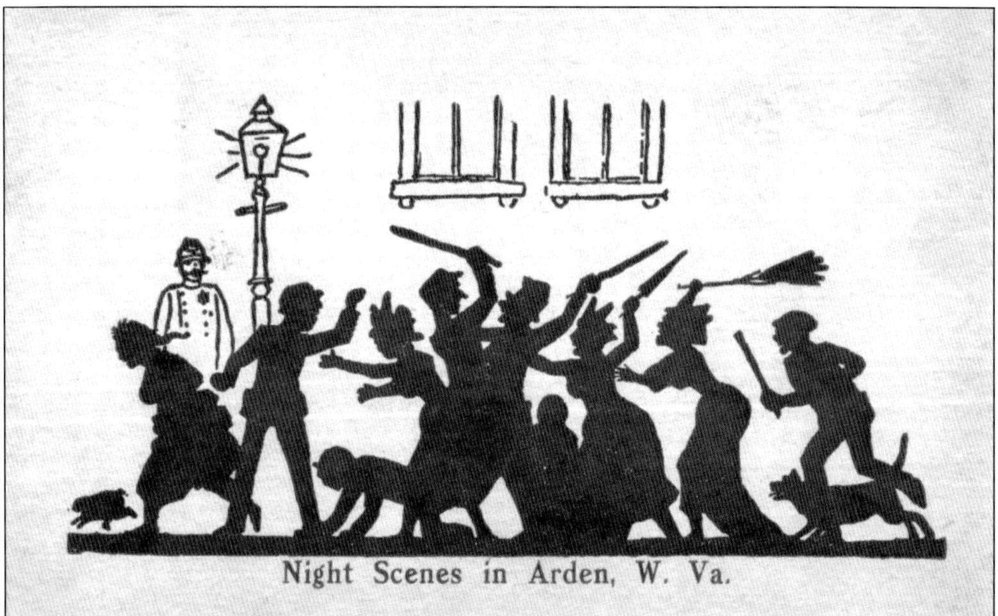

Then as now, postcards made good souvenirs to send to family and friends. This cartoon was mailed to "Miss Eva Johnson, Johnson, West Va." Miss Johnson, who was the postmistress in Johnson, apparently received the card in good order. It was postmarked in Arden on April 22, 1910. (Courtesy Peggy Robinson.)

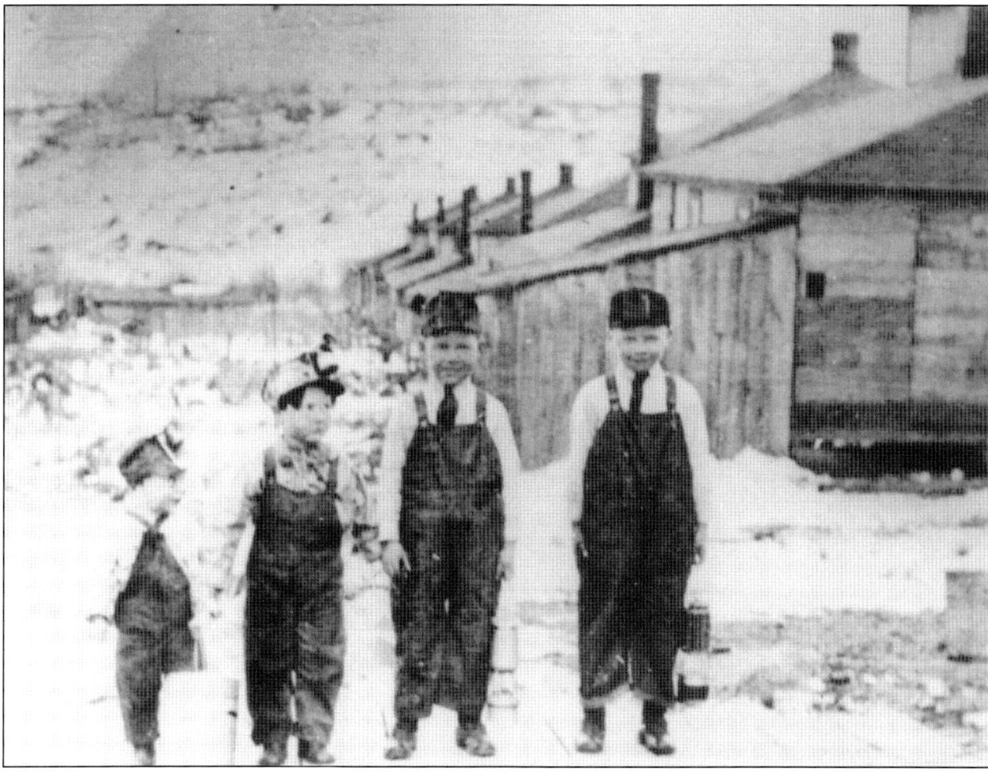

These Waddell boys, proud of their father's occupation, were dressed in coal miners' garb. Behind them are buildings typical of those owned by the coal companies and inhabited by the miners and their families. (Courtesy Joe Mattaliano.)

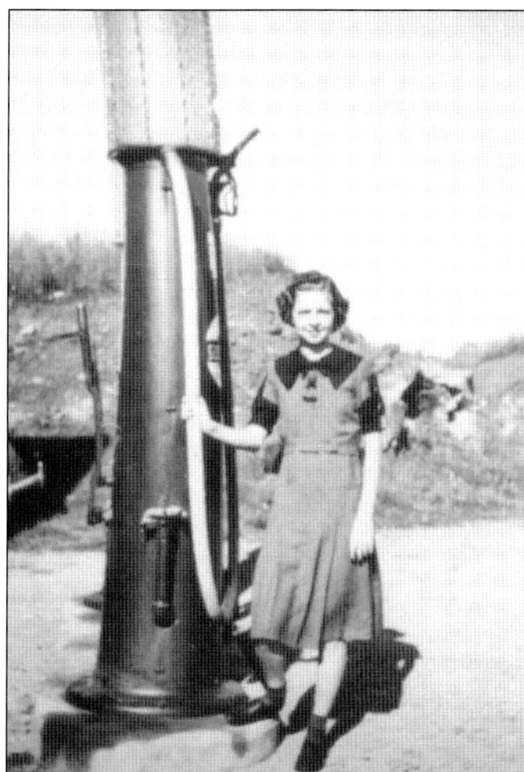

After Route 57 was completed in 1935, it brought business to the Elk City area. The first Benson store in Overfield was replaced by a more modern building and a filling station. Several members of the Benson family, including "Libby," pictured here, worked in the store and operated the gas pump. The store's soft drink cooler was cooled by 100-pound ice blocks brought from Philippi. (Curvature in the old photograph makes the gas pump look curved, but it was straight at the top.) (Courtesy Elizabeth Benson Talbot.)

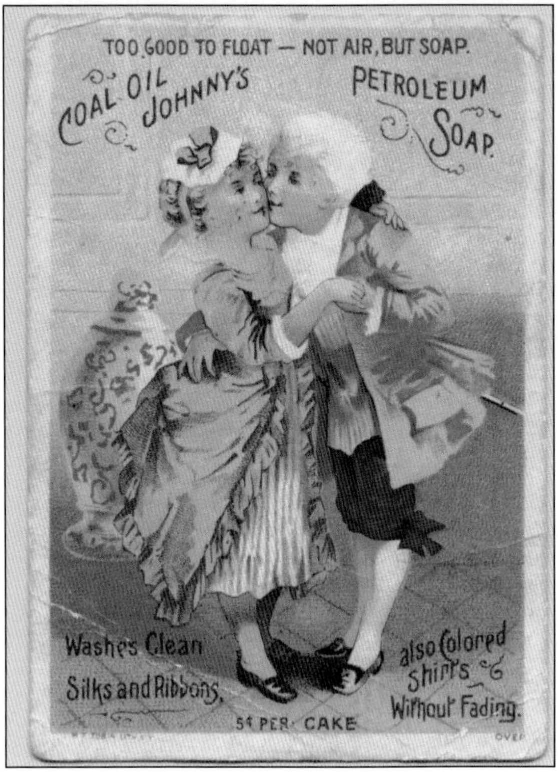

A byproduct of coal production was—and is—petroleum, which was processed to make a variety of products including soap. This advertisement and souvenir card describes Coal Oil Johnny's Petroleum Soap as "too good to float—not air but soap." (Courtesy Peggy Robinson.)

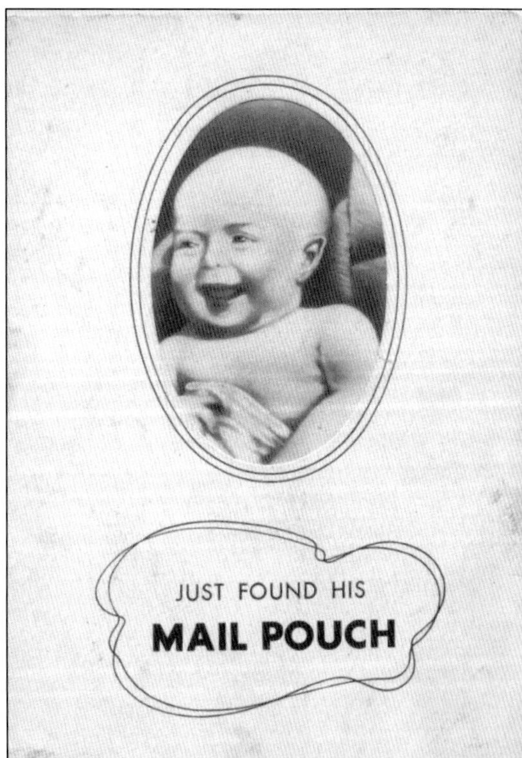

Another product widely advertised was Mail Pouch tobacco. The back of this "broadside" reads, "The original packaged ribbon cut chewing tobacco and the standard of excellence for over 58 years. TREAT YOURSELF TO THE BEST." (Courtesy Peggy Robinson.)

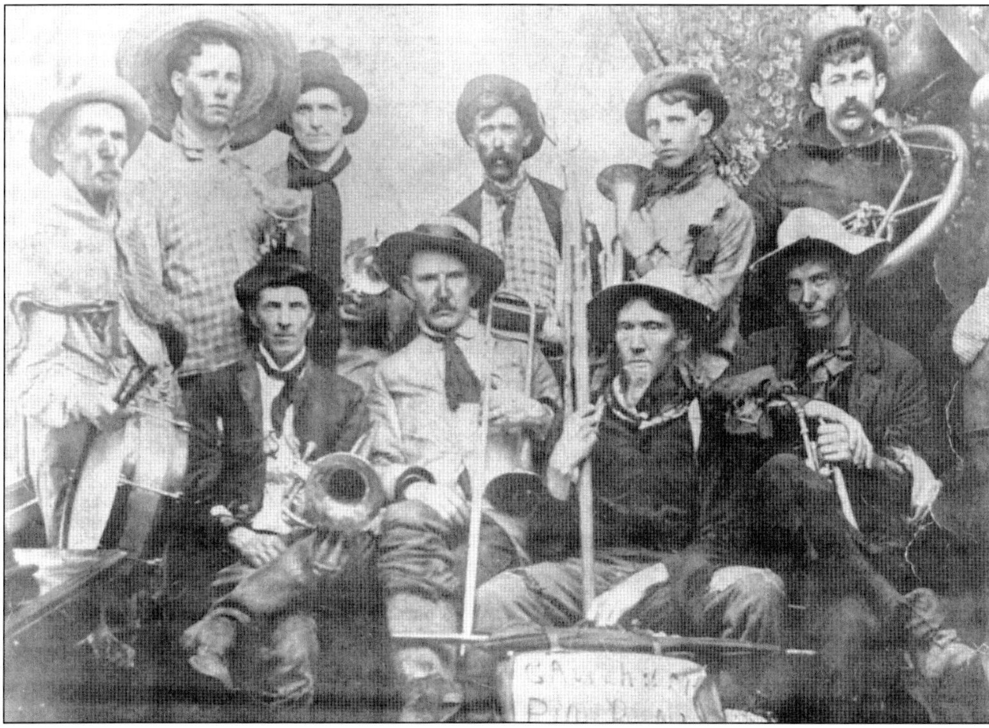

Whatever musical talent may or may not have been enjoyed by its members, this band was certainly colorful. Instruments included drums, trumpets, trombones, a tuba, and, apparently, a pitchfork and a few rifles. (Courtesy Joe Mattaliano.)

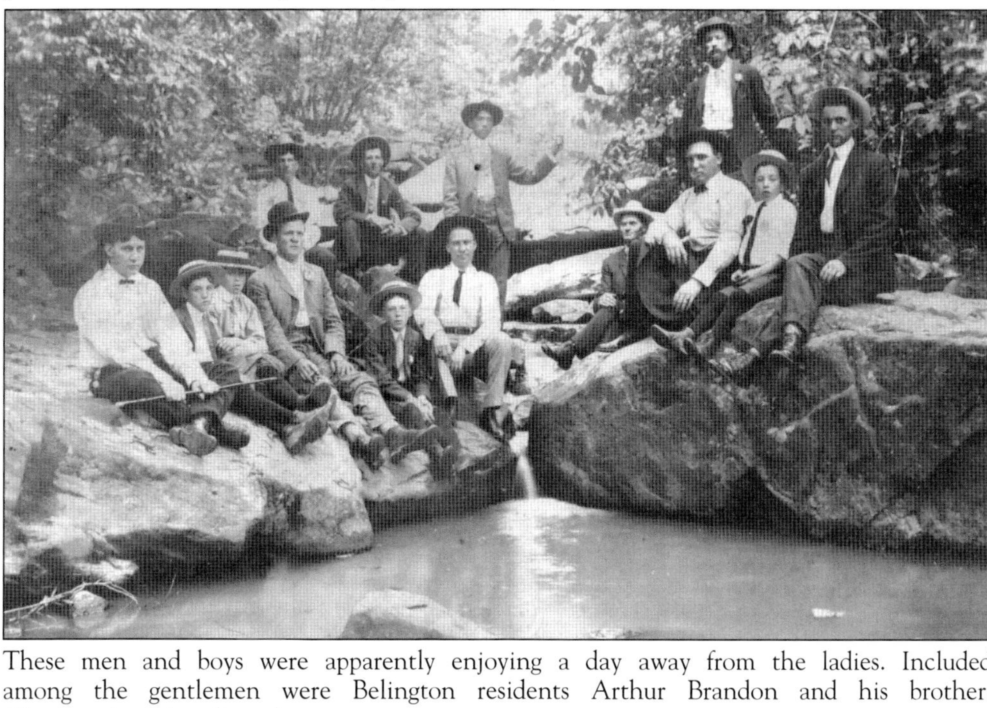

These men and boys were apparently enjoying a day away from the ladies. Included among the gentlemen were Belington residents Arthur Brandon and his brother. (Courtesy Joe Mattaliano.)

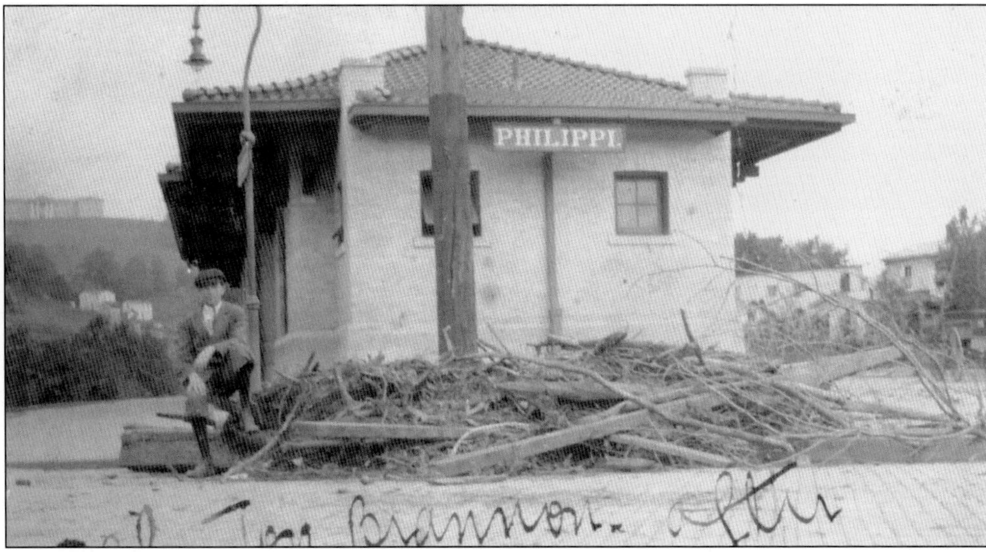

Debris from the flood of 1912 piled up against the wall of the Philippi railroad station. On the hill to the far left is four-year-old Old Main Hall on the Broaddus campus. (Courtesy James and Robert Califf.)

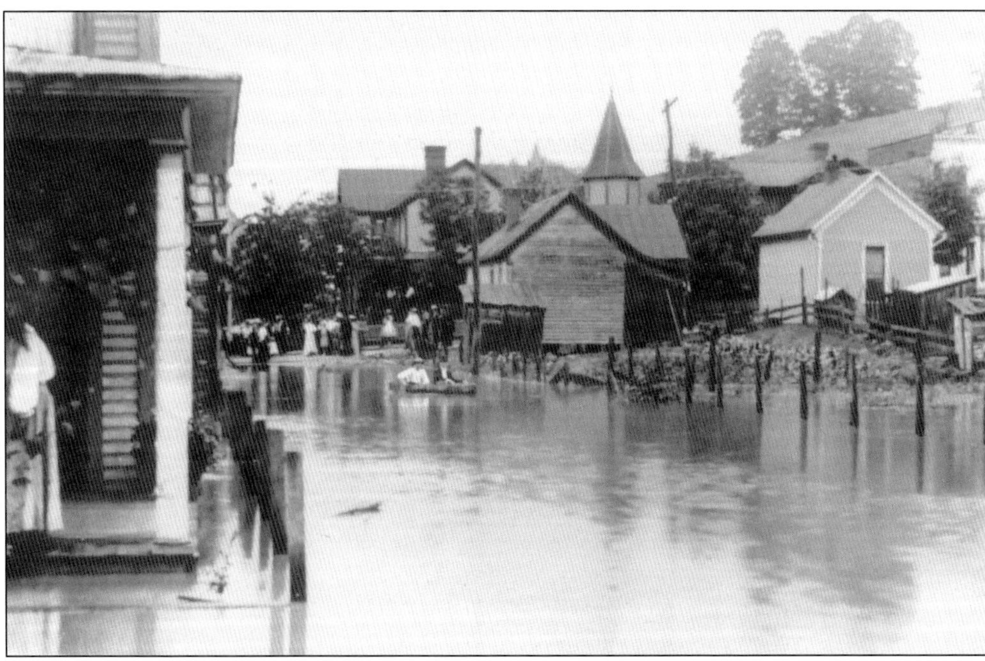

High waters were experienced all along the Tygart River in 1912. This photo was taken in Belington. (Courtesy Stephen Rautner.)

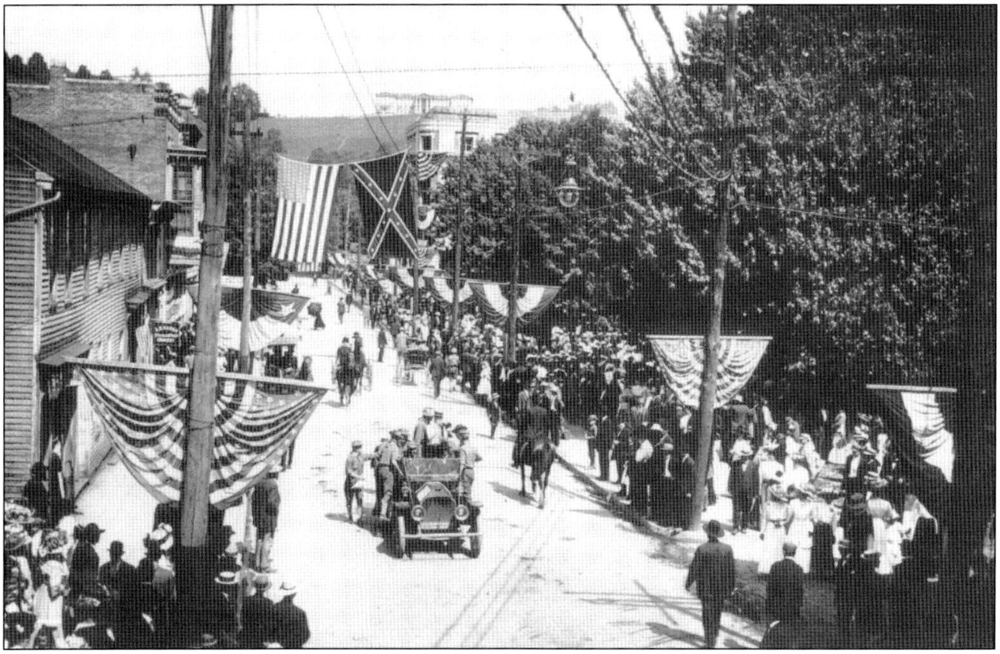

In commemoration of the first land battle of the Civil War, a Blue and Gray Reunion was held in 1911. The centennial of the battle was observed with another reunion in 1961. Since 1989, the event has been held annually.

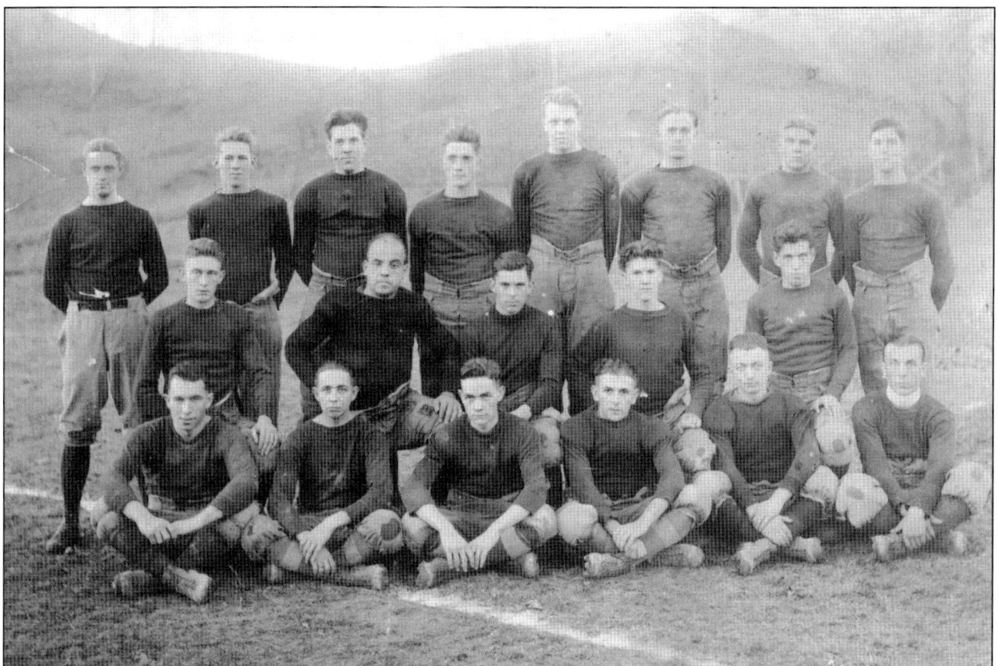

This 1921 photo of the Belington football team was taken by West Virginia Photo Company of Parsons. The photo belonged to N. Kennedy Black, who was probably a member of the team. (Courtesy Joe Mattaliano.)

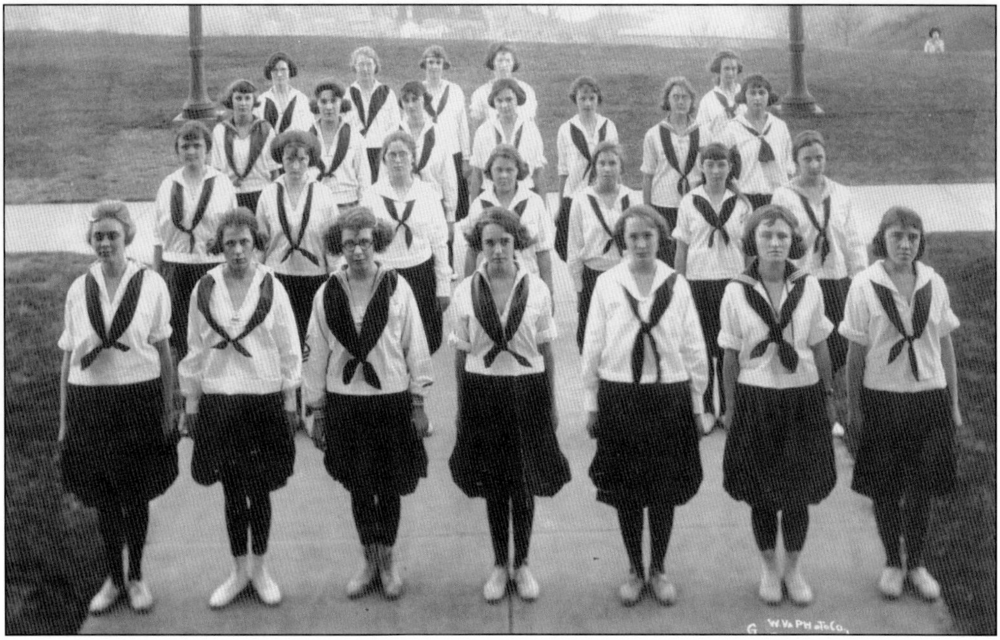

Taken on the hill behind Old Main, this picture portrays "The Broaddus Girls," including Avanelle Withers, who later married Hu C. Myers. (Courtesy Joe Mattaliano.)

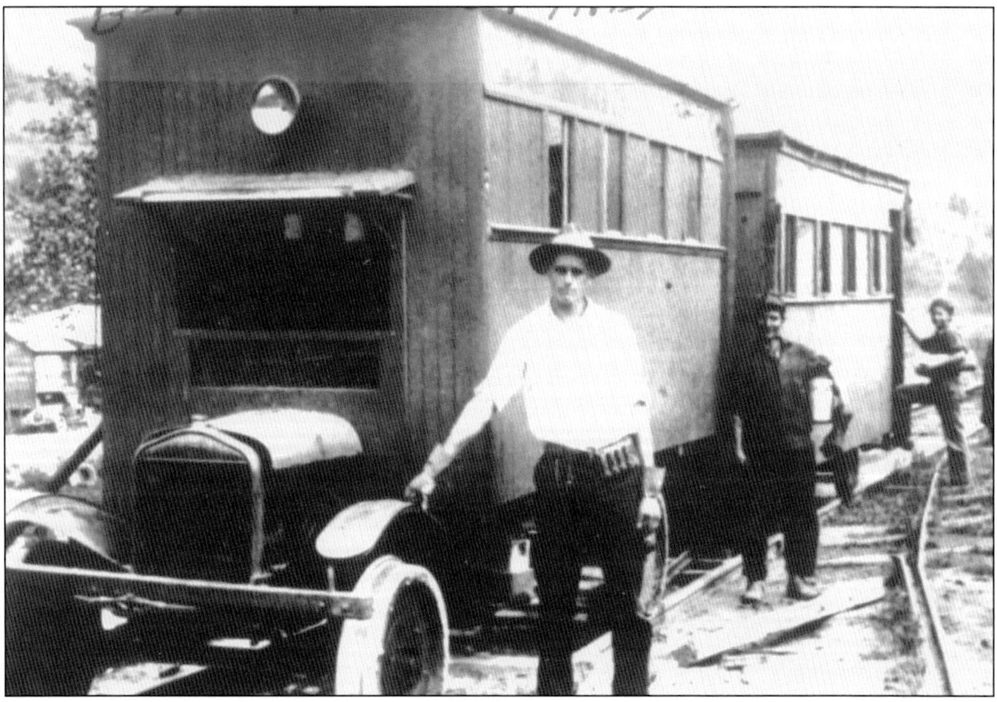

This jitney or trolley was created by Buford Cleavenger from old truck engines and cabs. It ran from Flemington (Simpson) to Galloway (Bear Mountain), hauling mail, freight, and passengers. Pictured here are the conductor, Leslie "Ick" Haddix of Philippi, "Shorty" Perk of Belington, Oris Cleavenger of Brownton, and the paperboy, Gordon Wright. (Courtesy Helen and Albert Gleza.)

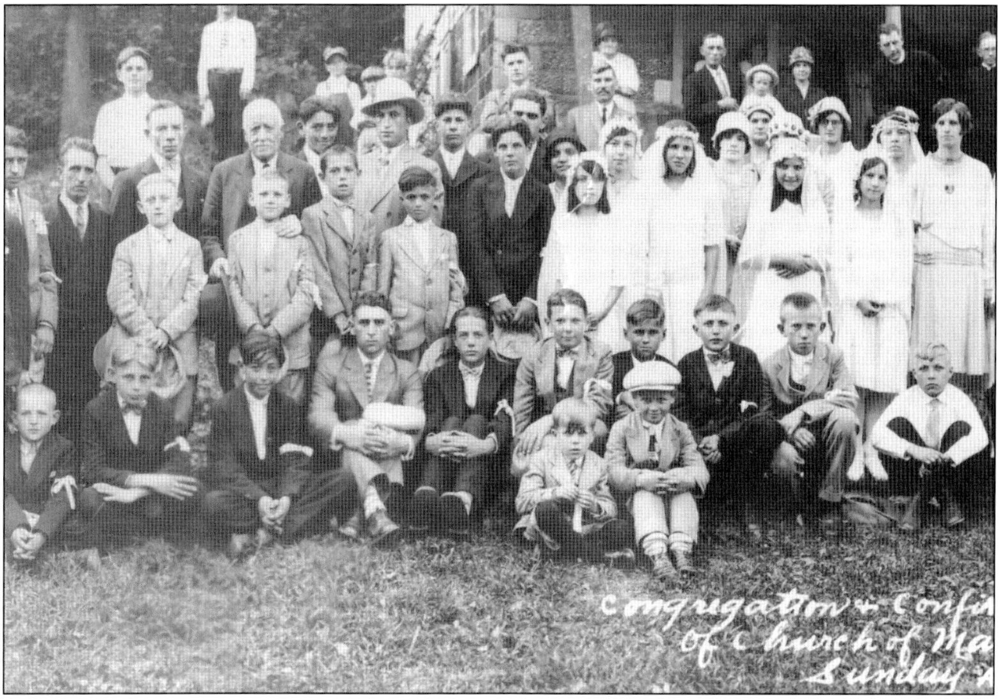

This confirmation class and the bishop who performed the ceremony in approximately 1925 give evidence of the strength and importance of Our Lady of Sorrows Church in Century. (Courtesy Nancy Streets.)

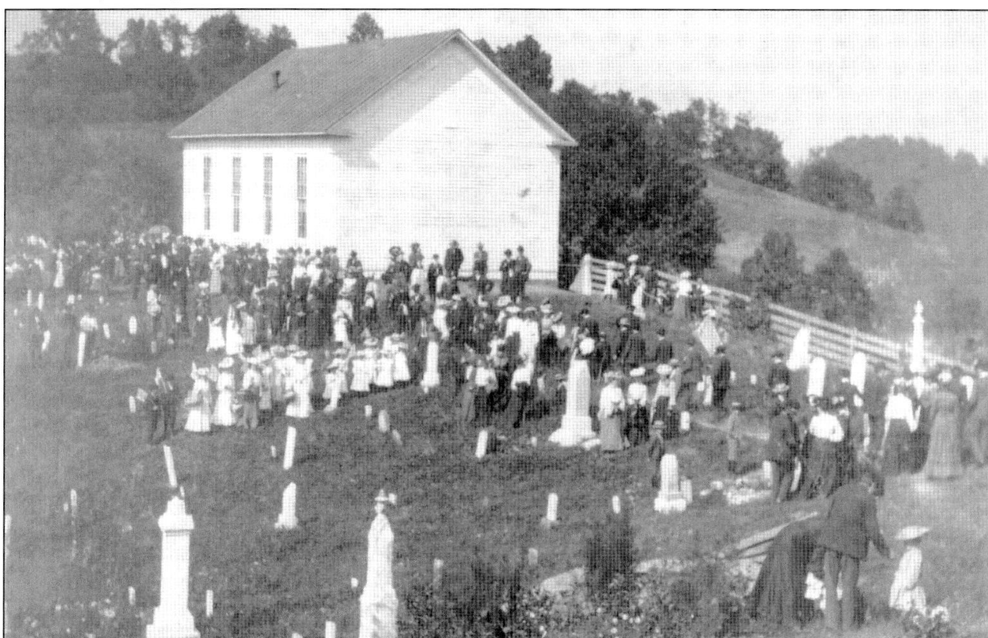

Decoration Day traditionally meant large gatherings at community churches and their adjacent cemeteries. Pictured here are the Mt. Morris church and graveyard sometime before the turn of the century. (Courtesy Peggy Robinson.)

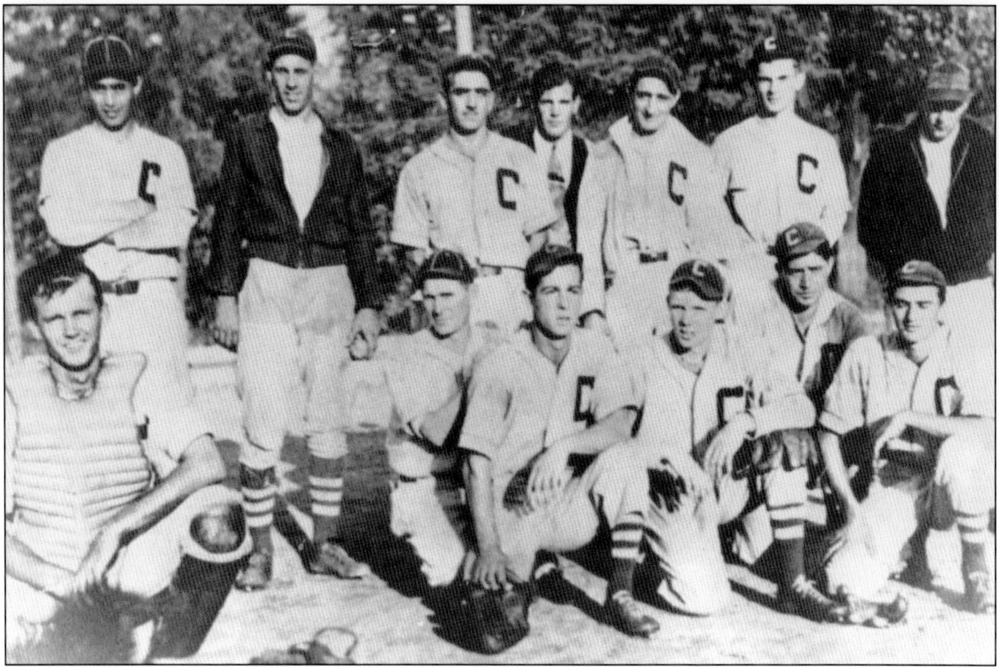

Baseball constituted a major recreational activity in all coal communities in the first half of the 20th century. Every community turned out to cheer its own team. Pictured here is the Century team of the early 1940s, which included Edward "Toot" Spotloe, Randall Bosley, "Bingo" Levicki, James, Pete, Albert, and Frank Zara, Mike Hunt, William True, William Bone, and Pete Zubas. (Courtesy Nancy Streets.)

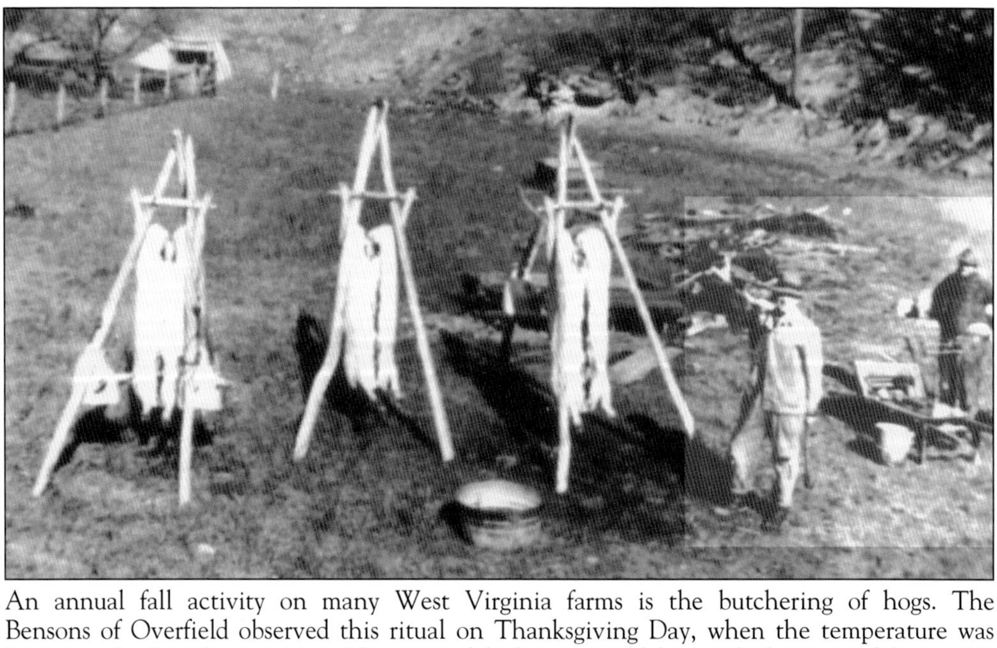

An annual fall activity on many West Virginia farms is the butchering of hogs. The Bensons of Overfield observed this ritual on Thanksgiving Day, when the temperature was low enough that the meat would not spoil before it could be smoked. Pictured here with three fine hogs are Bert Benson and Stephen Stuart on a "big day" in the 1930s. (Courtesy Elizabeth Benson Talbot.)

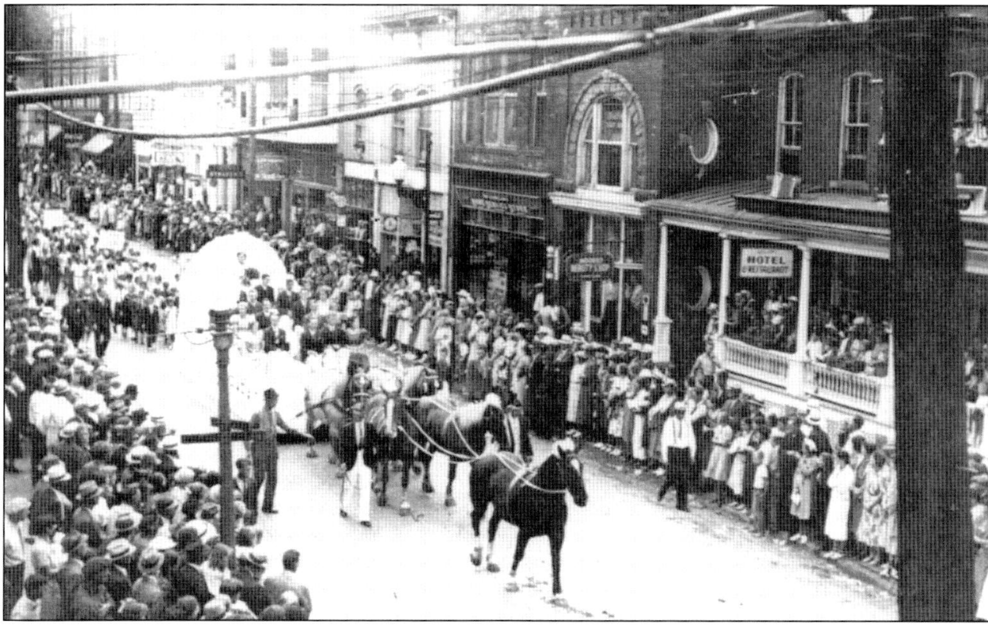

The annual street fair in Philippi included a Grand March or Grand Feature Parade. Pictured here are the queen's float and neatly ordered crowds along the street. Stores on the right include Strader's clothing store, the Rexall drugstore, Modern Beauty Shop, Home Service Store, and Wilson Hotel and Restaurant. (Courtesy Jane Mattaliano.)

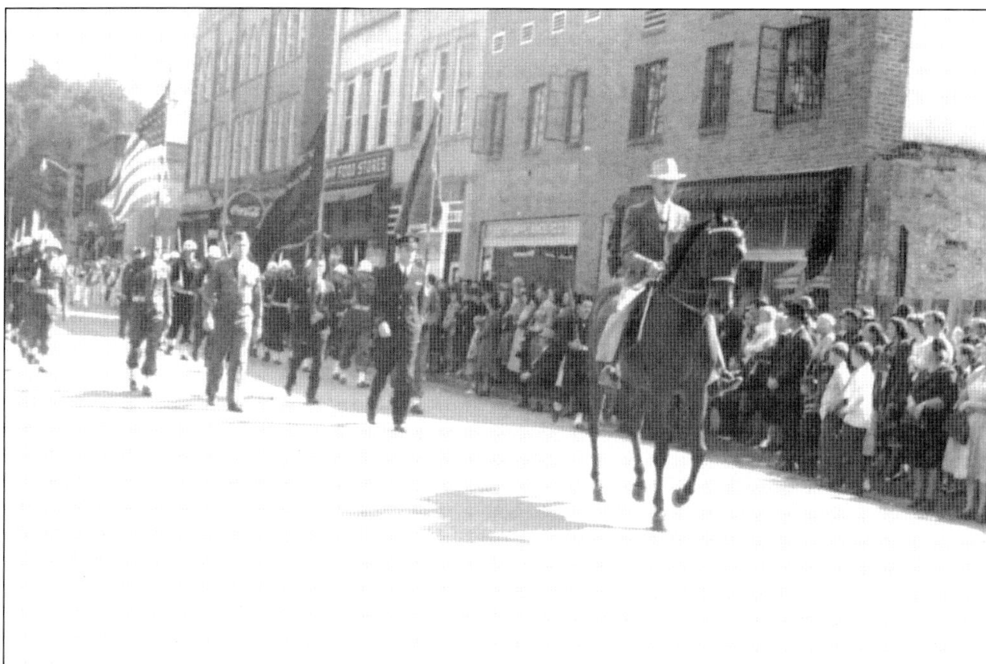

The marshal for this particular parade was Gordon Posten, a well-known and prosperous horseman of the area. The extensive Barbour County fairgrounds, established in 1976, occupy land purchased from Mr. Posten. (Courtesy H.A. "Red" Payne.)

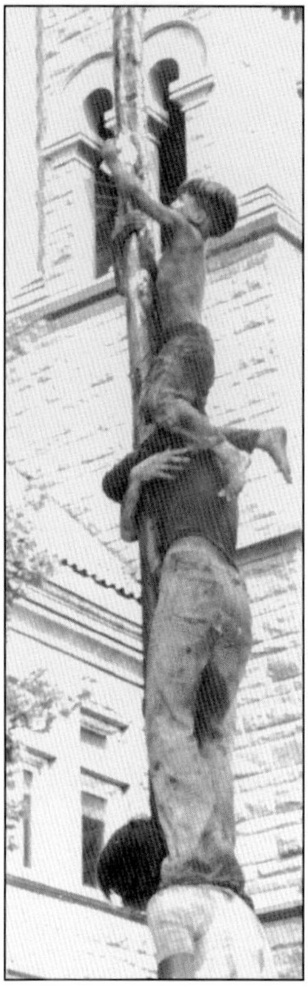

One of the most popular features of the Philippi street fair was the greased pole set in front of the county courthouse. With an opponent or supporter close behind, this daring adventurer was about to reach the summit. (Courtesy Joe Mattaliano.)

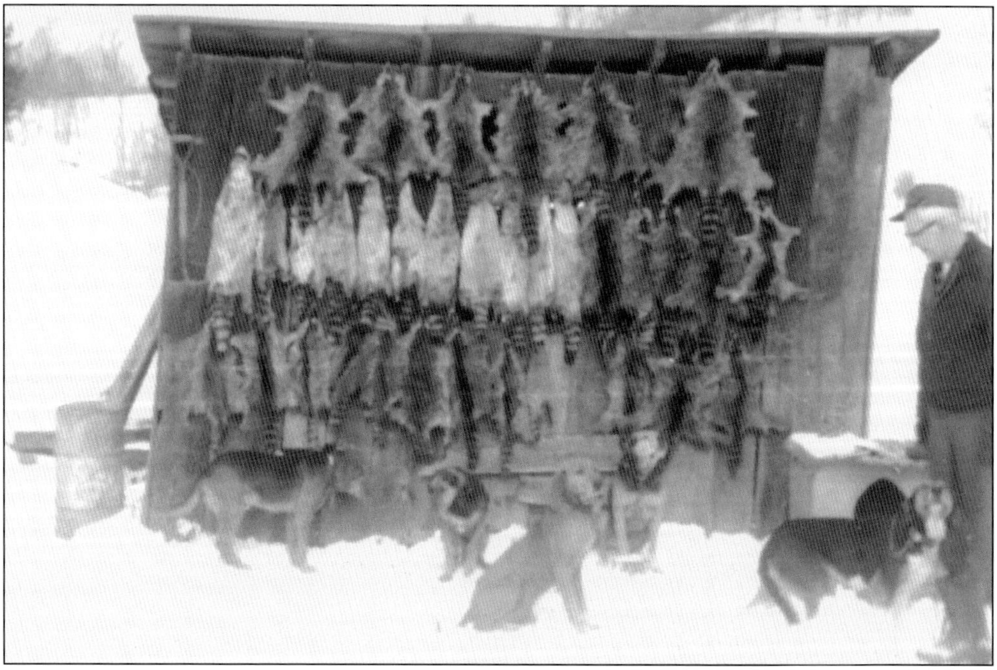

Hunting has always been a major activity in Barbour County, both as a sport and as a necessity. Forrest Brown's longtime hobby was coon hunting, evidence of which exists in this 1967 photo of Brown with some 40 raccoon hides. (Courtesy Retta Taylor.)

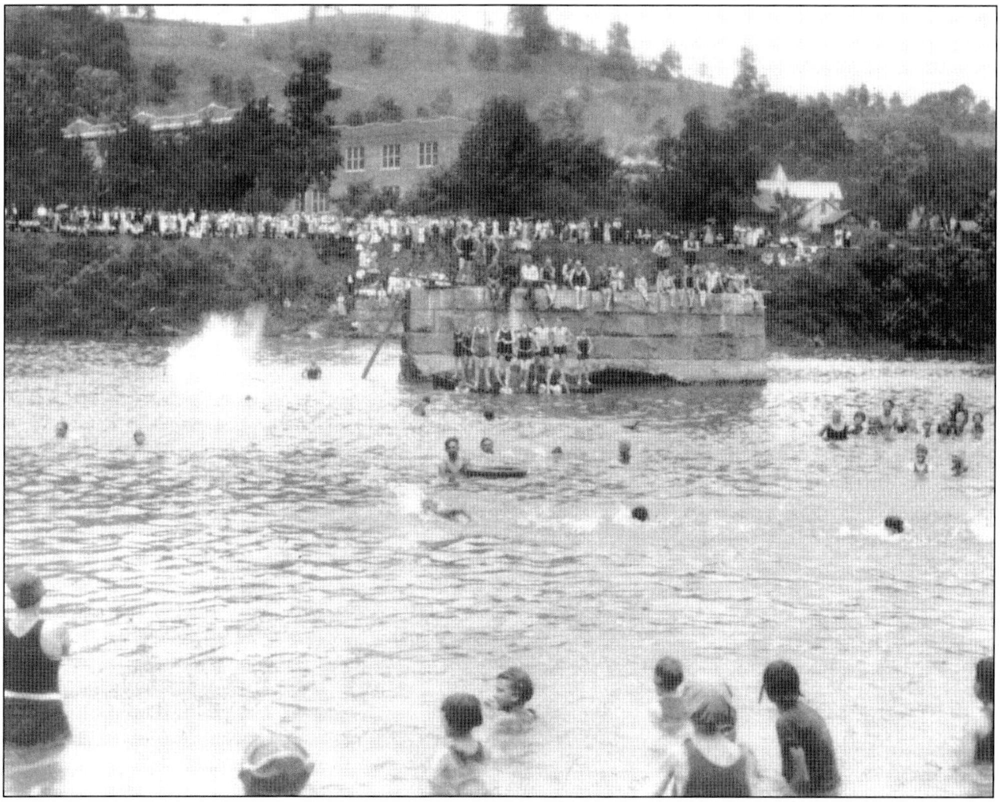

Major summer activities in the 1920s and 1930s were swimming and swim meets. The sandy beach behind the Philippi School was a favorite spot for such events. Participants reached the pier by swimming out, riding a ferry, or crossing a swinging bridge located upriver.

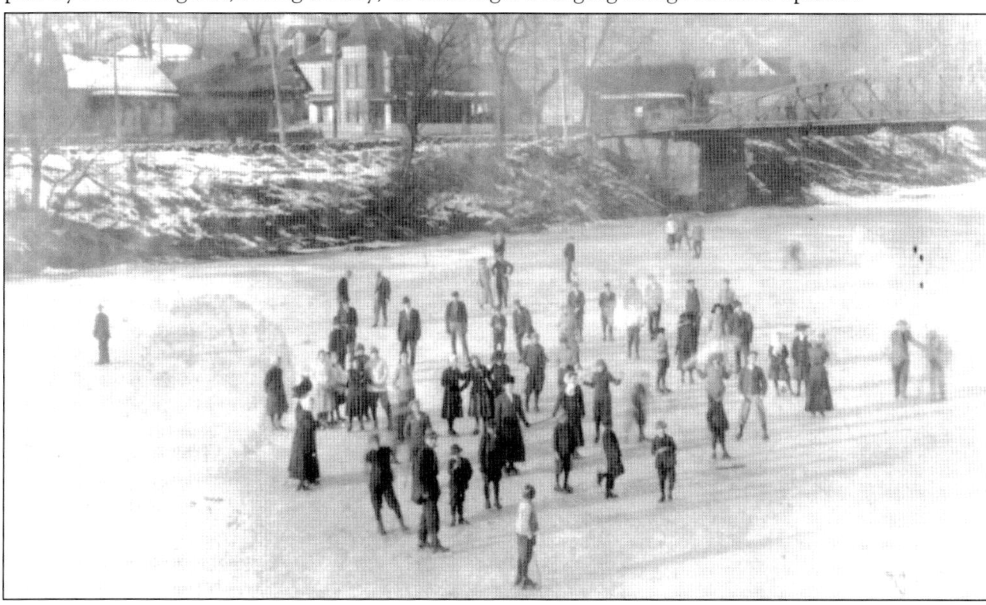

In the winter, the river became an ice-skating rink. This group of athletes was pictured upriver from the Belington bridge. (Courtesy Stephen Rautner.)

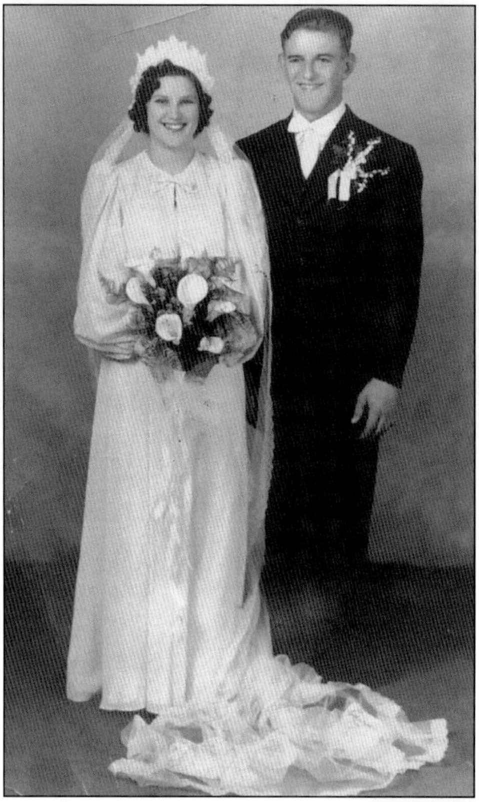

Helen and Albert Gleza, now living in Buckhannon, were married on December 28, 1940, in the Catholic church in Brownton. Helen reports that her veil cost $7.50, her gown $13. Soon after their wedding, Albert reported for duty in the U.S. Navy. (Courtesy Helen and Albert Gleza.)

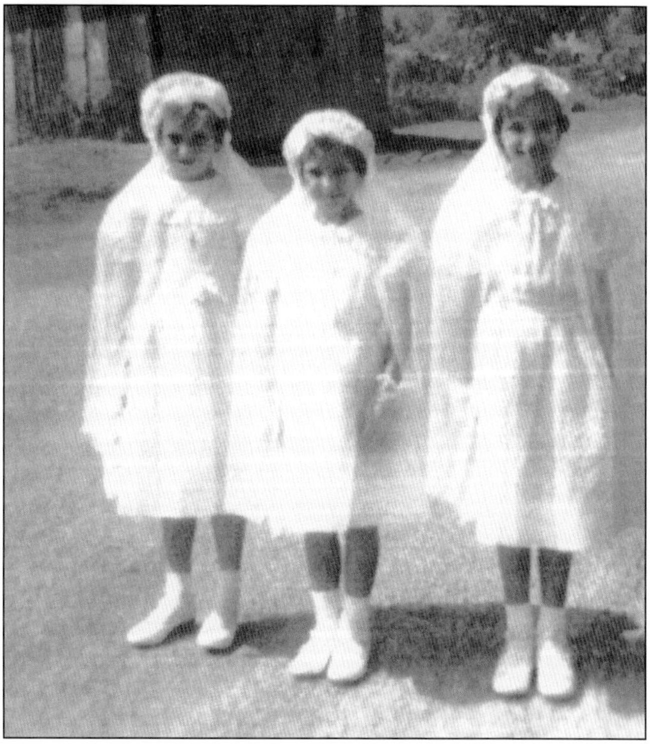

The Gleza daughters, Jean and Mary Ann, are pictured here with their friend Antonia Zbosnik (left) after their First Holy Communion in 1949. (Courtesy Helen and Albert Gleza.)

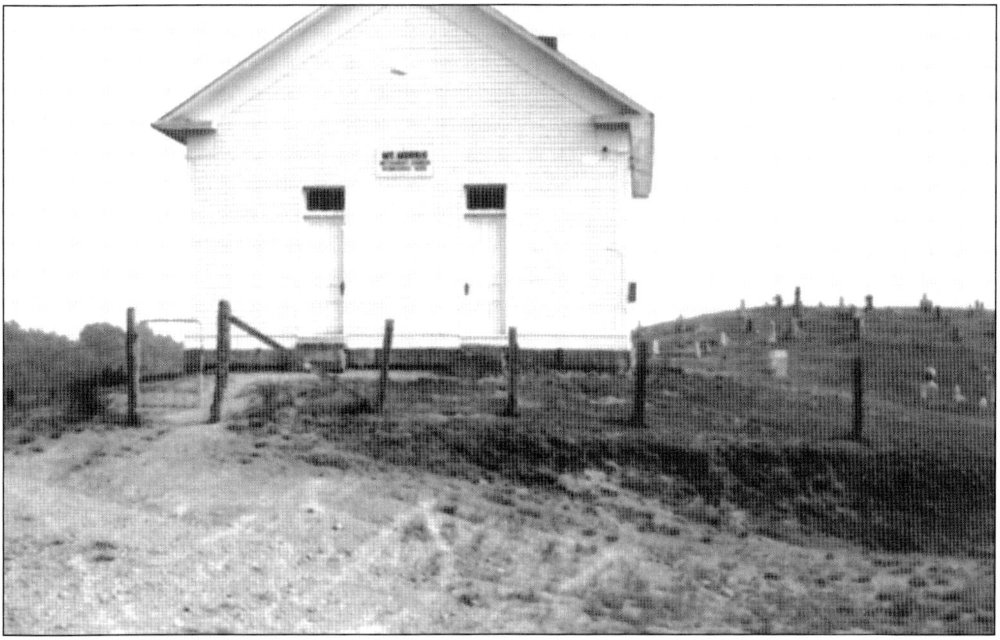

The two doors on the Mt. Morris church are likely to have been used separately by male and female members of the congregation. This church still stands. (Courtesy Peggy Robinson.)

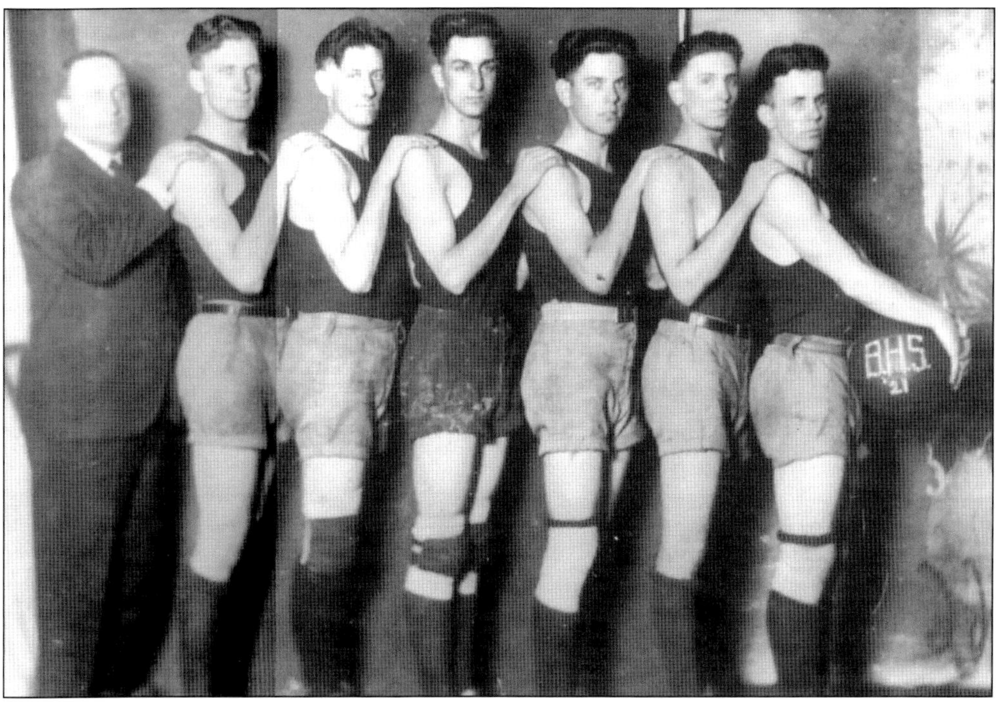

Basketball was—and is—an extremely popular sport in all of West Virginia. This fine-looking team played for Belington High School. (Courtesy Stephen Rautner.)

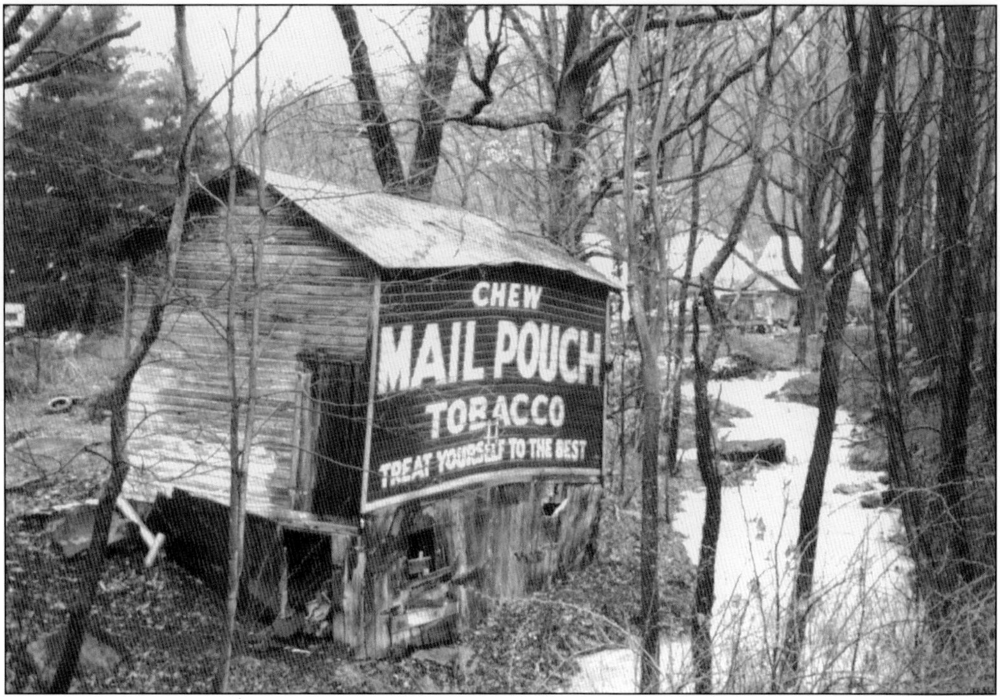

As the 21st century gets underway, only seven of the original hundreds of Mail Pouch signs remain in Barbour County. One can be found just south of Philippi on Route 250. (Courtesy Don Funk.)

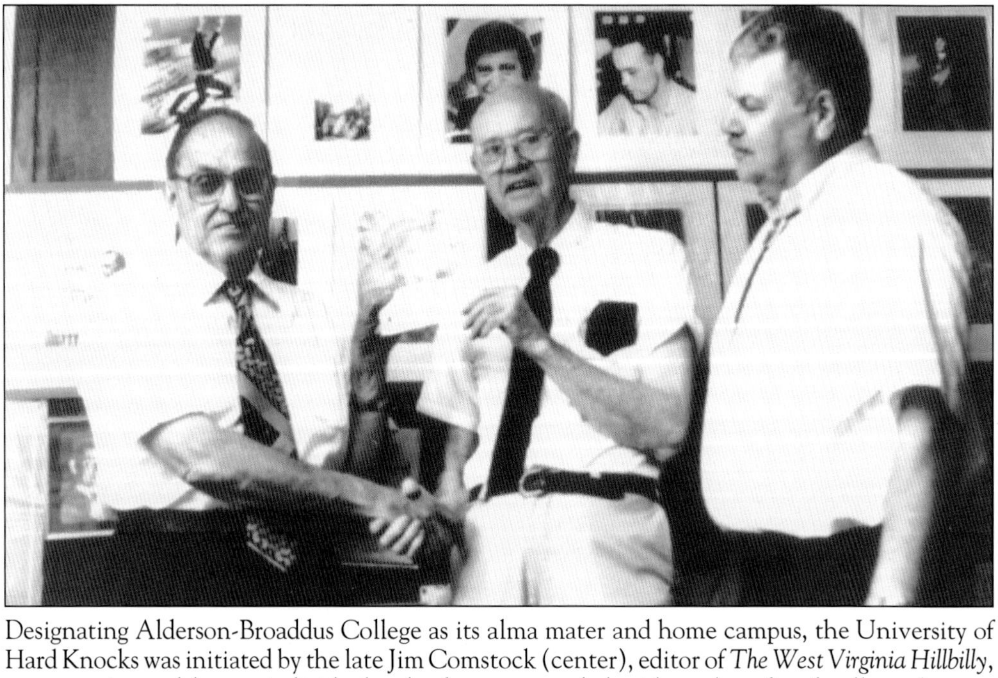

Designating Alderson-Broaddus College as its alma mater and home campus, the University of Hard Knocks was initiated by the late Jim Comstock (center), editor of *The West Virginia Hillbilly*, to recognize and honor individuals who have succeeded without benefit of college degrees. Leadership of the group has been provided by Dr. Elza Wilson (left) and Dr. Don Smith.